how i almost blew it

Sidharth Rao. Serial entrepreneur. Business builder. Angel investor. Author.

Sidharth's journey as an entrepreneur and founder began at age nineteen. A college dropout, he co-founded Webchutney with his partner Sudesh in 1999. As CEO, he led Webchutney to become India's most successful and award-winning digital creative agency, being ranked India's #1 digital agency for eight years by *The Economic Times' Brand Equity*. In 2013, Webchutney was acquired by the Dentsu Group, one of the largest agency networks globally. Webchutney was the most-awarded Indian agency at the Cannes Lions International Festival of Creativity in 2019 and 2021. In 2022, Dentsu Webchutney was named Cannes Lions Global Agency of the Year, a first for any Indian agency ever.

Sidharth served as Group CEO of Dentsu McGarryBowen before moving on to start Punt Partners, a marketing technology company with Madhu Sudhan. He was also a proud member of the global digital advisory board at Unilever and served on the jury of some of the most celebrated advertising festivals in India and around the globe. An active angel investor in several internet companies, he also incubated Networkplay, a brand ad network which was acquired by Bertelsmann AG. On 21 April 2023, Sidharth passed away at his farmhouse in Karjat aged forty-three. He is survived by his wife Shweta and his parents. *How I Almost Blew It* is his first book.

Praise for the Book

Written in an easy-to-read style, devoid of jargon and platitudes, this book does justice to some of the biggest start-up successes with plenty of history, context and in-depth research. Must read for students, practitioners and those interested in the start-up ecosystem.

—K. Ganesh, Serial Entrepreneur and Partner, GrowthStory.in

The book will give readers a new perspective and a rich understanding of factors that make or break start-ups. With detailed research and insights, Sidharth uncovers the inner lives of start-ups with their eye on the big prize. I wish every entrepreneur and even those sitting on the fence read the book.

—Ashish Bhasin, Chairman and CEO, Dentsu Aegis Network India

Riveting tales of celebrated and revered Indian entrepreneurs. These stories reveal hardcore lessons of ambition, hustle, dreams and blowing it all up. It shows how the gods of entrepreneurship are also mortals like us. It's hard to put down the book once you begin.

—Anand Jain, Co-Founder, CleverTap

Don't get trapped into believing that this book is only for tech start-ups. The learnings hold true even for the brick and mortar world. Sidharth has lived the lows and highs of entrepreneurship, not just tech.

—Anant Rangaswami, Editor of MELT on WION

how i almost blew it

Incredible lessons from India's most successful digital entrepreneurs

SIDHARTH RAO

First published by Westland Publications Private Limited in 2019

This revised edition published by Westland Business, an imprint of Westland Books, a division of Nasadiya Technologies Private Limited, in 2024

No. 269/2B, First Floor, 'Irai Arul', Vimalraj Street, Nethaji Nagar, Alapakkam Main Road, Maduravoyal, Chennai 600095

Westland, the Westland logo, Westland Business and the Westland Business logo are the trademarks of Nasadiya Technologies Private Limited, or its affiliates.

Copyright © Sidharth Rao, 2019, 2024

Sidharth Rao asserts the moral right to be identified as the author of this work.

ISBN: 9789360456719

10 9 8 7 6 5 4 3 2 1

Typeset by Jojy Philip, New Delhi
Printed at Saurabh Printers Pvt. Ltd

To Dad, who as a decorated Army General from the infantry successfully pursued BSc, MSc, BTech, MBA and then a Ph.D. Because of this, my sister Natasha who is now a pilot, and I had no guilt dropping out of college within the first year and pursuing our dreams.

To Mom, who is a national record holder for shooting, for ensuring she and dad kept footing the bill for my financial screw-ups through my entrepreneurial journey for a long time.

The role of parents is hugely underrated whenever entrepreneurship is celebrated.

CONTENTS

FOREWORD

Sidharth breezed into MakeMyTrip's office in 2001, with his trademark gold chain and open shirt setting the tone for how internet marketing would evolve in India over the next decade. Sid and his team invented viral marketing, and in its earlier days, the MakeMyTrip brand was largely defined by the work they did for us. In just twenty years Sid has founded and sold a company, been the CEO of a large agency, won multiple awards and judged a few more, written a bestseller and even built a farm. A few decades of work in just two!

I've known Sid now for more than twenty years, and he is among the handful of very, very close personal friends I have made in my professional life. We've had long chats at Toto's in Bombay and TCs in Delhi about work, books, investing and Jaggu Dada's latest utterances. Our running joke was that most companies we co-invested in went under, so to save the founder, one of us should say no to investing. Over the years, Sid has hosted me and many other friends and colleagues at his pad in Bandra. Each evening with Sid was special. I was happiest when Shweta and Sid told me they were seeing each other and I continued to enjoy their hospitality, along with their brood of dogs and cats.

When Sid first told me about this book, he wanted me to introduce him to some of the founders he wanted to quiz. I remember telling him to stop being his modest self and that all of them know him. Just ping them directly and they would love to be part of the book, I told him. And that's how it transpired.

Shweta and Sid's wedding in Goa was one of the most glorious weddings I have ever attended, and I look back fondly at the pictures now and then. Shweta made him beam and he looks his quizzical self in most pictures. The farm they built together was a culmination of years of hard work and it gave him much joy. The week before he passed, we had exchanged messages, promising that we'd meet at his farm soon. No one and nothing will fill this void, Sid.

It's been a long day without you, my friend
And I'll tell you all about it when I see you again
We've come a long way from where we began
Oh, I'll tell you all about it when I see you again
When I see you again.

—Wiz Khalifa

Sachin Bhatia
CEO at The Good Creator Co.
Gurugram, March 2024

FOREWORD

How I Almost Blew It is a book that stands out from other entrepreneurial books because it humanises the entrepreneurs that the media idolises. Sidharth wrote it because he wanted to show every prospective and struggling entrepreneur that the challenges they are facing, dire as they seem, form a well-worn path that every successful start-up has also been through and that it's possible to break out. As an entrepreneur who was at the brink multiple times and went on to scale the company he founded—Webchutney—to global accolades such as 'Agency of the Year' at the Cannes Lions 2022, he was possibly the biggest champion of the comeback story. Having been part of the Indian internet ecosystem from 1999, Sidharth had a ringside view of the rollercoaster a lot of the Indian internet companies went on before they became the household names they are today.

I first met Sidharth as an investor in his company Webchutney in 2008 and then worked closely with him on several projects. In 2014, Sidharth sold his company to Dentsu. He continued leading Dentsu's creative business and was an active angel investor. In the start-up bull run of 2014–20, money was flowing freely and start-ups were media darlings and could do no wrong. It was in this context that Sidharth felt that the representation in the media, where entrepreneurs were superheroes and always crushing it, was not the only side that aspiring entrepreneurs ought to know of. He wanted to show that all start-ups had multiple moments when they almost blew their chance. The book has lots of interesting nuggets, which have never before been shared in public, on decisions entrepreneurs made and the context in which they made them. *How I Almost Blew It* is a great read for any aspiring entrepreneur.

Sid was a warm, curious and deeply empathetic person who was always open to hearing about an entrepreneurial venture. He was the quintessential punter who was always excited about the next big idea or a person who was passionate about one. He was very generous, both with his time and money, and left a lasting legacy of entrepreneurs whose journey he was part of. While Sid's untimely passing left a huge void in the lives of those he inspired and cared for, his legacy of helping and championing young entrepreneurs continues to live on through his book. This note would be incomplete without acknowledging his wife Shweta's role in encouraging Sidharth to undertake and complete the book that you are about to read.

Madhu Sudhan
Co-founder, Punt Partners
Mumbai, March 2024

INTRODUCTION

'Building a start-up is very much an endurance sport.'
– Max Levchin

As the internet celebrates twenty-five years of being publicly available next year, there's never been a better time to be an entrepreneur. With more opportunities, a large amount of capital, an unprecedented scale of internet users, lower costs and a more level playing field than ever before, the Indian digital ecosystem is exploding. Fortunately, I have had the privilege of a ringside view of the industry from the beginning.

Much like dungarees, the internet has been in and out of fashion at least three times in the last two decades. Each time, it suffered because of excesses from investors, markets and entrepreneurs. The first one, in 1994, was rightfully called the dot-com bubble. After slowly recovering over eight years from 2001 to 2008, the second internet wave was sweeping the world again when it was stopped dead in its tracks by the Lehman Brothers' bankruptcy in 2008. The third moment, in 2016, mostly impacted India. It occurred right after giants like Tiger Global, Naspers and DST Global fuelled an investment frenzy in the ecosystem. Every venture capitalist rushed in, trying to match their investments, when the music suddenly stopped.

The first dot-com bubble began in 1994—fuelled by a fast-growing adoption of the internet and the possibilities of the new world order—and lasted for six years. During this period, investors were eager to invest in any internet company—at any valuation—especially if it had one of the internet-related prefixes or a 'dot-com' in its name. Venture capitalists, who were almost unheard of a couple of years ago, were easy to approach. Investment banks, which profited significantly from initial public offerings (IPO), fuelled speculation and encouraged investment in technology. A combination of rapidly increasing stock prices and confidence that the companies would turn into future profit-making machines created an environment in which many investors were willing to overlook traditional metrics, such as the price-earnings ratio, leading to a stock-market bubble. At the height of the boom, it was possible for a promising dot-com company to become a public company via an IPO and raise a substantial amount of money, even if it had never made a profit, or in some cases, realised any material revenue.

This hysteria then made its way to India, with investors—Intel Capital, Draper Fisher Jurvetson, Warburg Pincus, e.Ventures, Chrysalis Capital and JPMorgan Chase—ready to make the first big bets in the Indian market to replicate the success of their peers in the US. This era also witnessed the historic acquisition of the young company IndiaWorld, which operated a string of websites, by Sify, India's first private internet service provider, for a whopping ₹499 crore. This sent shock-waves through the entire business community. The investors who had just landed on our shores saw this as a validation of their decision to enter the Indian market. These investors went on to write the first cheques for companies like MakeMyTrip, Info Edge and BookMyShow, who survived the dot-com bubble, besides many more who didn't.

On 10 March 2000, NASDAQ Composite, a stock-market index, peaked at 5,048.62. In the coming days, a series of bad news poured in including that of Japan's recession, which triggered a global sell-off that disproportionately affected technology stocks. On 20 March 2000, a widely read Barron's magazine prophesied doom. Its cover article, titled 'Burning Up; Warning: Internet companies are running out of cash—fast', predicted the imminent bankruptcy of many internet companies. Investors began to rethink their investments. That same day, MicroStrategy, an electronic commerce software-making company, announced a revenue restatement due to aggressive accounting practices. The company had seen its stock shoot up thousands of per cent over the past year since it was considered to be an 'arms dealer' in the internet gold rush. Its stock price, which had risen from $7 per share to as high as $333 per share in a year, fell to $140 per share, i.e., 62 per cent in a single day. The bursting of this bubble was called the dot-com crash. India wasn't immune to the crash. Most revolutionary entrepreneurs ran back to the hills and never came back. Hyper-funded companies like Rupert Murdoch's Indya.com suffered deaths by a thousand cuts, and some like ChaiTime vanished overnight. But the few who stuck their necks made terrific comebacks four to five years later when, fuelled by a new optimism, venture capital firms started setting-up in India again.

The second wave of internet boom lapped against the shores. Internet companies began to thrive, only to crash again when the financial services firm Lehman Brothers filed for Chapter 11 bankruptcy protection on 15 September 2008, with over $600 billion in assets. That single incident threatened to bring the world economy to a halt. All the bets were off again.

Incidentally, 2008 also saw the birth of the next generation of start-ups in India. Flipkart, Zomato and a few more began their journeys and walked into the second phase of maniacal funding in 2012–13, catalysed mostly by Tiger Global. As Anupam Mittal, founder of People Group, said, 'Tiger entered and threw millions at start-ups at an early stage. All the limited partners at other VC firms were shouting at the partners saying, "See what Tiger is doing? Why aren't you deploying our capital faster?" The poor chaps did what they were told. When the music stopped and the dot-com graveyard became a reality, they started calling their partners again to inquire, "What the hell did you do with our money?"'

To add fuel to the fire, SoftBank jumped into the ring and joined the party by giving big cheques to growth-stage start-ups like Snapdeal, Housing.com, Ola Cabs and Oyo. The hundreds of millions of dollars that were pouring in turned almost every high-net-worth individual into an 'angel'. Youngsters—as fresh as hot bricks from a kiln—were raising money from investors who had missed the bus earlier. I had turned thirty-six that year and had two successful start-ups to my name. My first venture was Webchutney, a digital marketing firm I had co-founded in 1999, acquired by Dentsu Aegis Network in 2013. This was right after Network Play, an ad network we had incubated. It was acquired by Bertelsmann AG. I went on to raise a large sum for a proposed incubator that I had conceived, only to be told by a few potential investors that I was 'too old' to do this all over again. It seemed that if one wasn't an IIT graduate or a dropout and younger than twenty-three, there was slim chance of attracting the investors. The Housing.com saga came to a sorry end in less than eighteen months. And thankfully, for people like me, it brought relief that it was the end of the madness and things were going back to basics.

Throughout these years of ups and downs in the internet world, there are a few successful entrepreneurs who have acquired a lot of experience in navigating through tough times, scaling, almost blowing it up, fundraising and ultimately succeeding. They have lived lives that aspiring entrepreneurs can learn from.

The media celebrates fundraising and other vanity milestones in a start-up's journey, adding to the perceptions that start-ups are romantic stories. In reality, they are difficult journeys fraught with hardships. In my twenty years in the start-up cosmos, I haven't encountered a single successful start-up that hasn't had a near-death experience, almost shut down, almost sold itself too short and, therefore, almost 'blew it'.

In my freewheeling conversations with some of the most successful internet entrepreneurs in the Indian start-up ecosystem, I take a look at their exciting journeys, the differences in their approaches and how factors like pure dumb luck played a part along the way.

There are several success stories, including Flipkart, Paytm and Ola Cabs, as well as the stories of successful women entrepreneurs, that haven't made it to the book due to several unpredictable factors. As a start-up guy, I had to adapt to the situation. I sincerely hope that their stories will soon find space in books about their entrepreneurial journey. I have not attempted to present a formula for success in this book. Instead, my goal has been to present stories of a few entrepreneurs and prove that there is no framework for success except for sheer determination. As an entrepreneur who has been lucky a few times with start-ups, I wish I'd had the opportunity to learn from some of these success stories early on in my journey. As a reader of this book, I hope you get to learn from these stories and also enjoy reading them.

SANJEEV BIKHCHANDANI

Founder and Executive Vice-Chairman,
Info Edge (India) Limited [Naukri.com]

'I got five phone calls from Housing.com investors saying, "You've got the business" (because 99Acres was already generating ₹70–80 crore of revenue). They said, "We've got the product right with Housing.com. Why don't we merge?"
And my answer was, "If you've got the product, how come we have the business?"'

IT WAS OCTOBER 1996. AT THE IT ASIA EXHIBITION IN New Delhi, Sanjeev Bikhchandani gazed at the 'www' on the stall front. What did it mean? He had spent the last few years of his life searching for trademarks for big pharmaceutical companies and on salary surveys—he had been struggling for a breakthrough. The 'www' piqued his curiosity. He asked the stall owner what it meant and was told that it stood for 'world wide web'. This was the moment Sanjeev learnt about the internet. The promoter pointed out the Yahoo! website to Sanjeev and showed him how to search, browse, and check other sites. Intrigued, Sanjeev wanted to know how many users of the internet were there in India. The answer was, 'Fourteen thousand.''Wow! That's a lot of people,' Sanjeev told himself. He called his brother, a professor at the UCLA business school and expressed his desire to start a website and needed his brother to hire a server. In return for the server payment, Sanjeev offered his brother 5 per cent in the website and called it Info Edge. Info Edge eventually became a publicly listed company with a market capitalisation of ₹15,000 crore (about $2.3 billion). So, at $25 (₹1,000 back then) a month, his brother definitely got a good deal for the server.

SHEER DUMB LUCK!

I believe that dumb luck plays a huge role in a company's success. I always ask an entrepreneur whether luck and chance have played a role in their success. A chosen few disagree, but I genuinely believe that an entrepreneur's capacity for risk-taking can paradoxically lead to success.

That said, most of us have had chance encounters. Those who become successful in their chosen businesses are the ones who manage to keep an eye out for opportunities, believe in them when they show up and seize the moment. They intuitively understand where their control ends and the power of the universe takes over.

After a few years down the unexplored path, Info Edge began to take the shape of a business that could turn profitable for Sanjeev. In 1997, he launched the Indian job portal, Naukri. com as a subsidiary of Info Edge. By 1998, having reached extraordinary heights in the United States, the dot-com frenzy arrived at the Indian shores. Sanjeev says that his first round of dumb luck started around the year 1999 when he received calls from various investors inquiring about investing in his business. Sanjeev says, 'I was completely baffled. I had no clue about the dot-com bubble, valuation or venture capital. We made approximately ₹36 lakh in revenue that year. Things were moving fine and I had never thought of raising external capital. Still, I went for a couple of meetings and said, "Boss, I don't want to raise money." I refused!'

Sanjeev knew about building a business the traditional way—pay as you go by earning revenue and managing every dime as if it were a dollar. But having seen three cycles of investment frenzy in two decades—the first one in 1999, the next one in 2008 and then in 2014—as an internet entrepreneur and angel investor, I can tell you that it's not easy to hold back. Half the time, you wonder, 'What is it that others have realised but I haven't?'

A few months later, Sanjeev heard about a company called JobsAhead.com that was being launched as a competitor. JobsAhead.com's advertising budget for the launch itself was ₹75 lakh— twice the size of Info Edge's annual turnover.

Sanjeev and his team did a quick U-turn and raised $1.7 million (approx. ₹7 crore then) from ICICI ventures in late 2000. 'But by March 2001, the dot-com meltdown had begun. No one officially acknowledged it till September–October. Everyone kept saying that it's a technical correction. We received the funding on 8 April and put it in a fixed deposit. We had been in the business for three years and knew how tough it was to survive in the internet world, so when the market crashed, we knew that it was a real crash. We knew that six months before it happened, I told ICICI that this is a real crash and that the business should be built slowly. If we had raised the money six to eight months earlier, we would have spent it foolishly. Instead, we put the money safely in a fixed deposit just as the bubble burst. The timing was sheer dumb luck.'

When JobsAhead.com was launched, it created quite a buzz. It had better user experience and was hippier than Naukri.com. For some time, JobsAhead.com gave tough competition to Naukri.com. By 2001, it had raised ₹33 crore of funding in three rounds, their last round being valued at ₹11 crore. It continued to grow aggressively using sales and marketing techniques. Investors and internet companies had not even begun to recover from the 1999 burst when 9/11 happened. Similar to other sectors, the Indian jobs market also came under further pressure. While JobsAhead.com was expanding in a hurry, Sanjeev was building his business slowly and profitably.

Sanjeev says, 'The first thing we did was hire four sales guys in Delhi and asked them to go out, meet prospective clients and make sales. And we discovered that by employing a decent sales guy who would sell subscriptions within three months, we would make a profit of ₹50,000 per month. It's a fully loaded cost including his salary plus commission, conveyance, mobile phone expenses, depreciation on PC or laptop, office rent, air-conditioning, furniture etc. which came to about ₹22,000 then. We were still making ₹28,000 per sales guy. This way we had found our repeatable profitable unit—keep on adding more and more sales guys.

We had brand traction, we had the right strategy, and we had the most jobs. We had insider knowledge and learning curves that helped us. When 9/11 hit, JobsAhead.com realised that their last round of ₹11 crore funding would need to last a very long time, so they started laying off employees. And a lot of these well-trained people ended up at Naukri.com, further fuelling our machine. We made two years of losses and then we broke even and made a one-crore profit.'

Another Stroke of Dumb Luck?

I have been closely involved in two Mergers and Acquisitions (M&A) deals in my life. They are not easy to execute. The first one happened when I sold Network Play (a digital advertising network) to Gruner + Jahr (Bertelsmann & Co). It was the first acquisition deal of my life. The co-founder was an assertive leader who stayed back as the CEO to take the company forward. Afterwards, I sold Webchutney to Dentsu Aegis Network in 2013. The Network Play acquisition had turned into a disaster by then. The co-founder and CEO had quit and Bertelsmann was planning to resell the company and exit India. The managers of acquiring firms often overestimate their ability to assess the prospects of the target firms. When a merger goes sour, the executives explain their failure by saying that they didn't focus well on the human capital or that it was difficult to merge the cultures of the firms. What they mean is that they didn't combine human capital of both the companies as well as they combined the financial and organisational assets.

They are unable to manage them properly because they don't anticipate the disruptions to the human capital accurately. The underlying cause is that the leaders understand the art but not the science of merging the human capital. Like many aspects of conducting business, a successful M&A requires one to be equally creative and scientific.

Something identical happened to JobsAhead.com, Naukri.com's competitors. In May 2004, Monster.com, a US based employment website with global listings bought JobsAhead.com. This was a crucial moment for Naukri.com and yet another case of sheer dumb luck for Sanjeev. After five uncertain years between the 1999 meltdown and 2004, the acquisition of JobsAhead.com by a listed American company for over $10 million (approx. ₹40 crore then) was a hallelujah moment for the cash strapped start-up industry. For early investors, this restored their faith in the Indian start-up ecosystem.

But Sanjeev was worried about this acquisition. He says, 'We thought if Monster.com put together another 10 million dollars for JobsAhead.com, we would be toast! But a typical American company taking over an emerging small company usually has different plans. They believe that their brand has to be the mother brand. Therefore, Monster.com merged both the sales teams and they gave better sales territories to their employees. The JobsAhead.com sales team was actually a better team, but was left out in the cold because its territories had merged with Monster.com. Monster.com said that they wanted to keep both the brands alive for two years but they didn't invest any money in JobsAhead.com.' The chaos that ensued after the JobsAhead.com acquisition and reigned over both merging companies gave Info Edge two years to improve its game.

'We were still profitable during the Monster.com–JobsAhead.com acquisition and now, we were ready for an Initial Public Offering (IPO),' says Sanjeev. By 2006, Info Edge had grown from being just a ₹3.63 crore turnover company in its earlier years to an ₹84.05 crore company. In November 2006, the IPO for Info Edge recorded a listing gain of 94.93 per cent as it hit an intraday high of ₹623.8 on its debut. The issue price of the IPO was fixed at ₹320. Subsequently, it stabilised at ₹593.2 with a gain of 85.3 per cent over the issue price. Info Edge was now worth over ₹1,000 crore.

As the Monster.com–JobsAhead.com merger had gone wrong, Naukri.com was keeping a steady profit, which ultimately led to its winning this marathon. Info Edge ran a steady course instead of sprinting like its competitors. It was conducting business to remain sustainable in the long haul. This wise decision-making was a more significant factor in its success than its competitors' failings.

Battling Competition

Anyone even remotely interested in the Indian start-up ecosystem monitored Housing.com's spectacular rise and an even bigger flameout. I also followed Housing.com very closely till its end because my friends Deap Ubhi and Haresh Chawla (Housing.com's mentor and former group CEO of Network18) were its early investors. In its extraordinary journey, Housing.com raised several million dollars in multiple rounds, and I regretted not having put in a cheque early on along with Haresh and Deap.

In terms of pure PR and overall visibility, the co-founder and CEO of Housing.com, Rahul Yadav was dominating the classifieds segments of giants like Info Edge and The Times

Group after he raised an audacious $90 million from SoftBank, at the end of 2014. But he is also a character. He took potshots at the Zomato founder Deepinder Goyal on Twitter, wrote an immature email to Shailendra Singh of Sequoia threatening them with dire consequences for interviewing Housing.com's employees, resigned from his firm with a nasty email to the board and then went back to work as if nothing had happened. Manu Balachandran rightly called him the 'enfant terrible'[1] of the Indian start-up ecosystem.

There is an interesting story behind the conception of Info Edge's 99Acres which became a competitor of Housing.com. Sharad Malik, an NRI, and one of Info Edge's shareholders and advisors visited India every year on vacation. During one such visit, he shared his nightmarish experience of trying to sell a piece of property at Kashmiri Gate, New Delhi with Sanjeev and his team. According to Malik, one could never know the right market price of a property and had to depend on hearsay and real estate agents. It was Malik who suggested that they launch a real estate website that would cater to consumers directly. It was a largely untapped market in India. Info Edge's team studied the market and launched 99Acres.com in 2005, right after acquiring the matrimonial website Jeevansathi.com.

Sanjeev says, 'We knew that we had the better product. But there was a myth that Housing.com is better. There was an internet craze, and bankers found the perfect candidate in Rahul Yadav of Housing.com, who was the new player in the game. People believed it was a better product. The truth

---

[1] Balachandran, Manu, 'Rahul Yadav: The bad boy of Indian start-ups is finally acting like an adult', Quartz India, 17 May 2016. https://qz.com/india/684041/rahul-yadav-the-bad-boy-of-indian-startups-is-finally-acting-like-an-adult/

is that Housing.com was a better-looking product. It was art for art's sake.'

When Housing.com was launched, it had a map based interface rather than the standard text-based interface. Everyone hailed it as an innovation in user interface design. Sanjeev differed from day one, 'When you are buying a house, you don't look for the house on a map because you are not arriving here from Mars, and wondering, "Where do I buy a house?" You are driving by that place a hundred times in a year, thinking to yourself, "This colony looks reasonable. Maybe I should look for a house here." You are familiar with that area. You won't buy a house without being familiar with the region. It's not an impulsive purchase. You look at the options offered by the broker catering to your budget. People prefer text-based listings instead of a map-based interface. When we launched our own map-based interface, we discovered that only 12 per cent of traffic went there. As many as 88 per cent of our customers preferred text-based listings. So the better product is what the customer wants rather than what appeals to your aesthetic sensibilities.

'Other young competitors, like Commonfloor.com were managing things like Housing.com. When you invest a lot of money in a company run by a group of young entrepreneurs, they will build a great engineering product. But running a sales team is quite different. At Info Edge, we are a strong sales force consisting of 600 employees. We were churning out 70–80 crore of revenue around 2014–15, so our growth was being funded not by the investors' money but through our customers. I believe that the customers' money is a hundred times better than investor funding. If a customer uses your website, then it means that you have a good product. The investors' money will undoubtedly follow. But having the investor's money does not ensure that customers will follow. You may not have a good value proposition. If there is a *tezi* (speed) in the market, then more money will flow in. But market tezi comes and goes. Beyond a point, the investors might feel that there is no cash coming into the company. That's what happened to many other ventures. We don't know how much revenue is being generated by Commonfloor. What we do know is that we did a business of ₹120 crore at 99Acres. We did lose money, but we lost very little as compared to companies that were positioned at a revenue of ₹5 crore.'

Sanjeev puts it correctly. The core of any business is the value of its proposition and its ability to sell itself to its targeted market. Does it have what it takes for a customer to loosen his purse strings? Does the business have the viability to get a customer to pay up by reaching out to him with service and a sales pitch and then living up to the promise? Several real estate websites failed because they couldn't deliver on these fronts. They pumped in the money without ensuring a profitability model for generating revenue, which is a risky strategy, to say the least.

When Rahul Yadav raised the money for Housing.com from SoftBank, he called Haresh Chawla, one of its first angel investors and told him that SoftBank had assured him that investors don't worry about the revenue for ten years. This meant that 99Acres's competition had access to infinite capital, while 99Acres's business was completely revenue driven.

'I got five phone calls from Housing.com investors saying, "You've got the business" (because 99Acres was already generating ₹70–80 crore of revenue). They said, "We've got the product right with Housing.com. Why don't we merge?" And my answer was, "If you've got the product, how come we have the business?" I will tell you something interesting. You merge with the complementary product, not the substitute.'

Could the fact that all their competition self-combusted be attributed to dumb luck as well? According to Sanjeev, 'It wasn't dumb luck. That was our faith that we knew we were doing the right thing.'

Despite their conviction in the product and the belief that their competition would eventually die out, Info Edge raised ₹700 crore from QIP (Qualified Institutional Placement) as a war chest. Sanjeev adds, 'We raised QIP to essentially keep our watches ready and provide hints to the market that we are serious about the business. It wasn't like we were going to roll over and die.'

Everybody knows how it all played out eventually. Within six months of raising $90 million from SoftBank and Falcon Edge, Rahul Yadav was unceremoniously sacked from the company he founded in 2015. Within a year of that, the real estate website PropTiger (backed by News Corp) merged with Housing.com in an all-stock deal, bringing an end to the contentious saga. As a part of this deal, the combined entity raised $50 million from REA Group (an online real estate advertising company owned by News Corp) and another $5 million from SoftBank. Commonfloor had a similar fate. They were acquired by classifieds start-up, Quikr. Commonfloor founders Sumit Jain, Vikas Malpani and Lalit Mangal, having worked for ten years after founding the company, quit a year after the Quikr acquisition. On the other hand, 99Acres and MagicBricks (The Times Group) continue to lead the segment in real estate classifieds. Owing to Sanjeev's typical style of building a business, 99Acres is moving towards profitability, one rupee at a time.

A Public Apology

Despite its stellar success, 99Acres has had its share of controversies. One incident that could have potentially harmed its upward mobility was the breaking news on 8 November 2013. Vishal D'Souza, a property broker, had posted a classified ad for his client on 99Acres.com. The advertisement was for a 2 BHK flat with an asking price of ₹3 crore. Its description included 'with car parking' and 'no Muslims'. The ad caught the eye of social activist and lawyer, Shehzad Poonawalla who filed a complaint with the National Commission of Minorities against both the broker and 99Acres.

Sanjeev's team, however, saved the day by swift action and the issuance of an unconditional apology. They knew that their platform had been misused and they ensured that the ad was taken off immediately. 'It's important that whatever you do or whatever your opponents are doing to you, you pass the test of being a reasonable man. It was very sneaky for the broker to put up such a listing on 99Acres by pointing out a community and saying that we would not sell the house to a Muslim. It was against our core values. So I was there to clarify that we can't possibly check everything that goes up on our website, but it was possible for us to take corrective action, which we did. We discovered this on a Sunday, the day after Diwali, it was on a Facebook post. Within six hours, we had forwarded a response, produced a statement and removed the ad. Then I sent personal messages to everyone on Facebook. I put up the post and attached a public press note to it. People commented on it. I sent a private message to everyone who got involved with that post. I had sent 600 private messages myself, that too on a Sunday, saying, "Look, we are a responsible company. We are well-governed. This is something we don't approve of. It's just a mistake. It's not possible for us to verify everything, but we apologise for it. We are taking corrective action."'

Despite their best efforts, the issue did go viral. 'It was all over the news. There were discussions. Some people were really against us. I contacted several politicians and spoke on TV myself. I even went and met the head of the Minorities Commission.'

Eventually, the National Commission for Minorities accepted Info Edge's apology. Poonawala and Sanjeev met NCM Chairperson Wajahat Habibullah to discuss the issue. The Commission accepted their offer to develop policy recommendations against discrimination of minorities, particularly Muslims, on religious or ethnic grounds in the real estate sector. And finally, 99Acres committed to spreading awareness among real estate broker community to warn them against indulging in such discriminatory practices and introduced software to check if a listing is carrying the name of any religion, caste or community among other measures.

Funding frenzy

The 2013–15 funding frenzy in the Indian start-up ecosystem was like nothing ever seen before. It was estimated that over 50 start-up incubators and accelerators had launched in the first 18 months and billions of dollars were being readied to be pumped into some of the promising companies. That frenzy soon became a perfect shit-storm when most investors started getting worried about the fire they had fuelled and worried whether this entire mess was sustainable. According to Sanjeev, 'When money comes in too easily, there are all sorts of *pangas* (issues). Too much money came in too easily to certain entrepreneurs, so they were not compelled to build good business models. And when you are not compelled, your business does not prosper in the long run. Soon enough, the investor's money stops coming.'

Sanjeev has been witness to three such financial bubbles, but most of the crowd started to believe that this one is real for sure. He says, 'Nothing is real apart from profit. Valuation based on any other metric is unreal. In a year where financing is easy, you can probably use valuation for a company temporarily to raise money to migrate to profit. But you don't migrate to profit with just that.' Not everyone believed it to be the case. There were investors that Sanjeev approached who did not believe in his business model. Sanjeev says, 'I went and pitched to a VC before we took money from ICICI ventures overseas. He asked me why he should invest in my company. I told him that we were a profit-making set-up. We were not only breaking even but also making a profit. So he said, "If you're making a profit, then you have a vision problem. Nobody makes a profit in the new economy."'

Things are good for Sanjeev today. He is a billionaire and the owner of a consistent darling of the stock-market. All this makes it easy to forget the fact that he has been an entrepreneur for more than two decades with the first few ideas being complete non-starters. I remember a friend who had joined Info Edge almost a year before the IPO around 2004 to roll-out their advertising and education business. On his first day at the office, he saw Sanjeev driving into the office complex in a Maruti Alto. Baffled at this, my friend called me and asked, 'Do you think he is doing this to screw with everyone's head and set an example?' That's Sanjeev Bikhchandani for you. The one thing that stands out is his belief in showing fiscal prudence every day and spending every dime like a dollar. I once had a meeting with Hitesh Oberoi, co-founder and then

Managing Director of Info Edge at their office. I still can't get over the small size of that room. They were already a listed company and remained frugal. Sanjeev continues to be one of the most accessible mentors in the start-up ecosystem and yes, thankfully, he drives a Toyota Camry now.

KUNAL SHAH

Co-Founder, FreeCharge

'I am sure there are quite a few moments when I was quite paranoid about screwing it up. The fact that everything can go back to zero has stayed with me from day one. That's why I came up with the statement that 'horrible decisions happen when you are hungry, horny, or out of the runway.'

BEFORE STARTING FREECHARGE, FOR A DECADE SINCE 2000, Kunal taught computer science to school children and peddled laptops on eBay. Later, he joined Sandeep Tandon's BPO company, as a graphic designer. There, he went on to become the company's CEO and scaled its employee strength to 2,000 people. Looking for his next fix, he came up with the concept of marrying mobile talk time with coupons in the year 2010. Sandeep Tandon provided the initial angel investment and brought some key relationships from the retail industry to the table. Together, Kunal and Sandeep launched a simple website with a transparent value proposition—get free coupons equivalent to the amount spent on mobile recharge. Six years after launching FreeCharge, Kunal sold the company to Snapdeal for $400 million, in 2015. It was the largest buyout at that time in the Indian digital ecosystem.

When I first heard of FreeCharge around 2012, I thought that it was a lowbrow idea. It didn't make sense that pre-paid subscribers would drool over coupons! All of that changed when I bumped into Kunal while catching up with another friend Deap Ubhi, who had joined FreeCharge as the COO, in 2013. While talking about their company over a few drinks, I realised that they were operating at a staggering scale. I had never felt so foolish and presumptuous before. Anyway, we became friends and I constantly seek Kunal's advice on investing in start-ups and other spaces.

Raising Money

Within four months of launching FreeCharge in 2010, Kunal was being chased by some early stage VCs (Venture Capitalists).

Sequoia Capital was particularly persistent. Kunal kept avoiding all of them because he thought he wasn't ready and in all likelihood, would make a fool of himself. Shailendra Singh, a partner at Sequoia Capital, messaged Kunal on LinkedIn. Kunal didn't respond. Finally, the associates at Sequoia who were cold-calling him repeatedly prevailed and convinced Kunal and Sandeep to come to their office in Bengaluru for an exploratory chat. In those days, couponing was hot, thanks to the success of Groupon.com. Shailendra saw FreeCharge as a clever concept to sell a lot of coupons.

Kunal reminisces about their first meeting and says, 'We explained the business model to Shailendra and he asked us how many transactions we were doing at that time. I said, "14,000". He asked, "In a month?" I replied, "No. In a day. They are all credit and debit card customers." Shailendra jumped and said, "What?"' Kunal adds, 'His surprise confused me, so I had to recheck my data because he would have jumped with happiness even if he'd had that as a monthly figure.'

Shailendra's next question was about the CAC. For the uninitiated, CAC refers to Customer Acquisition Costs. Kunal had no clue what CAC meant. He says, 'I was trying to act smart but gave all the wrong answers, and then Shailendra understood that I had no clue what I was talking about.' Shailendra interrupted me and said, 'I am talking about marketing expenses.' I responded, 'What do you mean by that? I haven't spent on marketing yet so no CAC for now.'

Immediately post the Snapdeal acquisition in 2015, Shailendra Singh wrote about FreeCharge in a blog post, 'We found many of the soft ingredients we usually look for. An improbable set of founders with deep conviction in their approach. A product that needed zero marketing to get tens of thousands of transacting customers. An incredibly grounded, creative and open-minded founding team, willing to learn about building a mobile and internet business. I knew from my Justdial experience that customer acquisition engines could become very valuable. There were many questions to be answered but, by the end of that meeting, I told them that we would love to invest.'[2] Sequoia was ready to invest $3.5 million in Kunal's four-month-old start-up, FreeCharge, which had not raised a penny from angel investors or seed funds till then.

BUILDING TRUST WITH SEQUOIA

I have always had a great relationship with all my investors, which is why I am always surprised at the horror stories that I hear from entrepreneurs and investors about the trust deficit and toxic relationships that they face. Investors and business owners often compare their relationships to marriage. I believe that their relationship is somewhere between a friendship, a marriage and a business relationship. You have to like each other, you have to live with each other and you have to be driven towards the same goal together. Karan Mehandru (General Partner, Trinity Ventures) was right when he wrote, 'The organising principles for investor selection extend well beyond compatibility. Wartime trust is required; beer is optional.'[3]

While there is always pressure on entrepreneurs to raise capital by hook or by crook, I always advise first time

---

[2] Singh, Shailendra. 'How FreeCharge Found Its Mojo', *Live Mint*, 22 April 2015, https://www.livemint.com/Companies/r2ZIV9GJ 5PNTu97ZC87TnI/How-Freecharge-found-its-mojo-and-Snapdeal. html

[3] Mehandru, Karan. 'Investors Are Your War Partners, Not Your Beer Buddies', *Entrepreneur India*, 7 December 2017 https://www. entrepreneur.com/article/305584

entrepreneurs to conduct their due diligence before signing up an investor. Investors always ask plenty of questions from any entrepreneur whose venture they plan to invest in. Likewise, entrepreneurs also need to ask investors about their corporate structure, other investments, whether they've ever had to change CEOs, and if so, how they went about that process, etc.

There was mutual trust and respect between Kunal and Sequoia, which also led to both parties caring about and looking out for each other's interests. Kunal shares, 'Our conversations with Sequoia on negotiations were funny. On these calls, the negotiation bit would end in five minutes, and then the greetings would take thirty-three. The reason is that in the bigger scheme of things when you have set out on a very ambitious plan, small things like petty negotiations, a clause here and there, that have no large value over the long term, don't matter. Even during the sale to Snapdeal, we saw Sequoia give up on their liquidation preference out of their own will. Sequoia negotiated my employment contract after the deal. They had no reason to do that. On my part, there was an unclaimed ESOP (Employee Stock Ownership Plan) pool that I could have kept with the founders (Sandeep and me) easily. But we decided to distribute it within the team.' Kunal's decision to do so surprised Sequoia. But Kunal's ideas were clear. He knew that he would have personally gained ₹15-20 crore, making him wealthier. But he cared about doing the right thing. That's why Sequoia and FreeCharge always had a relationship of deep mutual respect.

GIVING UP THE ROLE OF CEO

The debate about who makes a better CEO—a founder-CEO or a hired professional has always intrigued me. I am biased towards founders and believe that they make better CEOs, probably because I am one myself.

Ben Horowitz of Andreessen Horowitz articulated a well-thought-out philosophy on why he and his fund prefer to back founder-CEOs and keep them in charge as the company grows. His essay, 'Why We Prefer Founding CEOs' has plenty of arguments supporting the idea but is fundamentally based around the advantage that founder-CEOs have over professional CEOs. Comprehensive knowledge, moral authority and total commitment to the long term are some of the most important factors.[4] It's hard to argue against the idea. Think of people like Jeff Bezos, Larry Ellison, Mark Zuckerberg, Michael Dell, Marc Benioff or the late Steve Jobs. Close to home, some of the biggest internet companies in India are still being led by their founders, namely Deep Kalra of Make My Trip, Sanjeev Bikhchandani and Hitesh Oberoi for Info Edge (Naukri.com), Vijay Shekhar Sharma of Paytm, Bhavesh Agarwal of Ola Cabs—the list is endless. Holly Liu (co-founder of Kabam, an interactive entertainment company) said, 'It is only a founder who has been there when the company was nothing. Therefore to go to a place where the company is at its nadir is something that is not new only for the founders. This is where the founding CEO gains her heart and strength to drive the company to its vision from whatever standpoint. They can see past circumstances and into their ultimate vision for the company.'[5]

---

[4] Horowitz, Ben. 'Why We Prefer Founding CEOs', *Andressen Horowitz*. https://a16z.com/2010/04/28/why-we-prefer-founding-ceos/

[5] Liu, Holly, 'Founder CEO vs. Professional CEO: What if Jerry Yang Stayed?' Medium.com, 1 August 2016. https://medium.com/how-to-raise-a-unicorn/founder-ceo-vs-professional-ceo-847c9a3e8c1b

The counter-arguments are equally strong. Many of the greatest internet stories have come from a combination of a founder as well as a professional CEO running the ship as partners. For instance, Timothy Andrew Koogle, who was previously with a lesser known company called Litton's, took Jerry Yang and Dave Filo's Yahoo! to its full glory. Meg Whitman worked with Pierre Omidyar on eBay to turn it into an e-commerce giant. Eric Schmidt helped Sergey Brin and Larry Page in building Google into a remarkable cash-generating engine from the search business that unlocked a series of bets that the founders continued to make. More recently, Joe Kennedy and Tim Westergren of Pandora, Dick Costolo at Twitter and Jeff Weiner at LinkedIn who joined as professional CEOs, helped to unlock true value in those start-ups. There are people in the industry who believe the opposite—that often, founders make terrible CEOs. They have their reasons to think so. Start-ups never have a linear growth curve, their progress is mostly bumpy, and sometimes founders are unable to segregate the business realities from their personal relationships with the teams. Founding CEOs rarely come in with professional experience but they build a specific set of skills that lead to intuition about their own business.

A founder is there to inspire creative thinking and turn a vision into reality. They listen to their teams and push others to be the best that they can be. It isn't that professional CEOs don't do the same things. It's that they do them within a managerial framework. The goals are more about ensuring that operations run smoothly, deadlines are met, and the business is running as it should. Starting a company from scratch is hard and founders often have to have a band of loyal followers in the beginning. The problem is that once a company scales-up, it usually needs very different talent.

Being both a good founder and a good CEO takes an incredible amount of dedication and drive. Not every successful entrepreneur naturally excels at shifting into an operational mindset. In a rather unusual and surprising move, FreeCharge announced that former redBus COO and Google veteran, Alok Goel was joining the company as CEO, taking over from Kunal in September 2013. It was unusual because FreeCharge was still in its nascent stage and it's not common for a corporate promoter to relinquish their CEO designation that early in a company's life cycle.

Kunal explains, 'Back then, it was an easy decision. We were going through a bit of a rough phase and I was sure that we needed to sort out a couple of things to start the next round of funding. We needed a stronger management team, we needed the product to evolve, and we needed growth. I wanted to focus on the company's growth completely. So, Alok's appointment as the CEO was the perfect decision from that point of view because it helped us to raise funds. FreeCharge didn't have a revenue model when Alok joined it. He was coming from Google who had gone through a similar challenge in its early days so I was looking forward to his perspectives on how we could do the same with FreeCharge using his experience at Google.'

Surprisingly, it wasn't Sequoia but Kunal who wanted Alok Goel as the CEO. Sequoia would have preferred retaining Kunal in that position and given Alok the title of COO but Kunal wouldn't have it that way. He says, 'When we brought in Alok and introduced him to the board, they suggested that we take him in as a COO. I told them that to get him as the CEO and if it doesn't work out, then I am still around. I have not disappeared since then.' Alok eventually left the company post its acquisition by Snapdeal. Kunal was reinstated the CEO

before he stepped down again to make way for Govind Rajan
of Airtel.

CREATING CULTURE

Hiring for a start-up is difficult at any stage of the company
because in the case of start-ups, it's a candidate-based market.
Every technology-based company is looking to hire developers,
sales and marketing staff. Any potential candidate is likely to
be considering multiple offers at any given time, which makes
it tough to find the right fit for any company, not just start-ups.

Deap Ubhi, who cofounded Burrp in 2006 was not
successful in raising the kind of money that he had wished
back then. But he had managed to build an incredible team
with some of the best talent available to him at that time.
Burrp was known for its idea, execution and even more so the
stellar team it had put together on a shoestring budget. After
few years of struggling with Burrp, Deap joined FreeCharge
as COO in 2012. He built FreeCharge's Bengaluru team
with a similar culture and vibe for which he had been much
appreciated during the establishing process of Burrp. Kunal
credits Deap for creating a culture that laid the foundation for
a strong team in Bengaluru. Kunal recalls, 'I think I met him
through many of our common connections. He was flirting
with several business ideas at that time. He helped in setting
up the Bengaluru office for us. He was with us for almost a
year. He got the culture at the Bengaluru office fixed for us.'
Kunal felt that Mumbai was cursed since they couldn't find
the right talent in the city, no matter what they did. Hence,
they decided to move their company to Bengaluru Deap also
brought in some innovative methods for recruitment. Kunal
says, 'I remember that this was our first hiring idea when we

went to Bengaluru. We booked a whole show for a Batman movie and asked all the candidates that we wanted to hire, to come for the film. We conducted interviews during lunch and coffee breaks. We had to do something different to make ourselves look cool.'

THE *PEOPLE* MAKE A BUSINESS WHAT IT IS

Kunal's success has mostly depended on his ability to build trust because of an innovative thought process. Talent retention is tricky and stressful business. It takes many hours of work to find suitable candidates. Companies are keen to ensure that once the candidates take up their offers, they stick with them. But this is not always the case. Prospective employees agree to join and then don't show up, possibly because some other large firm offers them more money. Kunal and co. came up with a unique way of ensuring that his selected candidates took the offers. He says, 'It is a classic Indian problem that candidates take an offer but don't show up on the joining date.' He believed that this would delay the overall process. In 2013 and even till now, many big companies practise a standard policy of giving each prospective employees, a sum of two lakh rupees with the offer letter.

Kunal says, 'We would do all the hard work of interviewing, shortlisting, finalising and the candidates would take the job in the big company. So we improvised a small hack. We would give a MacBook with the offer letter—no strings attached. People didn't know how to react to a company entrusting them with a MacBook before the joining date. They continued this practice despite scepticism from HR. The candidates could just as easily have taken the MacBook and never returned. But Kunal's philosophy, though unique, is not so incomprehensible.

He elaborates, 'Isn't it a better idea to lose one lakh rupees on a MacBook than hire an unethical person? It is probably cheaper in the long run. But no one ever ran away with a MacBook, so our joining rate became 95 per cent.'

It made sense to Kunal to spend on things like the MacBook rather than a flashy office. Even when they had the money, their office was basic at best. He says, 'How many customers will transact because we have a cool office? In case of an advertising agency, you have your client coming over and so you must be able to show that you are cool. But my customers are not going to come to my office, so why should I spend on it? We would give the team meals, snacks and home drop offs –all the necessities. But a cool office would only be for my ego. It doesn't help the company or the customers.'

CREATING WEALTH FOR OTHERS

Wealth equations are created not by keeping wealth but by sharing it. According to Kunal, conventionally, businesspeople don't do a good job of it. He says, 'We distributed a lot of money, but never disclosed this information because it felt unfair. The team had earned it for themselves, so it was wrong to announce it. For example, Infosys made the peon rich. I felt that the spin on this story one-sided. Because it is everybody's work that has made everybody rich. We never wanted to take credit for it.'

While a more equitable distribution of profits seems like a contemporary and forward-thinking principle to run a start-up like Kunal did as it could inspire some of his team members to start something of their own, one does get curious about the facts. How many of these employees who got a share of this wealth, actually started up on their own?

The answer might surprise you. Kunal says, 'About five or six of them. Many went on to be CXOs (Chief Experience Officers) for their new company. What they realised is that you don't necessarily have to create a start-up. You can also sign up for a big role in a small-sized company. None of them went to a large organisation. That's a huge achievement. I don't think that everyone should necessarily begin a start-up. If you get to be part of the initial team in a start-up and have large ownership as well, that's quite something.'

PAYTM AND OTHER COMPETITION

Kunal quips, 'There were quite a few moments when I was paranoid about screwing it up. The fact that everything can go back to zero has stayed with me from day one. That's why I came up with the statement that "horrible decisions happen when you are hungry, horny or out of the runway".'That's almost original. Rewinding the clock to the pre-wallet era, FreeCharge pioneered this sector. But soon, Vijay Sharma launched the same idea with better execution—a user-friendly interface, a sleeker look and an easier process, and called it Paytm. This is obviously a bittersweet story for Kunal but it validated his original idea with a revenue model as the winner.

He clarifies, 'It certainly made me realise that I shouldn't doubt my ideas. Even though I was raising my money from Sequoia, there was a level of doubt. At a certain level, you always think that perhaps, "I am being an idiot here, or an idiot there, but I cannot be a bigger idiot than this person". The Paytm story made me feel that I should have a lot more confidence in myself. The only thing is that I know that I can generate an idea a day and nobody can beat me to that. Even today Paytm has re-launched coupons on its platform. This goes to show that our concept was a winner and has stood the test of time. I often joke with Vijay (founder and CEO of Paytm) that I am the Chief Innovation Officer of Paytm, but I never felt the rivalry. Why should I feel competitive with him? I should feel competitive with small shops that are killing my business? People are stupid enough to get into such ego battles. Many people like competing, but I don't. I like to win together because there is so much more to be had. And not just Paytm. There were at least nine clones of our model in 2014. We were proud of the fact that we were the only Indian company that was being copied by other Indian companies as only western companies used to be copied at that time. If I could do it all over again, I would do this with a lot more confidence and aggression instead of doubting my every move because I saw the same move being made by others with much more confidence. Vijay was already making a lot of money in the Value Added Services business, so he was truly self-assured when he began Paytm. Vijay unlocked the confidence faster than me. That is the only difference and I think, a big lesson for me.

I remember sitting with Vijay in his Noida office in 2011. Webchutney used to do a lot of work with One97 Communications, Paytm's parent company. One97 was one of the largest players in the VAS (Value Added Services) space. They were partnering with mobile operators around the country and the world, churning out massive profits, and getting ready for an IPO when their biggest competitor, OnMobile (a public company), had some governance issues and the stock-market punished the entire stock severely. Vijay was annoyed about deferring his IPO because it had the potential to change his fortune and give his investors a well-deserved multi-bagger exit for their initial investment. This was indeed a disappointing scenario for all the involved parties. When I met Vijay when he was getting ready to launch Paytm, a recharge service similar to FreeCharge. I asked him why he was taking that up. Vijay told me 'I am not getting into the couponing business. I am going to use that as a customer acquisition channel to launch my wallet.' Back then, a lot of people, including me, didn't understand the magnitude of his plans.

Financing Frenzy

In 2013–14, armed with the success of selling Webchutney and Network Play, I began to work on a start-up incubator, a playground for ideas by other entrepreneurs and me. None of the entrepreneurs in the team was the traditional IIT or IIM alumni and we struggled to raise capital for our ideas. While a couple of them managed to make it to their next milestone, I was still looking at a graveyard of ideas. It was a frustrating period since there was a fund-raising frenzy across the town in Powai where the famed IIT Mumbai campus is located. Young boys and girls were pouring out of the campus as dropouts, starting companies and raising money. I was pretty puzzled since a couple of my start-ups were built on great ideas, or so I thought.

I asked a dear friend who was an active angel investor about the goings-on. According to him, 'If your team isn't straight out of IIT Mumbai, and is over 25 years of age, you have no chance in hell.' I knew that it was sheer madness because practically speaking, execution and experience trump ideas. Kunal has a unique take on the frenzy that had gripped the start-up world at that time. He says, 'I think the biggest realisation was that these smart, young people are like great fast computers, but they have no software or algorithms in them because they have had no exposure. Therefore, we just assumed that bringing these smart kids to the table would work. I understood why it worked in the US when I was a part-time partner at Y Combinator in 2016. I learnt that young entrepreneurs in the US have more exposure in life than the ones who grew up in India. So let's say that there are two laptops. One laptop comes with a variety of software but the other one comes with a blank operating system. The issue is that a lot of people just assumed that both the laptops were the same. Because they had the same specification—a super high IQ.'

The highlight of Kunal's story for me is his spectacular relationship with his investors, especially Shailendra Singh of Sequoia Capital, and his honest admission of not being able to develop and unlock confidence in his ideas faster than Vijay Sharma of Paytm even though the idea was his, to begin with. Kunal, who claims to be a keen observer of human behaviour and psychology, in April 2018, announced the launch of Cred, a members-only app which rewards its members with exclusive rewards for paying their credit card bill via their app. It is only available to members who have a specific credit score. Its seed round was about $30 million led by his good old friends at Sequoia capital. Coincidently, while FreeCharge was a play around pre-paid users and rewards, Cred is about post-paid users and rewards. In April 2019, it was reported that Cred has been in talks to raise over $100 million at a valuation of $300 million. Startups whose founders have been previously successful with other ventures tend to find it easier to raise funds regardless of the business model as investors trust the founders' skills. Like Kunal, one such example is Mukesh Bansal and Ankit Nagori's cure.fit, which has repeatedly raised significant investments since the launch. Mukesh had co-founded Myntra which was acquired by Flipkart for around

$350 million in 2014. He met Ankit, the CBO of Flipkart there and the two started cure.fit in partnership. It is currently on a success run, just like Myntra was. Similarly, Kunal's ideas are now paying off because of his previous track record. This makes me hopeful that this time, Kunal's ideas and confidence will both be bigger and bolder than what they were when he launched FreeCharge.

MURUGAVEL JANAKIRAMAN

Founder and CEO, Matrimony.com Limited

'Shutting down my other lines of business in classifieds, in 2008, was a low moment for me. We spent the money without proper planning and didn't spend it wisely. Getting into too many verticals, not focussing on the core vertical, led to spending of the money that could have been saved. On the other hand, if it weren't for all these verticals, I wouldn't have raised the money at all because matrimony had always been profitable.'

MURUGA IS A QUINTESSENTIAL GOD-FEARING MIDDLE-class Tamil Brahmin who was the first person in his family to go to college. I met him right after his first round of institutional financing, in 2006, to pitch creative and search-engine marketing to him. He is humble, speaks softly and has a classic Tamil accent. Six of us from Webchutney had taken a flight to Chennai. I still remember the opening slides that said, 'We are the perfect audience for BharatMatrimony.com because our workforce consists of 42 employees—94 per cent unmarried and a divorced CEO. We understand the consumer mindset.' He and his rather conservative team, who were sitting all uptight, broke into laughter. We did win the business! When I met him again, nearly twelve years after that first meeting, he was preparing for his IPO.

The Beginnings

In 1997, Muruga was working in the US as a consultant when he discovered the internet. He says, 'I knew I wanted to do something on the internet. As I searched online for offerings for Indians, I saw content sites like Sify.com, Samachar.com, and Rediff.com. I thought of starting with something familiar to me, which was my Tamil community. I designed and coded a website called sysindia.com in just a few days in 1997. I threw in features like the Tamil daily calendar, festival reminders, tips, etc. One could register their email address on Sysindia and choose the festivals for which they wanted reminders. We would email them before the festival with details regarding what is auspicious etc. If one wanted to book tickets to India, they could put up a request on Sysindia. We would send the details to travel agencies to do the customer's bidding. There was also a Tamil greeting cards section and finally, a matrimonial service.'

For two and a half years, Muruga continued to work on Sysindia as a one-man army along with a day job. He worked on the website after work as a hobby until, one day, he put his own profile on the matrimonial service. The man who is now his father-in-law reached out to him and asked for his horoscope. They had a match! That's when it dawned upon him that users of his site, mostly bachelors, were using the matrimonial service more than anything else and that there was an opportunity to build an exclusive matrimony service. Murugu adds, 'I initially launched only Tamil and Telugu matrimony because I was born and brought up in Royapuram, Chennai, which has a sizeable Telugu community. BharatMatrimony.com was available as a domain and that became the parent name.'

In less than three years, from a horizontal, community portal, BharatMatrimony went into the deep matrimonial vertical. As of today, it boasts of over 300 websites under that banner. It was a coincidence, or perhaps it was the right alignment of stars that Muruga got laid off in 2000 during the massive global recession. He returned to India to start his own office in a modest 300 sq. ft. facility at T. Nagar, Chennai. He hired a gold medallist from the University of Madras as his first employee. And so, BharatMatrimony was in business. Muruga created a pricing strategy only when he eventually converted the website to a paid model. For Indian customers, the cost was ₹300 till they found a partner and for US customers, it was $10. Today, the business model is different because the registration is free, but you can establish communication with prospective partners only by becoming a paid member. Muruga adds, 'Yes, today that's a hook. To get the contact details of the prospective partner, you have to become a paid member. Then gradually, from ₹300 per year, we changed the cost to ₹300 for six months and then to ₹300 for three months. Now the cost is ₹4,700 for three months.'

Raising Capital

Not many are aware that in 2004, someone from the famed investor Tiger Global approached Muruga and gave him a term sheet. Muruga had a small but profitable team by then and he found the clauses in the term sheet discomforting. Much like Sanjeev Bikhchandani's initial reluctance to take outside capital, Muruga refused to sign the deal. He cherished his independence too much and the business was also growing organically. Muruga modelled his company on InterActiveCorp (IAC), an American media and internet company which owns over 150 brands across 100 countries. Muruga was closely following IAC which continued its growth through acquisition, adding assets including TripAdvisor, ServiceMagic and Ask Jeeves in 2004–05. In August 2005, the company bundled together its travel-related sites and spun them off as a new public company, Expedia Group. Muruga was fascinated by this and began to create his network of websites. Clickjobs.com and Indiaproperty.com were launched in 2005. Indialist.com (local classifieds modelled on Craigslist), Loanwala.com and Indiaautomobile.com were next in line. Somewhere during that period, Yahoo! and Shaadi.com announced an exclusive alliance to launch a host of wedding and allied services channel called India Matrimony on Yahoo India's website. India Matrimony was going to give a one-stop opportunity to find life partners to its 29 million registered users.

It was a massive win for Shaadi.com. This happened during the display network era. Google hadn't appeared on the horizon, yet, and all vertical websites relied on Yahoo! and Rediff.com for traffic. This partnership meant that BharatMatrimony was getting locked out of the Yahoo! gateway. Since the only other search engine of significant size was Rediff.com, Muruga went to meet Ajit Balakrishnan in Mumbai to propose a partnership in exchange for some equity. Would Rediff.com subsidise the traffic costs and go exclusive with BharatMatrimony? Would Rediff.com not accept ads from Jeevansathi and Shaadi.com? Muruga says, 'Ajit liked the idea but wanted a majority stake in exchange for providing exclusive tenancy to BharatMatrimony on its portal. I dismissed this counter proposal and went back to building my business on my own. Then, in 2005, things started changing. Companies that had been around for a while and had survived the dot-com crash were seeing a lot of interest from investors again. MakeMyTrip, the leading travel portal, had raised $10 million in 2005 from SAIF Partners; Info Edge (the parent company of Jeevansathi) was rumoured to be preparing for an IPO in 18 months. And our biggest competitor, Shaadi.com, announced an $8 million venture capital investment by WestBridge Capital Partners.'

Given the environment, Muruga knew that if he didn't raise capital for BharatMatrimony and his other websites now, then he was going to be left out. He recalls, 'It wasn't an easy run because many investors came back with similar feedback that matchmaking is a one-time opportunity for monetisation since it is not lifelong. You need to acquire new customers every day. I met more than ten investors around that time but couldn't raise money from any of them. We were generating revenue of four million dollars then and some of the investors made lowball offers of $10 million valuations.' Muruga refused to entertain any such conversations. He adds, 'I remember 1 January 2006 because my investor's banker told me over a phone call that we had run out of options to raise money. That is the message I got on the first day of a brand new year. I told him that we should continue to put in our best efforts and something will work out. Suddenly, out of nowhere, the investment bankers organised a meeting with Yahoo!. I told them that there was no pointing in meeting Yahoo!. I didn't want a strategic investor because I wanted to run the company. I was extremely reluctant to meet the Yahoo! executives but the bankers insisted.' Muruga finally gave in. He went for the meeting and managed to persuade Yahoo! to join them as a financial investor rather than a strategic investor. Strategic investment had been Yahoo!'s initial intention because they had no need to invest capital to make money at that time, but they agreed with Muruga's proposal.

This was Yahoo!'s first investment in India. A few months before this, Muruga had also met Cannan Partners (a global early-stage venture investor). Cannan had set up their first office in India but hadn't shown much interest in Muruga's company. Anupam Mittal, the founder of Shaadi.com, told me that Cannan had been negotiating with his company for a while to invest. Things didn't end well between the two parties and Anupam walked out of the deal. Right then, Cannan got the wind that Yahoo! was considering an investment in BharatMatrimony and jumped in to participate in the financing round with them. In August 2006, BharatMatrimony announced an $8.65 million financing from Yahoo! and Cannan Partners as maiden investments from both. Muruga adds, 'Cannan had freshly recruited Alok Mittal (co-founder, JobsAhead.com) who was going to represent Canaan Partners on the board. I was looking forward to learning from his experience and expertise, which would give us a definite competitive advantage to BharatMatrimony's Click Jobs. Meanwhile, Yahoo! dumped Shaadi.com as their exclusive partner and replaced them with BharatMatrimony. Armed with fresh capital, Muruga began executing his plans across all verticals quickly and opened up many more fronts.

BLOWING IT ALL UP ... ALMOST!

The investments filled Muruga with the new ambition of dominating many verticals. He wanted to showcase successful business models to provide an array of world-class services including matrimony, property, automobiles, jobs, listings and SMS services. This lead him to rebrand himself as Consim Info Private Limited. He says, 'The new corporate name had been designed to represent the group's various business verticals—BharatMatrimony.com, Clickjobs.com, Indiaproperty.com, Indialist.com, Loanwala.com and Indiaautomobile.com—under a common philosophy. As a group, we had consolidated the online internet space and believed that the mobile interface would add value to internet businesses.'

The company announced ₹57 crore advertising budget in 2007–08. The spending would be divided between Clickjobs.com (₹25 crore), BharatMatrimony.com (₹20 crore), Indiaproperty.com (₹10 crore) and Indiaautomobile.com (₹2 crore). Further, the company planned to launch a portal for motorcycles that was to tap into the new and used motorcycle market by tying up with 1,000 bike dealers in less than a year. Muruga recalls, 'We spent most of the money on marketing within that year. Almost ₹15 crore had been spent on TV marketing in one burst. So, we had a play in all these classifieds like jobs, matrimonial, real estate and vehicles, with competitors in each. It turned out that $8 million was too little for the entire portfolio to grow and succeed.'

This was his first real setback. Thankfully, for Muruga, right before they ran out of cash in early 2008, they managed to raise another massive round of $11.75 million. This time, Mayfield Fund led the round and there was participation from existing investors, Yahoo! and Canaan Partners. In a press release during that time, Muruga said, 'Receiving investments from global players like Mayfield Fund, Yahoo! and Canaan Partners is a recognition to our company. We plan to leverage this fund to expand our matrimony business in the international markets and to strengthen our classifieds' offerings. We believe that the global knowledge and experience of our investors will help us scale our business strategically.' Evidently, Muruga was still hurting from how he had depleted the first round of financing. Thus, temporarily, he had dodged the bullet. The spending continued, but now, they were cautious.

CUTTING COSTS

The global environment was beginning to feel the headwinds of the financial market stresses, which became apparent in 2007. This resulted in sizeable losses across the financial system, the bankruptcy of over 100 mortgage lenders and the emergency sale of the investment bank, Bear Stearns, in March 2008, to depository bank, JPMorgan Chase. Some writers began calling the events in the financial markets, during this period, the 'Subprime Mortgage Crisis' or the 'Mortgage crisis'. Like many others, I also remember 2008 as the year of the sub-prime crisis. It killed so many start-ups and their ambitions. Webchutney and Network Play, the companies I helped build, nearly went under. There was a famous presentation that went viral immediately after the sub-prime crisis began. It was one which Sequoia Capital gave to its portfolio company CEOs. It was a long presentation with a clear message 'Get Real or Go Home.'

Muruga adds, 'The board members weighed in and asked me to keep a hawk's eye on expenses in the organisation. Also, they told me to cut down costs. We had to part with some of our associates and close some of our initiatives. Predictably, several issues cropped up in doing so. There were problems and rumours too. Before that, I had only focussed on the technology and product instead of other aspects of the business, so it was a challenging experience for me.' Finally, Muruga and the board decided that property and matrimony were businesses worth retaining. This was the time when his businesses went through death by a thousand cuts.

He recalls, 'This was a low moment for me. We spent the money unwisely, without proper planning. We got into too many verticals instead of focussing on the core vertical, which led to expenditures that could have been avoided. On the other hand, if it wasn't for all these verticals, I wouldn't have raised any money because matrimony had always been profitable.'

For a whole year in 2008, Muruga desperately tried to manage uncertain businesses like Click Jobs. His first instinct was to save it by getting hold of a strategic partner for Click Jobs. Uday Zokarkar, CBO of Click Jobs quit the same year and there was a lull for the next four-five months. Then in May 2009, Muruga tried to change the business model by incentivising job seekers by letting them upload their CV and charging them only for accessing a user's contact details. Companies would be charged only for contacting prospective employees and not for posting jobs. Click Jobs called this the 'Pay for Contact' model. The existing business model involved offering subscription packages to employers which would give them access to resume database. Muruga claims that he filed a global patent for this business model. At the same time, he continued to seek external capital to take Click Jobs to the next level.

Recovery and IPO

In Dec 2009, the company announced it had hived off four portals into a subsidiary called Perspi Interactive and kept only two of its top performing sites—BharatMatrimony.com and IndiaProperty.com under the parent company, Consim. Perspi would have ClickJobs.com, IndiaList.com, IndiaAutomobile.com and Loanwala.com.

An IPO was the way forward for the company. Muruga told Media Nama, 'Matrimony and property are high growth verticals for us and are profitable, while the others are emerging and require a different approach. You want to show profit and growth when you go to an IPO.' Was it a case of amputating a bleeding limb to keep the company alive? Muruga preferred a different analogy in a quote given to Media Nama, 'I have many sons. Some of them are growing and some have grown. They all need to be treated differently. I have to dedicate resources available to me and take care of their needs. We don't want some entities to suffer at the expense of others.' Muruga continued to spend on the bleeding companies for some time from his personal income, which of course, was not sustainable in the long run. He was reluctant, but he had to let go of those initiatives eventually.

Having unburdened himself of the weaklings, Muruga managed to free up bandwidth to focus on the profitable ventures with a promise that he was raring to start again. This proved to be the turning point that led him to launch more verticals—Assisted Matrimony and Elite Matrimony. They also established a strong leadership. He adds, 'That was strong advice from the board, which helped to focus better. I became more of an entrepreneur and a full-fledged CEO.'

In an interview to The Hindu BusinessLine in 2011, Muruga said, 'The first lesson I learnt is when you want to expand the services that you are offering to customers, it is important to stick to the core category. Though we were doing reasonably well in other portals, looking back, I think focussing on matrimony as a core area would have helped us scale faster. That is what we are doing now. We are aggressively expanding in this core area and already succeeding.' By the end of that year, Yahoo! had exited Consim by selling its 12 per cent stake to Bessemer Venture Partners, Mayfield Fund and Canaan Partners for ₹100 crore. The deal valued Consim at ₹900 crore. Bessemer Venture Partners acquired shares for ₹50 crore, Mayfield for ₹36 crore and Canaan for ₹14 crore. Interestingly, the deal came at a time when Yahoo! was itself struggling and there was speculation about it being taken over.

By 2012, it was clear to Muruga and his board that for them to be focussed and execute what they had to, they would have to make another choice between the matrimony business and the property one. But this was a more natural choice since BharatMatrimony was the number one website in its sector. By April 2012, they started the demerger process (which took a year to conclude). It ended up creating an independent management team which would provide a dedicated focus to their property venture.

Following the demerger, Indiaproperty.com raised $7 million (₹38 crore in 2012) in Series-A funding from Canaan and Mayfield with Ganesh Vasudevan as the new CEO in-charge. Finally, in the same year, Muruga got a significant burden off his back by selling Click Jobs to a completely unknown realtor from Delhi, Sanjeet Kumar Singh. The transaction size wasn't disclosed—which I suspect was to save everyone from any embarrassment.

In 2011, Operation 'Clean Up Consim' was finally over after almost four years of heartache. Rumours of an IPO started emerging again. In a report in 2013, Reuters said that the company was planning an IPO to raise between $100–125 million by the end of that year. BharatMatrimony had 20 million members by then and had found a place in India's Limca Book of Records for facilitating a record number of marriages. Its overseas operations now included the United States, the UK and Canada. The complete overhaul and shakeup had finally paid off.

On the Road to Success

In June 2013, after turning IndiaProperty.com into a separate business, Consim announced it had changed its name to Matrimony.com. 'We felt that when we are offering various matrimony services and creating so many matrimony brands, it is good to have Matrimony.com as the name of the entity,' said Muruga. It was almost as if he wanted a permanent reminder not only for himself but the entire team that this was indeed the core of their focus, their central and most important entity.

Having worked his way up in a similar milieu, Sanjeev Bikchandani is in a position to provide useful insight into Muruga's strategy of expanding rapidly after his first round of financing. He says, 'You have to have one solid profitable business. It's a bad idea to diversify without having one. So, we diversified only when we had Naukri.com making a solid profit for us.'

I met Muruga in 2018, he was two weeks away from his company's IPO. BharatMatrimony was planning to raise ₹500 crore at a valuation of ₹2,000 crore. He was visibly chuffed. He said, 'We are raising ₹130 crore in the primary because the company is profitable. We don't need much more. The balance is for the investors to get exits. Post that, our immediate goal is to get a billion-dollar market cap. Then we will look at what is to be done.' But this plan does not indicate that Muruga is ready to roll out other verticals as he has done in the past. He adds, 'Matrimony is a huge opportunity. We are now expanding the scope to include photography, bazaar, and mandap. Overall, it is a huge opportunity. We just got a 10 per cent market share in terms of organised markets, and while 60 million people are looking for life partners, only 6 million people come to online portals. I don't wish to let go of so much opportunity. It is better for us to focus on matchmaking and to expand our team and services.'

It is possible that Muruga is scarred for life as far as diversifying is concerned, but I think that it might be a good thing! On 14 September 2017, *The Economic Times* reported that online matchmaking firm Matrimony.com's public offering has been a success on D-street, with the issue being oversubscribed 4.41 times or 441 per cent at the end of the third and final day. Within twenty years of starting SysIndia.com, Muruga's company had been valued at about ₹2,225 crore.

Start-up journeys are tough. At one point, you are flushed with capital and enjoying the frenzy created by the media, and investors line up to invest in your crazy world dominating ideas and then immediately because of a 'black swan' event, every eye turns to cost-cutting costs, trimming plans and if anyone is willing to buy you, then the rallying cry from the investors is to go for that. I guess it is alright. Everyone who signs up for this journey, including Muruga and his investors are aware of these ups and downs. And while parts of such a journey can be ugly and difficult, the outcome can turn out to be magnificent as it did in Muruga's case.

AJIT BALAKRISHNAN

Founder and CEO, Rediff.com

'Life is difficult in the consumer facing businesses. The fact is that Google and Facebook own 90 per cent of a very small online advertising market, and we struggle to grab a share of the remaining pie. So it's a constant headache that makes me wonder whether we should be doing this at all.'

The Beginnings

UNLIKE MANY OTHER START-UP ENTREPRENEURS discussed in this book, Ajit Balakrishnan was not a white-collar professional who worked for someone else. By 1995, he had already co-founded and managed a very successful advertising agency called Rediffusion. Apart from this, Ajit's Bengaluru-based PSI-built custom microprocessor-based devices failed—mainly, because of the customs duties established by the government. Despite the failure of this idea, he was already searching for a new project. Long story short, as Ajit writes in his book *The Wave Rider: A Chronicle of the Information Age*, he ended his misery by selling his company to a German company who held a minority stake in it, packed up his Bengaluru apartment and returned home to Mumbai.

He then moved to London with his wife, Renu, who wanted to attend a short-term course at Oxford Brookes University. While in London, a chance encounter with the Mosaic browser (the web browser that debuted in 1995 and popularised the World Wide Web and the internet) helped him with his next big idea. As he writes in his book, 'When I got a look at it, I found it to be magical! I clicked around and got to the first few websites. It lets you see pictures, not just words, and there could be sound as well. A promise of safe, secure payment methods to come by simply and securely by entering your credit card number was right on the screen.'[6] He imagined many possibilities.

---

[6] Balakrishnan, Ajit. *The Wave Rider: A Chronicle of the Information Age*, Pan Macmillan, 2012

He immediately took a year's sabbatical from Rediffusion and returned to India, where he started developing a business plan. Armed with ₹1.5 crore capital of his own, he went on to hire a leased line and employed full-time writers. Rediff.co.in went live on Christmas Day in 1995.

It was a new and fascinating concept during the time. Rediff.com was envisaged as an online service provider with a dedicated editorial and research team. They had roped in Nikhil Lakshman as the Editor, UNI would provide them with the international news and there would be information on current events, news, business, personal investments, entertainment, sports, leisure and travel. He had launched it with a subscription model and by the end of the day, after pocketing just one subscriber from New Zealand, Ajit realised that his '₹1600 a year' fee strategy was DOA, i.e., dead on arrival.

He planned to build Rediff.com as a media company, different from Rajesh Jain's IndiaWorld. IndiaWorld had minimum staff and worked on the idea of being an 'asset light' company and the portal just fed off content from other providers. Ajit, on the other hand, had hired some of the best journalists and was setting out on his own to create a proper media company. Unlike IndiaWorld, Rediff.com was far from being profitable. And again, unlike IndiaWorld, which was happy catering to NRIs, Rediff.com envisioned itself as the gateway for Indians in India.

ALL THAT GLITTERS

I first met Ajit when I was going through one of the deepest troughs in my life. My enterprise, Webchutney, was staring at bankruptcy with no help in sight. Ajit, on the other hand, was on a high—Rediff.com and Rediffusion DY&R, an advertising agency he had started in the Eighties with his partner Arun Nanda, were peaking. Ajit had heard of me, but we had never met in person. We met in his office where I gave him the low, down on my situation, including the financial crunch and my lack of resources to survive it. I remember that he was quiet throughout and listened patiently to me till the end. Then he asked, 'How much money do you need?' I said, 'Four crore, minimum.' 'Take five crore. Build better infrastructure with the extra crore and create the best digital agency that this country has seen,' he said in an avuncular and magnanimous manner. I nearly choked. Everyone else had turned me down. I finally had a saviour. All he wanted in return was a 26 per cent stake in Webchutney and the promise that I would run the agency for the rest of my life without the thought of ever selling it. I was taken aback. I wanted the money, but I also wanted the flexibility to cash out at some point. After eight years of running the business, I had begun thinking about other bigger opportunities that I could explore. Not unlike Ajit, who had first built Rediffusion, the hottest creative services company followed by Rediff.com, a hot consumer brand.

It was for reasons such as this that I had idolised him. I wanted his success, wealth and the supreme confidence that came with it. These were my feelings nearly two decades ago when I had started Webchutney. Twelve years ago, when I met him for the first time, my opinion of him remained unchanged. I would have given an arm and a leg to be him. Today, however, I wouldn't say that. Over the years, Rediff.com failed miserably, even after making a strong second comeback, it had unwisely squandered away opportunities by mostly sitting on the fence and jumping in when it was too late. While I will always remain grateful to Ajit for his generous bailout offer in my moment of crisis (which incidentally, I never took), I no longer want to be in his shoes.

Quickly Finding Growth Drivers

The trouble was that barely any of the traffic to his portal was coming from India. Much like IndiaWorld, Rediff.com's traffic mostly comprised of NRIs. Ajit got together a market research team which figured that only one or two of Mumbai's internet users had ever visited Rediff.com. For Ajit, this was a painful reality to face. He describes the feedback he received from the hired market research team in his book, 'About 80 per cent of internet users check their email at one of the many free email websites. That's all they do. After they check their email, they close the browser and get on with other things in life. Only a minority of email users go onto chat sites; these are mainly people in their twenties. An equally small group goes to many of the search engines to locate information on the web. So between email, chat and search, you have covered just about all that internet users in Bombay do.'

It's around the same time that portals around the world realised that free email had to be the next killer app for the internet. Yahoo! acquired Four11 who had created RocketMail, in 1997, in a deal valued at $92 million. Microsoft was also playing catch up in the dot-com mania. Microsoft got HoTMaiL which had a sizeable lead over its competitor Four11 in membership and brand-name recognition, for a whopping $400 million. For Ajit, the writing was on the wall. He had to get Rediff.com's act together in the search, email and chat category. To his credit, he executed his plans at a rapid pace and that too, flawlessly. Rediff.com had launched Rediffmail by 15 August 1998—within 45 days of the revelation.

THE LAST SUCCESSFUL IPO

Raising capital for growth was far easier for Ajit and Rediff.com than Rajesh Jain of IndiaWorld. Ajit was seen as an entrepreneur with a series of successes, he had the IIM-C chops and understanding of acquiring great talent, exiting companies, acquisitions, etc. All the investors who had been speaking with Rajesh Jain eventually ended up investing in Rediff.com. With the vote of confidence from marquee investors—Intel, the world's biggest computer microprocessor company, Warburg Pincus and Draper Fisher Jurvetson, the legendary investors of HoTMaiL, who now owned 39 per cent of Rediff.com, its ambitions continued to grow.

Backed with cash that gave him enough headroom, Ajit had his eyes firmly set on growth. His competition wasn't just the local shops that had mushroomed, he was getting ready to compete with anyone and everyone including Yahoo!, eBay, MSN, AOL, Excite and Lycos, in short anyone that was looking East. Like King Leonidas from the film *300*, Rediff.com was Ajit's Sparta. Despite the investments, he was well aware that when the real fight began, the couple of million dollars he had raised wouldn't take him too far.

Early 1999, Ajit's investors told him he could go public at the NASDAQ. 'When they came to my office and said that I should make the company public, I said, "what public? We have 1,50,000 users on our portal and most of our users are not even in India. If we go public, we would have problems of user growth and revenue as India wasn't ready",' Ajit remembers telling them.

Nevertheless, investors prevailed and convinced Ajit to consider meeting bankers in New York to evaluate a prospective IPO. At this time, Ajit had little confidence that his fledgeling start-up could take on the expectations of NASDAQ, especially with revenues barely to the tune of $1 million and the company still incurring losses. But the stock-market was still in celebratory mode and a bunch of loss-making companies were regularly ringing the famed NASDAQ bell and raising hundreds of millions of dollars.

Investors were convinced that at least one internet company per major country would strike it big and when it came to India, Rediff.com was everyone's darling. Not in the least because it provided the full bouquet of services—a professional management team and a dominant share of the market. In New York, Ajit met everyone from Morgan Stanley, Dean Witter Reynolds and Merrill Lynch to Goldman Sachs and several others in-between.

Goldman Sachs was chosen as the lead underwriter with assistance from CS First Boston and Robert Fleming Inc. This coincided with Sify's announcement of its acquisition of IndiaWorld for a whopping ₹499 crore in November 1999. Rediff.com was larger in scale, size and vision than IndiaWorld and Ajit knew he could raise far more capital.

At the time of filing for the IPO, the offerings consisted of 17 interest-specific channels, community features, local language editions and Rediff.com's proprietary search engine. Rediff.com was also generating revenue from online advertising. Its page views had jumped from 13 million in April 1999 to approximately 70 million by March 2000. Portals with a first mover advantage aimed at specific geographic audiences had been well received by the markets. The markets, on their debut, had recently loved China.com, a Chinese portal firm and Starmedia, which targeted Latin America.

According to international Data Corp., about 1 million people used the internet in India in 1999. However, that figure was expected to jump to 17.2 million by 2004. Just around that time, the headwinds of the dot-com bubble had begun to blow. The NASDAQ index peaked on 10 March 2000, at 5048 and nearly doubled over the prior year. Right at the market's peak, several pieces of bad news began to trickle in. The first of these was that Japan had entered a recession. Then, Yahoo! and eBay ended talks of a merger and several other companies began to restate their revenue guidance because of aggressive accounting strategies. At the same time, media companies published reports of internet companies running out of cash fast. Together, these varied factors were too hot for the market to handle and it all spread panic among investors. Within a few weeks, the stock-market shed 10 per cent of its value. Capital began drying up fast. Rediff.com debuted on NASDAQ in the nick of time on June 20 with a share price offering at $12. It raised $55.2 million by offloading 4.6 million shares and the company trading under the ticker REDF was now valued at about $300 million. 'Ours was the last IPO before Wall Street crashed,' Ajit informs, 'The market tanked within the next two days of our fundraise.' Fortunately for him, he had successfully steered Rediff.com to an IPO on NASDAQ amidst a bloodbath in dot-com valuations. The IPO was oversubscribed nineteen times and the stock price climbed 61 per cent to $19.31 on the first day of trading.

THE STRUGGLE TO SURVIVE

While the successful listing was being celebrated, Ajit had bigger worries. With the global meltdown and the dot-com bubble burst, in India, a majority of Rediff.com's advertisers from the dot-com world found themselves in deep trouble. Ajit had not been off the mark in his predictions as revenues started drying up while the number of people using the internet rose at a very slow pace. While Rediff.com had money in the bank, its stock price was savagely hit, falling to $2.75 within six months. Its valuation fell over 80 per cent much like the meltdown that had hit Sify. There was no end in sight. Ajit knew he needed to grow the company and add real revenue. In March 2001, less than a year after being listed, Rediff.com announced its first acquisition of Think India, a privately held US-based portal focusing on Indians worldwide. As per the terms of the acquisition, Rediff.com Holdings Inc., a wholly-owned subsidiary of Rediff.com paid an aggregate of $3 million in stock to the shareholders of the website, Think India, and made it a wholly-owned subsidiary of Rediff.com.

Gopal Krishna, a graduate of Harvard Business School and a former consultant with McKinsey & Company, had founded Think India along with Gaurav Dalmia and Sandy Rekhi, a former executive at Oracle. It was a pure-play portal like its acquirer. With its help, Rediff.com would be able to monetise its page-views. At the same time, an experienced management team, an all-stock deal and Think India's low cash-burn, which was keeping up with Rediff.com's conservatism, made it look like the right acquisition.

In less than a month, Rediff.com acquired two other US-based companies, India Abroad Publications and Value Communications Corp to increase its penetration in the United States, a market which was easier to monetise because of higher internet penetration than India. Ironically, *India Abroad* was an offline newspaper, said to be the oldest and most profitable South Asian weekly serving the South Asian community in the United States, with a circulation base of 65,000 and revenue of $7 million in the December 2000. This was an all-cash deal worth $10 million.

Rediff.com also acquired Illinois-based Value Communications, a profitable communications company which focussed on internet-based marketing of international phone services to Indians in the United States. The 'earn-out' deal involved a down payment of $3 million. Earn-out refers to a deal in which the final acquisition price depends on the profit before tax over a said period of time. Value Communications had a user base of 45,000 with revenues of over $13 million in 2000. The company's acquisitions were focussed on creating 'a more stable revenue matrix by diversifying its revenue streams across multiple services, markets and businesses.'

Rediff.com also announced that it would raise its stake in Apna Loan which helped young, upwardly mobile Indians in choosing loans and credit card services. But the stock-markets were still punishing dot-com stocks. In December 2001, Rediff.com's share was trading at $0.65. Ajit's team kept its head down and focussed on increasing revenue and page views. By 2004, their work was rewarded with the company reporting its first profitable quarter.

On the Turnaround

The company had turned the corner and its profits did not go unnoticed. Rediff.com's stock price was back to over $12, the same price which existed at the time of the IPO, five years ago. And it kept rising. Within two years, by March 2005, it was trading above $25 per share. Ajit was not just a survivor but had come up on top with the company only $200 million shy of a billion-dollar valuation. He seemed to have succeeded where everyone else had failed miserably. Rupert Murdoch's Indya.com, Rama Raju's Sify.com as well as Rajesh Jain's IndiaWorld, were all in the graveyard or just inches away from it by then.

At the height of Rediff.com's glorious recovery, an investment banker in Singapore called Ajit on behalf of Naspers, the South African media giant. After its success with an investment in Chinese start-up Tencent, Naspers was looking to expand its base to other emerging markets. The banker, in his business-as-usual tone, asked Ajit what it would cost to buy out his stake in Rediff.com. Ajit asked the banker whether he was married. 'Yes, very happily,' the unsuspecting man replied. 'If you come to Mumbai to meet me, I am going to ask you what it would cost me to have sex with your wife,' Ajit is said to have famously told the man. Although, all these years later, he is far from proud for having said such a thing. 'One day, I'll call him and apologise,' he explains, 'although, I believe I'm a calm person, I guess it's natural to say something inappropriate in a moment of passion.'

THE ACCIDENTAL AMBUSH

Unfortunately, Rediff.com's glory was short-lived. The next two years saw Rediff.com clash with the global Goliath, Yahoo!, which challenged Rediff.com on its home turf by aggressively ramping up its team in India and localising content. Rediff.com found itself battling several newcomers and suddenly exposed on many fronts. There was CricBuzz which was generating a lot of traffic due to its sharply focussed attention to cricket. Finance, another one of Rediff.com's large verticals had to deal with the likes of Moneycontrol.com that had been acquired by Network18 and was being aggressively marketed on their hugely successful business channel CNBC TV18. Bollywood Hungama had gobbled up a large share of the market catering to celebrity gossip and film-related news. At the same time, newspapers such as *The Times of India* had started aggressively investing in building their own live online newsrooms. TV channels such as NDTV and CNN-IBN also started building their online presence. Even e-commerce began showing signs of life with Flipkart and Snapdeal, among others. Furthermore, with the rise of Orkut, followed by Facebook and Twitter where netizens began to spend a lot of time, these portals gradually became the single pit stop for discovering content. The utility of a gateway like Rediff.com had started to diminish. In an earnings call in July 2008, Ajit seemed in denial. He did not believe or at least refused to admit that he was surrounded. He says, 'We have only two competitors left in India: Yahoo! and Google. We have to match them in some of their core businesses. That is the real challenge.' He didn't believe that the online emergence of media companies posed any serious threat to his business. He adds, 'It hasn't worked anywhere in the world. It didn't happen for ABC, NBC and others. The user base online is completely different. NDTV is a great news provider, but going by any measure, they're a fraction—around 10 per cent, of what we are. Network18's Moneycontrol.com has a unique user base, less than our finance channel MoneyWiz (2 million). Our total unique users in India are 9.5 million and worldwide there are around 12 million.'

From being a pioneering leader, by the end of the year, Rediff.com was playing a desperate catch-up game. It launched iland, a poor cousin of the popular blogging platform, Blogger. com and created a separate social network called Social as a 'sandbox' for application developers to test their apps. MediaNama, a popular source for information on the internet and media space reported in October 2008 that the developer platform had only 11 apps in three months, with the most popular app having 133 users. Hot on the heels of every successful idea, in this case, YouTube, Rediff.com also went live with its video sharing platform iShare. With the dramatic rise of Google performance marketing, it launched its own pay-per-click platform called LocalAds, which barely took off. Rediff.com also tried its hand at investing in a start-up called Vakow, which it wrote off quickly.

The next few years saw a ton of other misses. Nevertheless, Rediff.com continued to be bullish about the future. It also kept its investors engaged despite a string of losses. By 2010, however, media observers had had enough. In August 2010, Nikhil Pahwa, the founder of MediaNama, wrote a scathing post titled 'Rediff.com: Still Drinking Its Own Kool-Aid' which highlighted how Rediff.com's strategy had gone horribly wrong. In the article, he says, 'LocalAds will take time, iShare will take time, Mobile and Wireless Broadband in India will be big, but will take time. Rediff.com may be readying itself for the future, but you have to ask— will consumers choose Rediff.com? Will telecom operators choose Rediff.com? And above all, will advertisers continue to choose Rediff.com?' Yahoo! had snapped up 47.5 per cent of India's internet users, Facebook users were proliferating at 35 per cent and even though Orkut, the incumbent social network, was sliding, it still had about 24 per cent of the market share. Rediff.com had been cornered at only 16 per cent of users. New players like in.com—launched barely a year ago—were already half the size of Rediff.com. Pahwa refused to mince words in his message to Ajit, 'Stop selling a future you can't foretell. It's like building a grand boat on the shore, waiting for the waves to come and take it to sea.' Ajit, however, attributed his challenges to the fact that he was a pure consumer player in India.

He admits rather sorely, 'Our business has two parts and one is a constant headache. The part of the business which does very well is our enterprise email service. We have 27,000 paying customers whose emails we manage. 19 out of 21 insurance companies are with us. Anyone who wants a secure India-based email comes to us. We have a few competitors, but we outmanoeuvre them with a slightly lower price and better customer service. Life is difficult in consumer-facing businesses. The fact is that Google and Facebook own 90 per cent of a tiny online advertising market, and we struggle to grab a share of the remaining pie. So it's a constant headache that makes me wonder whether we should be doing this at all.'

When personal computers had appeared in the Eighties, Ajit had taken time off from his ad agency Rediffusion to build India's first microcomputer. 'It was a consumer–facing business and we failed since the end consumer opportunity hadn't yet arrived in India,' Ajit admits. He had to sell the business to Groupe Bull, a French company. But the only ones who survived and thrived during that period were the body shopping companies—Infosys and Tata Consultancy Services—the enterprise service providers. The moral of the story is that Indian consumer markets are minuscule, particularly for newer technology. He adds, 'I think there are only about 3 to 5 per cent Indians who adopt technology early, who are aware and like to follow the rest of the world. It almost takes India 15–20 years to fully embrace new technology. I have seen it multiple times. Also, a seriously related issue is India's internet active user base defined by people who come online at least once a week, that number is about 22 million, not what's being quoted in the media.

He continues, 'For start-up founders who made it big like Sanjeev (Info Edge and Naukri.com) and even Deep of MakeMyTrip, it's not because of wisdom. They stumbled upon businesses which are not dependent on high internet penetration. For Sanjeev's business to succeed initially, all he needed was 3,000 to 5,000 HR managers who had internet access in their offices and could go to the website to find candidates. For that, they would pay Info Edge some access fee. And the students who put their resumes could go to a cyber café once in two months and update their CVs. Deep also had the same ease with travel agents. The travel agents were the original bookers. Now I think they have moved to consumers. But again, they never openly publish that data. I guess that 70 per cent of the bookings must be coming from organised or unorganised travel agents. The travel agents would buy e-tickets and then sell those tickets to their customers. Even in the United States, Monster.com was three times the size of the largest consumer portals in 1998. Consumer engagement in the US happened only after telecom companies laid the fibre and went broke. Though the fibre remained, consumer base exploded as a consequence of that.'

I tend to agree with Ajit's observation. The first publicly available internet service in India was launched by state-owned Videsh Sanchar Nigam Limited (VSNL) on 14 August 1995. It's taken us more than two and a half decades to get to 500 million internet users finally, and most of that traffic has been coming in the last two years, thanks to falling data prices. Historically, India has been a laggard in embracing technology. Having said that, nothing had stopped Rediff.com from aggressively investing in start-up businesses that seemed to be making better strides at revenue. Rediff.com sat on the cash and waited it out when it could have very well readied itself for a different avatar when the market was ready again.

How They Actually Blew It

Rediff.com became a prisoner of its past. The company participated in every new internet opportunity but failed to make a mark in any of them. The company's biggest asset continued to be its portal, Rediff.com which provided news and information on a variety of verticals such as movies, sports, current affairs, etc. But even these saw aggressive competition from players that were focused on their content and therefore, outperformed every one of Rediff.com's portals. Gmail and Yahoo! firmly owned the email space. Content verticals were the other rising stars. Rediff.com did try to get its e-commerce mojo back, but the industry had begun to already consolidate around the strongest players such as Snapdeal, Flipkart, and Myntra. It was a classic tale of being the jack of all trades and master of none. Despite being a pioneer, Rediff.com failed to capitalise on the opportunity for precisely this reason.

After a brief period of what looked like a great comeback in 2011 when the stock dramatically rose to over $25, it began another free-fall from which it never recovered. Rediff.com's cash reserves continued shrinking year on year by almost $6–8 million—it was a slow, drawn out and painful death. In August 2015, Rediff.com announced that it was moving its stocks which were then listed on the NASDAQ Global Market to the NASDAQ Capital Market as the company no longer met the stock-market's criteria of minimum equity levels for stockholders to remain listed on NASDAQ Global Market. It explained its reasons in a statement which said, 'The continuing listing requirements of the NASDAQ Capital Market are in the Company's opinion, more appropriate for companies at Rediff.com's scale of operation.' During the quarter which ended on 30 June 2015, Rediff.com's cash reserves were equivalent to $7.6 million—enough for its requirements for the next six quarters.

By the end of 2015, Rediff.com's stock price had fallen to below a dollar and in April 2016, Rediff.com announced that it was delisting its shares from the NASDAQ Capital Markets. It's been a roller coaster journey with more lows than highs but Rediff.com's portal is still live and Ajit's focus remains steadily on the profitable enterprise business. If he were able to turn back the wheels of time, there's a lot that Ajit would have done differently.

'I should have relocated my team and myself to San Francisco the minute we raised capital,' he rues, though one can't blame him for lack of effort. Ajit did move himself to San Francisco and stayed there for the next six months, but things weren't meant to be for him. While he was there, the markets collapsed. 'Nothing happened for the next two years. Otherwise, my team, which by the way is still with me, would have run a worldwide company. They are being wasted in this minuscule Indian market. You just can't do it from here. Our home base is too small. I should have moved in 1998,' he says, not without a trace of wistfulness.

What India Wants

Ajit has always pioneered trends, be it advertising, where he and his partner Arun Nanda built one of the biggest independent advertising agencies, Rediffusion to being a trailblazer in computer manufacturing and launching and Rediff.com. While he had comfortably accessed funds when he needed them, others—during the same time—found it challenging to raise capital. Over the years, this scenario has changed drastically and access to capital is now easy. It shows a willingness to encourage growth in the sector because as far as India is concerned, its time has arrived.

'Start-ups are a great thing for our country. Even at a policy level, the government needs to find more and more ways to encourage people to launch start-ups. Corporate employment is nowhere as luxurious as it used to be. The era of large companies with 10,000 employees is going to come to an end. In India, historically, the corporate and organised sectors never accounted for more than 12–13 per cent of all employment,' he says, still batting for his pioneering ideas. He may not be that far off the mark. Nearly 87 per cent of Indians have had to fend for themselves with a vast majority engaged in small businesses and farming. With the idea of re-skill, start-ups may be the only way that India can continue to grow.

Ajit's vision for the future reveals his astuteness, 'I wish the funding system were better. Look beyond our glamorous world at youngsters who are in their twenties, studying at a polytechnic, for example. Many of them may want to start a computer repair shop and will need capital. But the banks shoo them away. There is capital in the public sector banks but they won't lend it to the right people. They prefer to lend within their own circles.'

I wish I could spend a few years mobilising support from the government to step in. It's because the corporate sector can't provide jobs anymore. I am spending a lot of time with the government's Administrative Institute of Teacher's Training, trying to reform their curriculum in these polytechnics. We introduced android app development in the Sikkim government polytechnic recently. And not just polytechnic institutes, even engineering is facing the same fate. Hundreds of engineering colleges are shutting down every year. They were feeding off the IT services boom which created the phenomenon of substandard engineering colleges churning out substandard students. To make it worse, IT services were the first to get hit by automation. I am off to Tripura soon to tackle the same issue of curriculum upgrade. Students are very restive about the state of employment. Thinking of Ajit, I am reminded of every other entrepreneur from the late Nineties era. Everyone pays obeisance to Ajit because he was the pioneer. There would be a queue of entrepreneurs seeking advice, partnerships or potential funding from him. Rediff.com was to India what Yahoo! was to the Silicon Valley in the late Nineties. Sadly, much like Yahoo!, Rediff.com too blew it. A reminder that today's technology companies age in dog years.

ANUPAM MITTAL

Founder and CEO, People Group

'Look at our history. This is the first time in India that people have started believing they can pull something off on their own. The previous generations of entrepreneurs needed licences, government approvals, capital, etc. So what did the best talent do at that time? They believed that the only way they could create some value for themselves was by becoming the best doctors or engineers of the world and that's what they did. They became the best in the world. This is exactly what is happening with entrepreneurship.'

ANUPAM MITTAL WAS ON A PERMANENT HIGH. BY 2006, People Group (the mothership of all of his ventures) looked like it could do no wrong. Their star attraction, Shaadi.com along with other verticals like Makaan.com and Mauj.com, had raised truckloads of money from venture capitalists. It also had a dating and social networking site called Fropper and an astrology website called AstroLife. People Group was looking to become a diversified internet conglomerate and was locked in a battle for the classifieds space along with Info Edge, BharatMatrimony and the Goliath, Times Internet, which woke up late to the threat and had launched TimesJobs, SimplyMarry and MagicBricks, hot on the heels of Info Edge's Naukri.com, Jeevansaathi and 99Acres and BharatMatrimony's Click Jobs and IndiaProperty.com. At the peak of all the fundraising frenzy, People Group looked like a likely winner, if not the numero uno. It was inevitable that People Group would take the number two spot behind Info Edge. But then things began to unfold differently for Anupam.

Somewhere in 2006, he had also invested in a large worthy competitor of Webchutney called Interactive Avenues. Back then, it was arguably the highest-value angel cheque to be invested in India. By 2011, he had also invested in an idea that he initially didn't believe in. Two IIT graduates had pitched him an on-demand cab service. After initially passing on the idea, he had eventually returned to them with a cheque. This company was Ola Cabs. Ola is now valued at $5 billion. Anupam had a multi-million bagger on his hands. On the other hand, his investment Interactive Avenues was acquired by a global network in 2013, returning more than thirty times his investment. Armed with this ammunition, Anupam has gone on to invest in over a hundred start-ups till date. What's more, he is one of the most sought after angel investors in India.

THE BEGINNINGS

As a commerce student at Jai Hind College in Mumbai, Anupam didn't like to attend lectures. He believed that Indian students weren't studying to become qualified but to turn into desirable matrimonial matches. His father's textile manufacturing business was the only reason for him to take up commerce. While in college, he realised that he could easily pass the exams by studying for only a few weeks before their commencement. This gave him the liberty to pursue other interests, but eventually, he ended up joining his father's business. He was content with his work but fate had other plans for him. He ended up making some bad decisions, which caused huge losses in the business within two years. He decided that the job wasn't for him and never returned to his father's factory in Mumbai's suburbs again.

After travelling around Europe and the US for six months, Anupam realised that he needed to invest in his higher education to develop his faculties. He received an MBA degree from Boston College in the 1990s and in 1996 he joined MicroStrategy, a software company that developed business intelligence software when the internet was just taking off. Yahoo! had been launched in 1994 and Netscape had announced its IPO in 1995 and turned out to be a complete blockbuster. This changed the technology and start-up landscape forever.

In the meantime, MicroStrategy had become a poster boy for start-ups. Riding the frenzy, the company's valuation shot up from \$100 million to \$40 billion in just two years. Anupam had generous stock options in the company and by the time he was in his mid-twenties, his stock was worth millions of dollars and growing by the week. Around that time, he was visiting his family in India and began to think about the implications of consumer internet business in India, where it was still early for the dot-com business. The first era of portal wars hadn't even started.

He chanced upon the idea of a matrimonial website when he was under the lens of a traditional matchmaker himself. Meeting the man with the bag full of files which listed details of prospective brides became the prototype for Anupam's website. He explains, 'I discovered that the number of choices for me were limited according to the matchmaker's capacity to carry those files. He carried around fifty biographical data files with him at a time, which became the extent of my options.' Anupam began to think of ways to get over the geographical and numerical limitations of finding a match. This was the germination of the idea. He says, 'I started the site, hired five engineers and four designers whose salary was about ₹7,000 and ₹5,000, respectively. I was making a six-figure salary in the US so it didn't matter. I booked a domain name called saagai.com and we kicked off. I was remotely managing the team from the US.'

However, on 12 March 2000, his company MicroStrategy announced an accounting irregularity. Their stock crashed 66 per cent. NASDAQ fell from 5500 to 1100 points and their public perception quickly changed from being Wall Street's darlings to its devils. Anupam had become a multi-millionaire in his twenties—a time during which he admits to having gone crazy with the spending. 'We bought Ferraris and Porsches, but soon lost the shirt off our backs,' says the risk-taker. Fortunately, he already had a back-up option waiting for him in India.

In the year 2000, the dot-com business crashed and the internet was no longer a good space for building a business. Surprisingly, this is when Anupam's website began to pick up a steady pace. He adds, 'There was traffic coming in from the US because NRIs had internet access. And as they were geographically isolated from India, the website met their demands. Indians, on the other hand, were yet to have any regular internet access.'

Anupam's team was also taking up one-time projects of building websites for others. This way, the operations of Sagaai were cross-subsidised by their web development assignments. Around 2000–2001, Anupam decided to buy the domain name 'Shaadi.com' after the dot-com bubble burst because domain names which cost thousands of dollars earlier had become cheaper. Anupam was sure that the name 'Sagaai.com' wouldn't work. He says, 'We needed something short, a name that could strike a chord and be easily remembered. Sagaai.com didn't have that ring to it. People also spelt it differently. I was convinced that Shaadi.com was a great name for a matrimonial website but the man who owned it was demanding $25,000! Since the bubble had already burst, I thought that if I wait it out, he reduce the asking price. The negotiations started when I offered him $5,000, but two months later, he assured me he wasn't going to budge. So, I trusted my instincts and decided to use most of our savings to buy the domain name for $25,000. At that time, everyone thought I had lost it.' Over the years, the new domain name 'Shaadi.com' proved to be a turning point for Anupam. People started talking about the name, the media fancied it and even global media companies like BBC and CNN remarked on the use of the internet in the context of a unique culture of arranged marriages.

How He Nearly Blew It: A Series of Unfortunate Events

Anupam believes that his first crisis was losing everything he had earned at MicroStrategy. This unexpected series of events led him to turn his side gig into a full-time occupation and he moved back to his home country in 2002–2003. He raised his first round of external capital in 2006 but made the rash decision of quick diversification. 'In hindsight, I didn't learn anything from the 2000 bust. I thought we could do anything,' he says, about his imprudent decisions.

He launched a bunch of different businesses using external capital. There were some 10 million internet users in India in 2001 and by 2008, the number had risen to about 12 million. 'We raised all that money with the ambitions of scaling up, but there was almost no growth in the user base. With that handicap, we were challenged to earn meaningful revenues on the one hand and continue scaling-up on the other. At that time, we believed that we had to work on multiple platforms. In 2008, I had a contractual agreement with a venture capital to use the investment of $10 million in people interactive interface. Based on that, we got into various areas. We wanted to use that to build the next level. Soon after, the Lehman Brothers bankruptcy brought about a global economic freeze. All the VCs vanished and I was facing bankruptcy all over again,' he ruminates. The company was in debt because Anupam had borrowed money to fund the company's operations and was confident of the $10 million investment. Their expansion plan depended on it. With no other options left, Anupam had to hunker down and go through his first round of lay-offs. Some initiatives like Fropper (the networking site) were put on the backburner and a decision was made to focus on the company's profitability over the next few years. This decision came at a price. They lost the race in the matrimony website business to BharatMatrimony, in real estate to 99Acres and later, to MagicBricks and their Makaan.com and had to settle for the third position. He reveals, 'We lost our competitive position in all the businesses because we were not investing. We were just cash optimising when everyone else was investing heavily. The investors were keen to shut down everything else because even though Shaadi.com was profitable, its money was getting sucked in by Makaan.com.'

The investors understood that Makaan.com had accumulated crore of liabilities, was heavily dependent on Shaadi.com and not carrying its weight at all. Anupam agreed to spin out the company, recapitalise it and let it have a chance to grow on its own. Anupam had cashed out on his largest investment by then. He had made investments in Interactive Avenues, a digital marketing start-up in 2007 which had been acquired by a global advertising network, Interpublic Group (IPG), in 2012. It was the largest investment in the digital space at that time with a rumoured enterprise valuation of ₹350 crore. Anupam owned a third of the company. His angel investment came to his rescue at the right time. He chose to invest ₹12 crore of that money into Makaan.com and ended up owning 100 per cent of the company. After recapitalising the company, he also created a 20 per cent ESOP (Employee Stock Ownership Plan) pool. Aditya Verma, the business head of Makaan.com, became the CEO and co-founder of Makaan.com. Anupam admits, 'I had almost blown it again. We had nearly reached the point where we may have had to sell these companies for a song. But because I could exit Interactive Avenues in 2012, by sheer dumb luck, I was able to hold on to my companies.'

CROUCHING TIGER, HIDDEN ANGEL

Real estate classifieds are known to be bloodsuckers before becoming profitable. Anupam's key competitors in the classifieds space included two giants. One was the Info Edge group with its cash generating machine Naukri.com and another was the publicly listed Matrimony.com (whose flagship brand is BharatMatrimony) which claimed nine times more traffic than its nearest competitor. All three of them started with a similar ambition of growing their tentacles in several classified verticals. Info Edge launched Jeevansathi in the late Nineties. Matrimony.com led by Muruga, rapidly expanded after fundraising. Both Sanjeev Bhikchandi and Muruga had paid heavy prices for stepping up their verticals and had to scale down rapidly to ensure that they didn't lose everything in the process. Keeping their track records in mind, Anupam's spinning out with Makaan.com was nothing short of playing with fire. He could have ended up in a similar situation if not for a fortuitous turn of events in April 2015. Real estate portal PropTiger.com, backed by Rupert Murdoch's News Corp, approached him and quickly acquired Makaan.com for an undisclosed sum to create a common platform that would offer property services and solutions to homebuyers, real estate developers, property brokers, banks and private equity investors. Prop Tiger was typically a digital real estate marketing and transaction services provider that helped customers buy homes. With Makaan.com, it ventured into the secondary market where buyers could choose from resale properties as well.

It proved to be a win-win situation for Anupam. He had gambled by throwing in a large chunk of his personal capital into an industry that had never seen a profitable business before. Fortunately for him, the gamble paid off. 'I knew that the industry was going to get more capital intense but there is a window for such things. Timing is critical. Sometimes, you see reality playing before your eyes like a movie before it becomes reality. That is what happened with Makaan.com. It was a risk because I was putting in a large sum but the reality played out exactly like the movie that I had in my mind. I couldn't have written a better script. I made a lot of cash in that deal and additionally, I am a large shareholder of the combined entity of Housing.com, Makaan.com and Property Tiger, which is valued at $250 million,' he chuckles.

A Decade Too Early?

Anupam started Shaadi.com in 1997 and more than twenty years later, he is still waiting for a great outcome for the investors. I started Webchutney in 1999 and I often wonder if my company's outcome would have been different if I had started it a few years later with a little more experience in advertising. A good idea before its time can be a trap, guzzling the time and resources of the early explorers since the market isn't ready. Similarly, perhaps, Anupam also ventured out a decade too early. He reflects, 'It's essential to keep things within context in our business. It's easy to get carried away to try to be the next hot thing but you lose your way quickly. One has to remember that there are cycles due to which everything is about the right timing. One develops an instinct for it with experience. So if you look at People Group's history, whether it's Mauj.com, Makaan.com or Shaadi.com, you know that we started very early but we've had investments come into the company. We haven't been very aggressive about raising capital but we've been growing very well. We merged Makaan.com with Prop Tiger and created a lot of value for the investors. I think the journey has just begun. If you look at the western world, Match.com, after fifteen years of being in this business and owning some of the largest names in the world, like Tinder, finally went public only a couple of years ago. Today, its market capitalisation hovers somewhere around $10 billion. Yes, we were very early, but I think that's also given us a lot of time to learn. This is not e-commerce as we're not simply selling products at a discount. There is a second layer of complexity to our business—the recognition of people's behavioural patterns to match them together and get them to use interfaces intuitively.'

The speculation whether People Group's fortunes would have been different had it started its operations a few years later has lost its relevance now. Today, it is alive and kicking with a thirst to expand further, which is what matters in the end.

FROM AN ENTREPRENEUR TO A PROLIFIC ANGEL INVESTOR

Investors have different reasons for being angel investors. Some look at it as a way of diversifying their portfolio to include a high risk, high return asset class; some just want to give back to the ecosystem that made them wealthy by supporting entrepreneurs; some want to stay current and relevant and keep learning about new technologies and trends; some view it as a networking opportunity; and some have a combination of these reasons. Every reason is laudable and altruistic in its own way. Anupam has invested in over a hundred start-ups till 2018. In fact, he was one of India's very few angel investors when he started investing in 2006. He is also a limited partner in Kae Capital and Orios Venture Partners—early stage funds that invest in start-ups. Having invested in twenty start-ups myself, I sometimes wonder whether angel investing is a poor use of my time given the time spent and the relatively high failure rate. Even though angel investing looks like it's a casual, easy and fun activity, those who want real returns end up spending a lot of their time on the start-up in tasks like finding deals, vetting companies they are interested in, and post-investment, working with them to ensure that the start-up is successful. An angel investor is lucky if he lands himself in a team that doesn't need him after taking the cheque. Evaluating the strength of a team based on a few meetings is a risky proposition in which the dice can fall either way. No investor knows how the cookie crumbles, so investing in a hundred start-ups must have been a Herculean task.

Anupam remarks, 'Look at our history. This is the first time in India that people have started believing they can pull something off on their own. The previous generations of entrepreneurs needed licences, government approvals, capital etc. So what did the best talent do at that time? They believed that the only way they could create some value for themselves was by becoming the best doctors or engineers of the world and that's what they did. They became the best in the world. This is exactly what is happening with entrepreneurship.'

He is absolutely right. The last five years have been transformational for India's entrepreneurs. Indeed, Anupam believes that 2010–2020 is 'the foundational decade for creating incredible value for our future generations' and I agree because it is decade of democratisation of entrepreneurship in India. It is a decade that ought to go down in history as the fear of failure has been replaced by confidence, resilience and the ability to dream and believe. These traits were elusive a few years back but today, these are the Indian entrepreneurial ecosystem's strongest suit. This change in attitude, coupled with funding options has made it into a thriving, viable ecosystem.

Therefore, investors like Anupam must be credited for bringing about this gradual but welcome change. Of course, this has also created opportunities for immense profitability for him and made him rich. His investments in Ola Cabs alone, for which he cut a cheque of ₹50 lakh, have grown to ₹200–300 crore over seven years. Ola's refusal to be crushed by the arrival of the global giant Uber has been surprising. I also had this fear when Ola first raised institutional money. My theory was simple: YouTube India *is* YouTube, just like Tinder India *is* Tinder. I didn't think Ola stood a chance given the technology and execution experience that Uber had already garnered.

Anupam felt differently. He recalls, 'Firstly, Uber was just a black car booking service in San Francisco when it started, so it wasn't comparable. It would be unfair to call Ola a knock-off. From an investment point of view, I admit that it was a lucky stroke. The first time I spoke to Bhavesh (Bhavesh Agarwal of Ola Cabs), I refused to invest. It wasn't about Uber but the idea hadn't made sense to me till then. Our experiences often shape our realities. For someone living in Mumbai's Cuffe Parade, taxis are not a problem. When I met Bhavesh for the first time, I told him that I couldn't understand the problem that he was trying to solve.'

Despite his early reservations about the idea, Anupam couldn't forget about it. He admits that he would ring up Ola's call centre every week because they did not have an app then. Invariably, the phone was answered by Bhavesh himself, unaware that he was being tested. Anupam would show frustration or anger as a potential patron or launch into a diatribe against the service. The way Bhavesh handled every situation impressed him. He says, 'He used to listen very patiently. It reminded me of myself, of how I used to answer all the customer queries myself. I knew that Bhavesh was committed to his idea. As luck would have it, I was in Delhi and experienced exactly what Bhavesh had been trying to explain all along, that there are no taxis available by the roadside in Delhi! You can't just hail a taxi because you must call to get one. It dawned on me that it was a real problem. I was already sold on the founding team's conviction and maturity and this personal experience sealed the deal for me. It made me think this was a risk worth taking. The rest is history.' When I met Anupam in 2018, Ola was valued over $5 billion. And yet, Anupam is still not ready to sell his stake to other eager investors. He adds, 'I think it's very rare in an investor's life that you hit upon companies that end up becoming multi-billion dollar enterprises. If you're really lucky, it may happen once in your life. Ola is outperforming Uber in many ways with a massive market size. It makes sense for me just to sit back. Besides, I wouldn't know where to place my money if I took it out! I would most certainly earn lesser returns.'

Today, India needs more entrepreneurs to turn into venture capitalists as Anupam did. He has more early stage start-up investing experience than most VCs. Even though he is aware of the fact, Anupam is a reluctant venture capitalist. 'You're never quite free as long as you are a promoter of a company whether you are a CEO or not, so that's a fallacy. Unless you are in a mature industry where you are like a Marico, you cannot take your eyes off the road. While I do think about becoming a VC from time to time, the more I think about it, the more I am convinced I should never become one,' he feels. While Anupam's disinterest may seem at odds with his circumstances, he does have a point. Becoming a venture capitalist is a thankless job. He says, 'Look what happened when Tiger entered and threw millions at start-ups at an early stage. All the limited partners at other VC firms were shouting at the firm, asking why their capital wasn't being deployed faster. The poor chaps did what they were told and after the music stopped and the dot-com graveyard became a reality, the limited partners again called up their firms to ask what happened to their money.'

He does have a point when he says that the days of selling are over and one has to be in the demand creation game. Whether Indian markets can see the current trends or not, demand creation is the need of the hour. Entrepreneurs need to be able to tell investors why they ought to invest. With changing global trends, it remains important to create previously unforeseen demands and desires. No one thought that they would have any use for an iWatch till Apple thrust it upon the world. It continues to be one of the company's most steadily selling products. Likewise, the future belongs to the internet of things and trends such as 3D printing, which, according to Anupam, would be the 'next big disruptor'. Digitisation is only in its third decade of existence and nobody knows what is going to hit us next.

Losing a boatload of money at MicroStrategy accelerated Anupam's full-time entrepreneur role. As an entrepreneur, he raised a ton of money but his empire nearly crumbled. With his investments and eventual success of Makaan.com, he is now rebuilding Shaadi.com. He has recently appointed a full-time CEO for Shaadi.com which suggests that he is running the race one lap at a time. His stint is undoubtedly an example of how a setback might be a blessing in disguise—not only for the entrepreneur but for the entire industry.

ASHISH HEMRAJANI

Co-Founder and CEO, BookMyShow

'A unicorn is a fucking mythical animal. It doesn't exist. It's a horse with a horn and it's ugly. When I am asked whether BookMyShow will ever be a unicorn, my response is that I don't know. But what I know for sure is that we are cockroaches. We are survivors, we can survive a nuclear holocaust— you put us in the microwave and we will make it. I couldn't care less about anything else.'

ASHISH HEMRAJANI WAS A PART OF THE *MAD MEN* world long before the show became a televised sensation. He was living life in the fast lane as an account manager at J. Walter Thompson but lived in constant fear that everything could go up in smoke any day. He needed to get out of the jaded and uninspiring environment and recharge so he booked a vacation to visit South Africa, Zimbabwe and Botswana in 1999. He had no idea that the journey would alter the course of his destiny. As he sat under a big tree in the Storms River Valley, the idea of BookMyShow struck him, quite like the Newtonian apple. A radio commercial selling rugby tickets online on the portal Computicket.com helped him gravitate towards the idea. Computicket.com was the original avatar of Ticketmaster and the inventor of event ticketing. The idea was quite straightforward. It did away with pricing arbitrage, made ticketing information accessible and was convenient for users. This was a novel concept for the Indian market where the purchase of a simple movie ticket meant queuing up outside cinema halls to try your luck at pigeonhole-sized windows without the assurance that your patience would be rewarded. Moreover, black marketing of tickets for popular films was rampant and the *paan wala* sitting opposite the box office was more likely to have tickets to the show than the man sitting at the window and was sure to charge you four times the cost of the ticket. It was usually a huge gamble because the cinemagoer had no idea whether tickets would be available, and if available, then how many they'd be able to purchase and whether they would even get seats of their choice. Cricket fans had to face bigger challenges. They not only had to not stand in long queues while getting drenched in the pouring rain or fainting in the sweltering heat, they also had to escape random policemen who carried *lathis* and took immense pleasure in beating up restless ticket buyers.

Hence, the idea of an online ticketing service stuck with Ashish who was well aware of these issues. While in Stellenbosch—the Napa Valley of South Africa—he had a few too many glasses of Merlot and woke up with a searing headache and an awful realisation that at some point during the night, he had sent a text message with his resignation to his boss. Caught between a rock and a hard place, Ashish had no option but to try his luck and hope that the start-up idea which had germinated in his head would bear fruit.

THE FIRST ROUND

Ashish was only 24 at that time—the age when one has more enthusiasm and confidence than caution and experience. He formed a company with two of his college friends, Parikshit and Rajesh. Together, they wrote a single-page business plan about online ticketing and faxed it to Chase Capital Partners (CCP). This happened during the dot-com boom in India when things were moving fast for some key players in the market. Sify announced a massive ₹499 crore acquisition of a company, which many assumed to be just a few pages on the internet called IndiaWorld. Despite the misgivings of naysayers, Sify's market capitalisation at the NASDAQ was climbing to almost $1 billion every month. Rediff.com was also preparing for its IPO. By 2000, there had been investments in almost a hundred pure-play internet companies. Leading this pack was Chase Capital Partners which had invested $26.6 million in 12 companies.

CCP had tasted success with its investments in North and Latin America and unlike other private-equity funds which tend to concentrate on a single industry or country, CCP was spreading its tentacles everywhere. CCP requested a meeting with Ashish and his partners within a week of that fax. They landed a million dollars faster than they could say 'dot-com'.

Within six months of this generous funding, News Corp also came knocking on Ashish's door. They also wanted a piece of the pie and handed over another two million dollars to the unsuspecting entrepreneurs. The company expanded its business at a rapid pace, spreading it to eight markets and employing 150 people within months of setting things in motion. Ashish explains, 'We were selling tickets for movies, plays and concerts. Today, the cash on delivery (COD) option has become conventional but we were the first call centre company in the world who included that option in our set-up.'

Even so, it was not a very sophisticated system. The group used Ashish's personal number to receive the calls. They did set up a website for online bookings but it was seldom used. 'That's because the ecosystem for such bookings didn't exist till then as internet penetration was low. Debit and credit cards weren't widely used either,' Ashish explains. Tickets were bought on the phone which made BookMyShow more of a call centre service rather than an online portal. Ashish adds, 'Customers would call us to book tickets and we would pick up the live inventory from cinema halls.' It was a simpler time and yet a difficult task. Movie tickets formed the largest chunk of their business but cinema bookings were not automated then so the company made deals with the multiplexes. They would buy the inventory in some multiplexes and block it in others. This way, they kept their risks diversified. That was the upside but the downside was that whenever they didn't take risks, they lost opportunities. 'The beauty of running an internet business is that your costs must start tapering off when your revenues rise. But our system was so inefficient that it was exactly the opposite,' says Ashish. He finds it easier to see the humour in the situation in retrospect. The reasons for their inefficiency were often beyond their control. If a well-hyped or significant film released over a weekend, they would surely be inundated by a barrage of calls which required more hands on deck to prevent their Net Promoter Score (NPS) from falling. Selling more tickets also meant having more people with vehicles to be able to deliver those tickets. 'Our model just wouldn't scale efficiently and we could never see us making a profit in this manner. It was a massive problem,' Ashish recalls. 'We could never outsource our deliveries because we were worried about inventory theft so we took care of them ourselves. One person would go to the cinema, buy the ticket and deliver it. At this rate, we could handle 15 transactions every four hours. So with a call centre and delivery work force, every time there was a demand uptake, we would bleed more money,' he adds.

Learning the Ropes

Like Zomato and Delhivery, BookMyShow's work involved physical delivery of tickets and in cases of COD, the receipt of payment as well. One doesn't need to be a rocket scientist to deduce that such a model can be a logistical nightmare. This was the pre-smartphone era, which meant that even the basic technology that we are highly dependent on today was still in the making. Putting it euphemistically, Ashish and his partners had more than their fair share of last mile challenges. For instance, in 2001, Bryan Adams was going to perform in India. Tickets for the concert were selling like hot cakes but there was panic in the company's back offices. They had booked and sold their entire inventory of tickets but the money they received just didn't seem to add up. They dug deep and found out that they had thousands of undelivered tickets. There was a problem on the ground. Ashish could never have predicted since it was his first encounter with such a situation. Movie tickets are cheaper at about ₹100 or ₹200 apiece. Even if someone orders five to six tickets, the amount would still be around ₹500 or ₹600 and the buyer could always pay the cash upfront on delivery. Concert tickets, on the other hand, cost around ₹1,000 per ticket. The customers going for the concerts usually book them in a bunch of five to six tickets. This meant that the person booking the ticket would have to pay around ₹5,000 or so upfront. Since no one carried that much cash in their wallet, several times when our delivery guys went to drop off the tickets, the buyer would take time to make the payment by collecting it from friends or by going to the ATM. But the delivery guys who were on a tight schedule couldn't wait and would simply leave. We had all those NDRs (Non-delivery receipts) which came back to us,' Ashish narrates.

During such moments, the core team had to go into the muck and get their hands dirty. 'We split into teams. Some of us handled the calls at the call centre and the rest of us took the tickets in our cars and delivered them ourselves. All hands on deck! It was situations like these that prepared us for the worst and turned us into professionals,' Ashish recalls.

Start-up founders need to get their hands dirty. That's the only way to build a sound and successful organisation. They cannot be problem-solvers or fine tune the system unless they become aware of the problems hitting the employees on the ground. Inexperienced founders can't even learn to delegate work until they have worked on all the stages. It doesn't have anything to do with being a blue or a white collared employee. It's about constructing the DNA of the start-up as these things cascade from downwards. Founders have to be willing to step into the thick of the situations, pick up the phones and delivery cartons whenever needed which demonstrates the strength of the leadership and the desire to succeed. It sends the right message to the employees because it also stokes their desire to constantly learn and remain vested in the organisation's growth. Ultimately, the buck stops with the founders but unfortunately, there are also certain founders who confuse delegation with abdicating their own responsibility. However, Ashish and his co-founders don't belong to that ilk. They knew the need of the hour and were always willing to roll up their sleeves and focus on getting the job done. BookMyShow's eventual success is a testament to these traits.

Since it was a novel business model, the hiccups in the system were also unprecedented. The team had to constantly improvise and much of the learning was done on the job itself. They didn't have a GPS tracking system, camera phones or even the ability to a purchase a complex Customer Relationship Management (CRM) system. Difficult customers were challenging to deal with, and in the absence of reliable technology, they had to devise their own methods of tracking customer behaviours and patterns. 'Sometimes, customers simply denied that our delivery boys had tried to reach them, especially in Delhi. With no means to prove that the customer was wrong and that we had indeed gone with the delivery and the customer wasn't at home to receive it, we came up with our own *jugaad*. We told our delivery guys to make a note of the description of the door. If a customer called and denied the delivery attempt, we promptly described the colour of the door, the type of bolt on the door and certain other specifics of the entrance of the particular address. The customer didn't lie again,' says Ashish, grinning at his own ingenuity.

But that wasn't all. Worse problems were showing up. Customers like a certain Pappu Pehelwan from Paharganj would always snatch away the tickets and shut the door on the delivery boy's face during every third transaction. They had to make a note of such errant clients and blacklist them to prevent losses. There were also moments of amusement at the client's expense. A certain Mr Khanna (name changed, of course) would always buy four tickets for family films and have them delivered to his house. However whenever he bought the tickets for a sleazy film, he would purchase only two and have them delivered to his office. 'We didn't really need a data scientist from Israel to figure out that Khanna was having an affair,' Ashish laughs.

How They Almost Blew It

While different struggles kept Ashish and his co-founders fully occupied, they failed to notice the larger monster lurking in the vicinity, waiting for the kill. By the time they lifted their heads, the dot-com bubble had burst globally, had wiped out billions of dollars of wealth and made the revolutionaries run for the hills. Everywhere, investors were withdrawing from their commitments. When Ashish and his co-founders were informed by their investors, their first concern was their employees. 'I was sure of one thing that if we went belly up, I wanted to be able pay severance to my employees,' he says. The investors, of course, wouldn't hear of it. This forced Ashish to do some arm-twisting. 'I had to threaten them. I told them that I want severance pay for all the 144 employees. All of them had quit their well-paying jobs to follow an entrepreneur's dream.

When the bust happened, I went from city to city for the closures. In Mumbai, I took the employees to a tiny green space opposite Shivaji Park. Our office used to be in Prabhadevi and I didn't have the money to take anyone to a proper conference room. I could see the disappointment, tears and the emotions ranging from sympathy to anger. I told them the truth that I couldn't do anything about their jobs but that I had strongly negotiated to get them all a severance package. This gave them a six months cushion to find jobs. We even helped many of them with their placements,' adds Ashish.

It was a classic case of the mighty having fallen. The six remaining members, which included the three co-founders, bought the company back from CCP and News Corp. They winded down their 2,500 square feet office in Prabhadevi and moved to a 136 square feet office space in Bandra. Despite the odds stacked against them, they were determined to not give up on their dream. In this sense, Ashish and his co-founders were the spitting image of Tyson Quick, the founder and CEO of Instapage who bootstrapped his company to $11 million in annual recurring revenue without any traditional venture funding. He slept in his car because he couldn't afford rent. When things seemed impossible, he reminded himself of what Steve Jobs had once said, 'I'm convinced that about half of what separates the successful entrepreneurs from the non-successful ones is pure perseverance.... Unless you have a lot of passion about this, you're not going to survive. You're going to give it up. So you've got to have an idea, or a problem or a wrong that you want to right that you're passionate about; otherwise, you're not going to have the perseverance to stick it through.' It took Quick another two years to get there but today his company has an annual recurring revenue of over $10 million with an employee strength of 130 people.

Ashish and his co-founders decided to shut down their consumer-facing business because the market wasn't ready. They figured that they would go back to the roots and build software that made ticketing more efficient for cinema owners. Their software allowed cinema owners to access e-ticketing through their website. BookMyShow began to handle electronic ticketing for all kinds of events including concerts. Ashish explains how they implemented their new strategy, 'We would run their box office and do the home delivery. The customers buying tickets didn't know we were powering it or that it was an outsourced operation, much like a BPO for the entertainment and ticketing business. We were the ghost event managers working behind the scenes. No one saw us, no one heard us.'

It was hard and often, unrewarding work. In those days, the small team of six would often sit in their Bandra office, 'twiddling thumbs' because there wasn't enough work to keep them all busy. All the money had dried up and they were beginning from scratch all over again. They couldn't even afford an STD connection on their telephone and would use the public phone to make calls to movie theatres and multiplex chains like PVR who they were targeting as clients. 'There would always be an ambient noise during the calls and prospective clients would often ask us what that was. I had to improvise on the spot so I usually told them that ours is a busy office,' chuckles Ashish. He continues, 'The worst would be stray dogs getting into a fight right next to the booth. Anyway, I would try and organise several meetings with prospective clients in a city and then take the train. I'd stay in the place for a couple of days, finish all my work and travel back to Mumbai in the train.' Rationing was not limited to travel expenses. Ashish talks about how they would only use air conditioning if they made some money, always reused pens, and wrote on the back of printed sheets. In short, they did everything within their means to keep expenses to the minimum. In fact, they are so used to their penny-pinching ways and saving up on the petty cash that 'even today all the office, except for the design team, uses only black and white printers.' Ashish reveals, 'We still reuse paper clips, envelopes and the back of printed sheets of paper. Those early habits have stayed with us. Those tough times taught us the valuable lesson that good times and bad times are both temporary. This knowledge has always kept us grounded.'

Most promoters had humble beginnings. They scrounged and saved to create a company. Azim Premji, the billionaire chairman of Wipro, is legendary for asking people to turn the lights off in the office. Infosys's Narayana Murthy still lives in the same apartment in Jayanagar where he first started out. David Cheriton, the Canadian-born Stanford professor—who lucked out by being an early investor in Google and is now a billionaire—said that he finds the idea of living lavishly disgusting. 'I'm actually quite offended by that sort of thing,' he told the *Edmonton Journal* in a 2006 interview, 'these people who build houses with 13 bathrooms and so on, there's something wrong with them.' In a *Forbes* piece, Cheriton said that one of his biggest expenditures was his 2012 Honda Odyssey which costs about $33,000. Ashish also speaks for his co-founders when he says, 'Some of our employees now drive to office in Mercedes, Audis and BMWs, but we all still drive our old beat up cars.'

Relaunch and More Fund Raising: Rising from the Ashes of the Dot-Com Crash

By 2006, however, Ashish and his team knew that they were ready to re-launch their original consumer-facing portal again.

In the last five years, internet penetration had grown, speed was better and payment gateways had lower failure rates. Even if personal broadband connections were still uncommon, most offices provided good infrastructure through which transacting clients could place their demands. Low cost carriers had arrived and the Indian railways had already launched its online ticketing service spawning an audience that was slowly getting comfortable with the idea of online transactions. Bigtree entertainment, which was BookMyShow's parent company, returned to the market in search of funds and soon enough, it had raised money from the Network18 Group which was quickly creating a portfolio of internet companies by acquiring, investing and building them. It was an impediment for Ashish that funding was hard to come by. He was patient and persistent. 'I've had investors not being convinced (of the idea of BookMyShow) in 1999, 2002, 2007, 2012, 2014 and 2016. But the good thing is that there has been one yeasayer for every naysayer. This is why my advice to budding entrepreneurs is to never get disappointed or elated in these matters,' he says, sagely.

It was a done deal between BookMyShow and Network18 from the moment Ashish met Haresh Chawla, the group CEO of Network18. While he had a couple of investors already willing to fund his enterprise, he went ahead and met Chawla anyway. He explains, 'I knew that this would be a better partnership. I pretty much agreed to the deal because I thought that working with Haresh would be a great experience and it did turn out that way.' In 2012, BookMyShow went on to raise its next round of funding from Accel amounting to $18 million, $25 million from SAIF partners in 2014, followed by $81.5 million from the Stripes Group and the last $100 million from the private equity player, TPG Growth. This last round of funding sent the valuation of the company soaring at about $850 million. However, it still remained shy of turning into a unicorn which seemed surprising given that start-ups like Ola Cabs, Paytm, Flipkart and Snapdeal had all raised enough money to be valued at billions of dollars. Ashish quips, 'A unicorn is a fucking mythical animal. It doesn't exist. It's a horse with a horn and it's ugly. When I am asked whether BookMyShow will ever be a unicorn, my response is that I don't know. But what I know for sure is that we are cockroaches. We are survivors, we can survive a nuclear holocaust, you put us in the microwave and we will make it. I couldn't care less about anything else. Being an entrepreneur is like being a mongrel that wakes up every morning and says to itself, "Where is the scrappy fight today?" When you are out in the street, you fight, you bite, growl and snarl and quickly consume the food before someone else shows up to try and take a bite off your plate.' If this is a classic case of grapes being sour, nothing in Ashish's demeanour let's that on.

ON COMPETITION AND INVESTOR CONFLICTS

Things went well for the next four years but in March 2016, Paytm—the largest wallet in India, backed by marquee investors like SAIF partners and Alibaba Group—announced its foray into movie ticket business via its platform. Vijay Shekhar Sharma, founder and CEO of Paytm, said in a press release, 'Launch of movie tickets on Paytm is in line with our overall strategy of bringing more and more payment use cases online. Today, online platforms penalise customers for paying in advance digitally as they are asked to pay a fee and surcharge. We will eradicate this practice and enable customers to purchase popcorn and other confectioneries thereby reducing queues as well.' BookMyShow was used to having competition but this was one of those awkward moments where Paytm and BookMyShow had common investors. Ravi Adusumalli, an MD from the venture capital SAIF partners was on Paytm's board and Deepak Gaur, from the same VC, was on the board for BookMyShow. Such conflicts are not new in the Indian start-up ecosystem. Sequoia Capital is a large shareholder in Ola and globally, is also an investor in Uber. In the case of Paytm and BookMyShow also, both the investors and the invested managed to avoid any large conflicts. It is quite admirable that they could reach an understanding in a dog-eat-dog world. Ashish notes, 'My equation with Ravi goes beyond BookMyShow. I have full faith in him and Deepak. When Paytm forayed into ticketing, Ravi asked me whether I would like for them to walk away. I really value them because of this. And there is absolutely no discomfort because they have created a Chinese wall that safeguards both our interests. So, that's where we stand today. We continue to be friends.'

On approaching investments in India versus China

India is arguably the most promising internet market in the world. We have attracted billions of dollars in global venture capital from China, Japan, Silicon Valley and Europe. It is also the largest user base for Facebook, Google and WhatsApp. The country's mobile penetration has already crossed the billion mark with over 400 million smartphones and the cheapest data access in the world. Yet, give or take one or two great examples of success, most Indian start-ups falter. Haresh Chawla—partner at True North, a private equity fund, an active angel investor and a friend and mentor—wrote in *Founding Fuel* about start-ups hitting a glass ceiling around 2016 and the fallacy of the 'one' market despite the hyper funding that everyone witnessed in the 2013–15 era. He argued in detail about the existence of three kinds of India. According to him, *India One* composed of the top 15 per cent of Indians, i.e., about 150–180 million, earning an average of ₹30,000 per month. They are the ones who have money left over after buying necessities. These 15 per cent of Indians control over half the spending power of the economy and almost its entire discretionary spending. *India Two* is the middle 30 per cent or 400-odd million Indians, earning an average of ₹7,000 a month. This would be a country about three times the size of Bangladesh with a similar level of purchasing power. *India Three* are the forgotten 650 million who subsist and don't have the money to buy even two square meals. Their incomes rival that of sub-Saharan Africa. He argues that the failure to distinguish between 'internet users' (*India Two*) and 'internet consumers' (*India One*) has messed up every estimate of the market. This destroyed the Total Addressable Market (TAM) calculations that have driven most VC funding and valuations. In a real sense, TAM—of people who can afford to actually habitually spend on current offerings of our internet giants—is not one billion people, it is about 150 million people[7].

Ashish built BookMyShow profitably in a scenario where others were interested in the buying growth and not focussing on profitability. Before the battle with Paytm began, BookMyShow had been consistently posting profits year-on-year. The maniacal funding era pushed everyone to drive growth and increase the market size. He is well aware of Chawla's

---

[7] Chawla, Haresh. How India's Digital Economy Can Rediscover Its Mojo, *Founding Fuel*, 30 August 2016. http://www.foundingfuel.com/article/how-indias-digital-economy-can-rediscover-its-mojo/

premise of the three types of India and is clearly disappointed in investors for their lack of understanding of India's economic story. 'Investors have to recognise that India is not the US, and certainly not China. USA has 300 million people, all with some equitable income. They can all afford a smart phone. No one is struggling for food, clothes or a roof over their head. Most of our population, on the other hand, is struggling to get by on a daily basis. What are they going to do with a 40 per cent discount on a pair of jeans? So, *India Three* feeds on *India Two* which feeds on *India One*. We always knew it's not a 1.5 billion population, that TAM isn't there even though there is a theoretical universe of 1.25 billion population. It's going to take time for the TAM to catch up with the universe.' With the price of data crashing and content consumption shooting up and YouTube usage surging seven times, the tectonic shift has already been set in motion.

According to Ashish, 'Content first kicked-in and now, it should naturally progress to commerce. But for that, *India Two* and *India Three* audiences need to be making more money. It's not happening at the pace at which the access to internet is growing. Money is still not flowing down fast enough.'

That kind of growth has happened in China but it hasn't yet happened in India. India is different from China. There is no YouTube, Facebook, Uber, Gmail or WhatsApp in China. It is a completely controlled environment and all the companies are given a runway of 15 years to build dominance and most of them have been supported with investments by China's Ministry of Culture. All quasi-government agencies and their sub-holdings are completely in cahoots with the government. If you want to succeed in China—get close to the government, if you want to succeed in India—stay away from the government.

Ashish couldn't be more right about China. That country is like a multi-lane super highway you can zip through at top speed till you bounce completely off the road because it doesn't go all the way through. 'McDonald's learnt it the hard way when they hit about a 100 stores. Suddenly some new government rules cropped up. Ticketmaster went in just two months before the Olympics and the government said they could sell their tickets but were forced into a joint venture with a local entity. Disneyland also learnt it the hard way when the land on the opposite side was given to a competitor at a subsidy. India is different because here, you must navigate the crowded roads with the autorickshaw, scooter, cows on the street, ditches and potholes before you can hit the Expressway, but once you get on it, you can drive at 120 or 130 km/h with nobody to stop you.'

That said, according to a McKinsey Global Institute (MGI) report released in 2018, between 1990 and 2013, China pulled out 730 million people out of poverty. India was at 170 million. There can be little comparison between China and India. While one is a booming $11.3 trillion economy, the other is not more than a $2.1 trillion upstart. The opportunities that our populations hold can't be compared.

On the Duties of an Angel Investor

By 2018, Sachin Bansal and Binny Bansal of Flipkart had invested in seventeen ventures with a total funding of $26 million and $32 million, respectively. Kunal Bahl and Rohit Bansal of Snapdeal are said to have made over 28 investments. Anupam Mittal of the People Group has over 30 investments including Ola. Ashish, on the other hand, prefers not to actively angel invest. His only known investments are DishCo, an app that allows users to book tables at different restaurants and discover signature dishes, Juspay in the payments arena and Invideo, a video automation company. He shies away from investing more aggressively and explains, 'I can't invest in 20–30 companies because that would be unfair to BookMyShow. If I am investing money in a venture, I like to put in the time and effort as well. For now, if I just want returns then I have other instruments of financial planning. Start-ups ask for investments for two reasons: the money and the expertise. If I have a portfolio of 40 companies and they all seek my time then I won't be left with any time for BookMyShow. That's not right. This is why I restrict myself to only two to three companies a year.'

The Advice is to Not Take Any Advice

Indians love to give advice. Everyone in this country has pearls of wisdom to impart on everything from how to raise your baby to how to run your company. Ashish has also met his fair share of wisdom gurus. He shares, 'You aren't going to believe this. Someone actually said to me that since I am into ticketing, I should also work on travel ticketing. He thought it all to be the same. He suggested that I should expand into the travel and hotel booking industry.'

'What did you think of it?' I asked.

'I thought he was total dickhead.'

From a drunken text to his former boss to survival tactics to being a persistent but cautious entrepreneur, Ashish has done it all and created space for himself as one of the biggest players.

Nothing seems to deter him, neither detractors nor competition. In that sense, he is truly the hard bred street mongrel, always ready for his next scrappy fight.

BRIJESH AGARWAL

Co-Founder, IndiaMART InterMESH Ltd.

'So we realised with Tolexo that a very long drawn high capital investment game would play out. We were burning through almost a million dollars a month with no end in sight. One cannot predict why an Amazon or an Alibaba won't encroach the space tomorrow; these are companies that come with loaded guns, ready for the long haul. This wasn't a battle we wanted to engage in. We would have sapped all of IndiaMART's resources and capital built over 20 years trying to fund this. So we pulled out.'

The Beginning of a New Era

Brijesh was introduced to the internet in 1994 when he was eighteen years old. A relative passed away and the family found shares of a British company tucked away in his belongings. They called up stockbrokers in Calcutta and Mumbai to make enquiries but eventually, reached a dead end. A few weeks later, Brijesh mentioned these mysterious shares in a phone call to his older brother, Dinesh, who was working with HCL in the US. Dinesh placed the call on hold. While Brijesh was sweating over the cost of the phone call, around ₹100 rupees per minute in the Nineties, his brother returned with some exciting news. He gave Brijesh all kinds of information about the company, including its founders, directors and the status of their relative's shares. 'Obviously, I was surprised,' recalls Brijesh. 'How do you know so much about this company?' he asked his brother. That was when his brother told him about the internet. 'My first impression was: you can find anything in the world on this. It sounded exciting. But we left it at that. I was still in college back then,' adds Brijesh.

Dinesh brought a computer for Brijesh in 1995 when he returned to India. The brothers began to discuss the possibilities that could open up through the use of the computer and the internet.

Brijesh says, 'Dinesh's first idea was to start an internet service provider in India, but we soon realised that the process required licences and given our lack of access to capital and poor understanding of government regulations, it would be complicated for us.' So they began to evaluate other businesses, and eventually stumbled upon the Yellow Pages for exporters. Here was an idea! People searched for services and product providers in the Yellow Pages but the internet was a far more efficient way of doing this. 'Our trading background helped us in realising that this idea was right up our alley. I saw how exporters at trade fairs would benefit from websites since there was very little information about Indian traders on the internet. That was how IndiaMART was born … for showcasing Indian businesses,' he says.

The Reality Check

While the two brothers were excited about their idea, they soon realised that this idea might have been born before its time. 'Hardly anyone knew about the internet and so, very few people cared about our service,' Brijesh reveals. Their next step was to scan the government data and the directory of the Federation of Indian Exporters to get the names of different businesses in sectors like garments, handicrafts, spices, gems and jewellery. 'We made forms and sent them to these companies asking them to fill in the information regarding their products and the contact details. We were sending thousands of envelopes around the country. The problem was that barely anyone returned our requests. The response rate was less than two per cent.

Nevertheless, we listed whatever information we received on the IndiaMART website.' It wasn't the first time that the brothers wondered if they had begun too soon. This was a classic case of pioneers lying face down in the mud with arrows in their backs. 'Over the years, I have come to believe that the first mover advantage is mostly a myth engraved in a start-up playbook,' says Brijesh, still not convinced that their first move was ever an advantage. In reality, nearly half of the companies that go *first* fail. The ones who succeed are the companies that entered the market early but not first. They learn from the proverbial arrows in the pioneer's back and ride the wave of market excitement to success. Companies defined as *first followers* have a mere eight per cent failure rate.

Brijesh confesses, 'We considered going back to Nanpara, our hometown, near the Nepal border. Our family owned a gas station there. We spoke to our grandfather and told him that we were losing money because our customers treated us with suspicion and usually, kicked us out of their office under the assumption that we were fly-by-night operators.' Fortunately, their grandfather was made of sterner stuff and asked them to take a long term assessment of the matter. He asked them to consider whether the system that they were building would be useful to any business in the future. 'We were 100 per cent sure of that. Exporters were spending lakh of rupees in every trade show. It would certainly be worth their money if they listed their company on our website and made their information available 24x7, 365 days a year to a global audience. We knew we had reached early, but surely, this idea's time would arrive just as soon as more people understood what the internet was,' Brijesh adds. Their grandfather's support and insistence that Brijesh and Dinesh walk the whole nine yards if they believed in the idea was also backed by his financial support, which helped them tide over the tough times.

It was time for the two to reconsider their strategy and approach to the services that they were trying to sell. 'Maybe businesses were not ready to believe in our online service directory, but exporters surely needed a website that showcased their capabilities, with pictures of their infrastructure and an online products catalogue. And while at it, we could keep enriching our database. This was an easier sell as awareness of the internet was growing. We also began charging the customers for building their websites,' Brijesh explains.

IndiaMART closed the financial year of 1997 with a revenue of ₹6 lakh. In 1999, the revenue grew to ₹52 lakh. The internet euphoria was on the rise. Just as the brothers were warming up to the idea of venture capitals to accelerate their plans, the dot-com bubble burst. Despite it being a year of global gloom and doom, their revenues stood at a cool ₹1.25 crore. The brothers knew that while their web development business was profitable, it was a commodity business. Hundreds of small shops that could make websites for cheap had begun to mushroom. Dinesh and Brijesh knew that the only way to pull away from the clutter was to go back and invest in their original business information platform for exporters. They ploughed the cash generated from their services business to incubate the directory business.

Reinvention

By 2006, IndiaMART had clocked in around ₹18 crore in revenue. Then, a couple of external factors forced them to reinvent all over again. The lesser known 'Crocodile of the Yangtze River', Alibaba had got an investment of $1 billion from Yahoo! and emerged as the go-to platform for source suppliers and manufacturers, globally. When the rupee appreciated in 2007–08, exporters were badly hit. The major export sectors that were directly in the eye of the storm were IT and services, textiles, leather, sugar and pharmaceuticals. All kinds of exporters from India lost their competitive ground. However, currencies of major competitors in China, Vietnam, Pakistan and Bangladesh did not appreciate in comparison with the Indian rupee. US was the biggest market for the textile sector, which suffered a slowdown along with the decline in US growth as it had gone down to 0.6 per cent in the first quarter. This factor, along with the appreciating rupee, was a double whammy. The Agarwal brothers knew that they needed to mould their product according to the market situation. 'This time, we also needed more capital to get some breathing space,' says Brijesh. But the stock-market was in bad shape. After meeting many naysayers in the venture capital community, IndiaMART finally raised $10 million from Intel Capital in January 2009. They also pivoted their business model from being export-oriented to domestic businesses. 'India was not making strides in exports, but the domestic market was getting bigger. By then, the internet audience had also increased and people knew how to utilise the medium properly. Our twelve years of hard work before this felt like a net practice on the cricket pitch. The real match had just begun,' Brijesh grins.

FROM A FAMILY BUSINESS TO A CORPORATION

As a young start-up, from 1999–2007 until Webchutney raised its first round of institutional financing from Capital18, I never thought of having a formal board of directors for my company. Once the board was established, I wondered why I hadn't done that sooner. I realised that their experiences in strategic decision-making across multiple businesses were a boon. As entrepreneurs, we often go through the constant struggle to be operators and manage the day-to-day operations, while simultaneously keeping the big picture in mind. The trouble is that most first-time entrepreneurs don't have the experience in processes and effects of long-term strategic planning. By instituting a board of directors, you can select participants who have unique experiences in hiring strategies, capitalisation, resource allocation, etc. They can be singularly dedicated to guiding you in developing and executing your long-term strategic goals. Additionally, their power to be impartial is irreplaceable. Entrepreneurs can often get emotionally attached to their ideas and efforts, so much so that they often miss the forest for the trees. A good board is comfortable telling the entrepreneurs not to obsess over something that isn't working.

In an interview to MediaNama in March 2009, three months after raising the capital, Dinesh had said, 'We were a highly cash flow-positive business, and towards the end of 2006–2007, there was a market frenzy. Our costs were going up unnecessarily and the whole business model started to look non-feasible. If costs were to grow at 30-40-50 per cent, I didn't see the businesses flourishing in the long run. That is when I decided to raise the money. We would never have thought of raising money otherwise.' After the investment, Sarayu Srinivasan from Intel Capital got into the act and built a formal board for IndiaMART. He roped in Deep Kalra of MakeMyTrip, P. N. Vijay, Country Head of Citibank India and Nachiket More, the COO of ICICI Bank, as board members.

'This was a blessing for us. The board reshaped our working style from being slow, fearful and orthodox to being bold and confident in our vision. They had a significant contribution in making us the company that we are today. We experimented a lot while changing gears and in that process, everyone knew that we would have to invest tonnes of money. They were very adept at guiding us in terms of where to invest, where not to waste money etc. That helped us a lot, because left on our own, we would have either wasted the money or not spent it at all. The first board worked with us for three years, and it was the best learning phase of our entire life and career during that period,' Brijesh admits. By 2011, IndiaMART had opened

52 offices across 20 cities. In that fiscal year, they touched a hundred-crore turnover.

The Big Leap and the Mighty Hard Landing: How They Nearly Blew It

By 2014, IndiaMART had grown into a business of ₹350 crore —listing 26 lakh suppliers, 2.6 crore products across 80,000 categories and a database of around 12 million buyers. The brothers were studying the online commerce space. They always had their ears to the ground regularly communicating with suppliers and buyers listed with them. 'One constant feedback we received was that if crucial issues such as payment, packaging, logistics, and on-time delivery are taken care of, then the e-commerce marketplace can be more efficient than the physical one.' Much like what was happening in the e-commerce space for B2C consumers. IndiaMART had provided a business discovery platform for products and pricing information and was generating boatloads of business leads every day. Transactions and fulfilment centres seemed like the obvious next step to close the loop.

The idea was to provide a single platform to any number of buyers and sellers for transactions. Tolexo was launched in January 2015 and IndiaMART announced it would invest ₹100 crore to build it. It was committed to putting in $1 million per month for the next 100 months or more, using its balance sheet and internal accruals to do so. Tolexo was targeting ₹1,000 crore revenue by 2020. It was IndiaMART's most ambitious bet. Within a year of Tolexo's launch, IndiaMART raised fresh funds from Amadeus Capital Partners with participation from WestBridge Capital and the Accion Frontier Investments in addition to Intel Capital, their existing investor. A significant portion of the raised funds was allocated to Tolexo. And then, for the financial year 2015–16, Tolexo reported a net sales of ₹4.69 crore and losses of ₹72.9 crore. Its work force stood at 350 people. Something was going wrong.

'We didn't realise that to bring the entire ecosystem of suppliers online would be a humongous task. It wasn't going to be easy for anyone as the market wasn't ready. Companies that wanted to play this game needed ten years of runway to continue burning through cash. We certainly weren't willing to do that. Also putting IndiaMART, the demand generation engine on the back burner didn't mean that Tolexo would automatically become the transactional and fulfilment platform. To develop customer loyalty all over again is a time-consuming affair. One has to build it slowly. If you try and speed it up—behaving like Amazon or Flipkart—you need to have more capital. So we realised that Tolexo was going to be a very long-drawn, high-capital investment game. We were burning through almost a million dollars a month with no end in sight. One cannot predict why an Amazon or an Alibaba will not invade the space tomorrow. These are companies that came with loaded guns and were ready for the long haul. This wasn't a battle we wanted to engage in. We would have sapped all of IndiaMART's resources and capital built over 20 years trying to fund this. So we pulled out.' By March 2017, the media was reporting mass layoffs at Tolexo.

Getting Knocked down and Getting up Again

It's back to the basics now for Brijesh. IndiaMART reported around 4.7 million suppliers and 60 million buyers transacting on the website, in 2018. In March 2018, the company posted a revenue of ₹410 crore, and turned profitable at a cash-flow level, earning ₹182 crore from operating activities.

'We are growing 30 per cent year-on-year revenue and have recently launched a payments facilitation and an escrow programme. The adoption of digital technologies and digital payments has improved considerably post-demonetisation,' he explains.

The company is planning an IPO soon. IndiaMART's existing investors and promoters plan to sell around 4.2 million shares through the listing, according to the company's draft red herring prospectus filed with the Securities and Exchange Board of India on 29 June 2018.

When the company goes public, the brothers will cumulatively hold over 55 per cent of it, the largest ever for an internet IPO in India. Late Eddie Cantor, the comedian, dancer, singer, actor, and songwriter once said, 'It takes twenty years to become an overnight success.' For Brijesh and Dinesh Agarwal, it has been twenty-two.

JITENDRA GUPTA

Co-Founder, Citrus Pay

'Cube was trying to be a challenger to Paytm and in hindsight, I think that was a big mistake.... We were trying to be BillDesk, Paytm, FreeCharge, CCAvenue, all at the same time. So, I decided that I won't allow a single rupee to be spent on Cube. As the financial in charge, I turned off the tap on it. Satyen wasn't pleased with the decision and raised the issue with the board.... I was surprised that the board decided not to invest a penny further in Cube and asked Satyen to leave the company.'

IT IS FASCINATING THAT SO MANY BIG INDIAN start-ups were born not out of brilliance but unemployment. In that sense, perhaps necessity *is* the key to invention. Jitendra Gupta had been unemployed for nearly eight months and the period of uncertainty had done little to help him figure out his next move. All he knew was that he could no longer work in a nine to five job. Having worked as an investment banker for ICICI for seven years, he was done with that job. There were two reasons—one, the financial slowdown had set in and two, he didn't feel enthusiastic about his job anymore. He didn't want to spend the rest of his life being unappreciated and unrecognised for his hard work. But did he feel that he was on the cusp of something monumental? No.

After quitting his cushy job, Jitendra spent his time on lucrative freelance assignments to pay the bills and spent his free time in soul searching. The only thing that he was sure about, during this transition was his USP (Unique Selling Proposition). People valued his opinion on payments. This trait, coupled with his acquaintance with Amrish Rau of First Data, whom he knew from his banking days, led to the germination of an exciting idea of starting a financial technology company that could provide mobile and app-based payment solutions. He explains, 'I realised that most of the assignments that I received were related to the financial services sector, especially payments. Incidentally, I met Amrish at a party and told him that I was thinking of creating something in the payments space. Amrish said, "Go ahead. I'll write you the first cheque." This gave me a lot of confidence because Amrish was quite known in that space.' And so, Citrus Pay was born.

On Funding

Jitendra started the company in April 2011. He knew that he wasn't bringing anything new to the market but he was confident that his idea would stay afloat given the sheer size of the market. He understood that he would be able to earn enough revenue and grow organically. Amrish eventually became a co-founder in Citrus and introduced Jitendra to Mohit Bhatnagar from Sequoia Capital. Mohit showed great enthusiasm for their project. 'I wasn't looking to raise funds yet because we hadn't even launched the platform, but I met Mohit out of courtesy. He asked all the usual questions, but what really got him going was the fact that I'd already signed five bank contracts to work with our platform,' recalls Jitendra. Mohit was taken aback because Jitendra was still a lone ranger with no team, no office, no technology or infrastructure but he had already signed contracts with ICICI, HDFC, Axis Bank, SBI and Citibank. He asked Jitendra to swing by his office the next day, which also happened to be Jitendra's birthday.

When it rains, it pours. Jitendra would tell you that this is true. He met with no less than six partners from Sequoia who threw a range of questions at him. Later, he received a call from Mohit who enquired about Jitendra's capital requirements. He says, 'Amrish and I had projected a requirement for half a million dollars, but I decided to go a little further and said that we needed a million dollars.' Jitendra, however, was not prepared for Mohit's response. Mohit said, 'Think again. You are asking for too little. I will give you two million dollars.

Think big.' It's very unusual for founders to raise money before their product has been rolled out. Most first-time entrepreneurs need to raise money from family and friends, get some traction with customers and only then can they go out to raise institutional capital.

Of course, there are exceptions like Mukesh Bansal of cure.fit who raised a boatload of money pre-launch. He was able to do so only because he was not a first-time entrepreneur, having already launched and sold Myntra to Flipkart. Similarly, Kunal Shah received financing for his yet to be launched Fintech start-up, Cred. Kunal had sold FreeCharge for nearly $400 million to Snapdeal. Both men had great industry credibility, so things were easier for them, but pulling off a large-seed investment pre-launch when the conviction is built purely on instinct rather than metrics or traction was unheard of. Compared to that, investments at a later stage are easier because they often rely on metrics, cohorts, and other empirical evidence of traction.

Non-Tech Founder

Mark Suster, a famous entrepreneur and venture capitalist who is currently a managing partner at Upfront Ventures, believes 'If you don't have somebody inside your organisation who is setting the technological direction, then I'm convinced you'll never head for greatness.' Jitendra, on the other hand, had been working the unconventional way. He set a minor trend by outsourcing the entire technology build-up for his platform. Having spent two decades in the industry, it was the first time that I had seen something like this. Jitendra decided to work with ElectraCard Services, which is no longer operational, but it used to provide a payment gateway to ICICI then.

He reached out to its founder and told him that he required that gateway. Since the company was only working with banks, its services were quite expensive. He quoted an amount that meant that Jitendra would have had to cough up over a crore per year just for the technology. Jitendra says, 'I convinced him to work with us on a per-transaction basis initially. Our outflow to them in the first year was hardly ₹12 lakh. But within eight months of going live, we realised that it was not going to work in terms of stability, flexibility or what we wanted to deliver. So we hired Talent Pickup, an IT services company based in Pune. The company hired staff dedicated for our tasks so we could directly allot work and manage them ourselves. The best part was that I didn't have to handle the replacement or recruitment! We continue to work with them to date.' However, Sequoia was concerned about this method. 'I asked them how it mattered whether they were on-rolls or not. It was still my team and worked closely with me. Fortunately, our business was growing and investors don't care when things are working. We had a good uptake every month. So eventually, they were okay with it,' Jitendra explains.

Start-ups usually don't outsource their tech stack. Although many successful start-ups—MakeMyTrip, Naukri.com, IndiaWorld and Rediff.com—didn't have a tech co-founder. Nevertheless, it continues to be a hot topic of discussion for VCs. It's one of those beliefs—like the myth that a single founder has low chances of success—which many founders have struggled with.

Differentiating

There were ten payment solution companies in India, in 2011, when Jitendra started his venture. E-commerce industry was not a formative idea till then. Only urban dwellers were warming up to the idea of paying their utility bills online. Paying online wasn't a smooth process either. The process of online payments is such that each transaction has to go through different entities or hops (issuer, acquirer, card schemes, payment gateway etc.) Each entity must be able to smoothly connect and share encrypted data, which in turn, must meet the strict and unique security requirements of the receiving body. Sometimes there is a security failure because some issuing banks have an aggressive fraud detection mechanism. There are certain transactions that they recognise as unusual, for a particular clients. This recognition is usually based on past purchase behaviour and transactions. The purchasing transaction that does not conform to your past spending behaviour gets flagged as fraud. It is not an exact science or a perfect method of evaluation and sometimes, genuine transactions also get flagged and rejected as frauds. That said, I believed that payments were a commodity business with a better user interface wherein bugs could be fixed if the need arose. So what was Citrus's value addition to the market?

'Since I had a lot of experience in payments, I knew all the processes and most of them were unnecessarily manual. Every player was operating in the same way—by taking the bank's pipe, consolidating and providing it to the merchant at a single entry state. That's all. My experience had helped me learn how things were changing in the US and European markets. So that was an inspiration. I was certain that we could automate several of these payment methods. I was aware that we could substantially improve the customer and merchant experience and get a solid foothold in the market,' Jitendra says.

To explain, Citrus was trying to create a convenient and easy-going experience for the users. For instance, till 2012, India did not have the 'card save' option in which the user could save their card details on the portal for future transactions. The market believed that this was an impossible idea to execute in India because the RBI guidelines didn't allow it. Jitendra dug deeper and figured out that it had nothing to do with the RBI. The issue was with the Payment Card Industry's security standards which decided where and how the card information is to be stored and provided guidelines on how a card needs to be encrypted, retrieved and transmitted. Since none of the banks in India around that time were compliant with the guidelines, this facility was unavailable to an Indian user. This gap in information and knowledge meant that inefficiency existed in the process. Jitendra realised that the pioneering payment gateways that were built in the past decade had not kept up with the dramatic changes in the dot-com world. It was a sitting duck.

Citrus's USP, therefore, would be to provide a faster checkout for users by storing their card information on their server. This meant the merchants wouldn't have to do a PCI gateway and could use a single account to retrieve data. As luck would have it, Cleartrip launched its expressway in the same month as Citrus and everyone looked to Cleartrip for their user experience. Once Cleartrip established the avenue, it became easier for Citrus to follow suit. Merchants who had initially refused to be a part of the plan because they thought it would not be safe began to call up Jitendra with a demand for the card save feature. The tide had finally turned in his favour.

Citrus provided another advantage, which was an automated switch to a different gateway in case a bank's payment gateway went down. In case such an error occurred indefinitely, a team of two or three people would be permanently deployed to monitor the situation in real time. In the event of a shutdown, the team had to switch the gateway. Citrus provided software that made this switch automatic. They had no immediate takers for the service till ICICI's gateway went down for six hours, causing the Jet Airways site to go down. The PVR multiplex site was also down for the whole weekend. 'My sales team was flooded with calls from Jet, PVR and Inox. We had pitched to these businesses in the past but it took an adversity for them to recognise what we were bringing to the table,' Jitendra says as he recalls the moment when Citrus Pay became a prominent player in the market.

On Scaling

Citrus went on to gain fifty customers within two months of launching. Jitendra personally directed the product and sales teams while coordinating with the technology team. By May 2012, the company began to establish a good momentum, churning out a revenue of ₹1 crore per month. That same year, in July, Ticketnew.com, an equivalent of BookMyShow in South India, which catered to single screen theatres, signed up with Citrus, and became its largest customer.

But relatively speaking, they still weren't playing in the big league where they could claim to process tens of thousands of transactions every day for one single client. Then in November 2012, Citrus bagged a deal with redBus. Citrus's competitors played aggressively to land these plum accounts. As Jitendra recalls, 'It took us many meetings to convince them to choose us.' However, Citrus's real big catch was Airtel. It took Jitendra and his team over a year to convince them to sign on. Airtel was their first mega client, with 50,000–60,000 transactions every day. As Jitendra puts it, 'Everything in the company changed the day we signed on Airtel.' Signing a deal with such a large customer can generate meaningful revenue, especially for an early stage start-up, provide validation that you are 'enterprise grade' level and make it easier to land other big clients. Citrus was now ripe for new big businesses.

ON CO-FOUNDER ISSUES

In 2012, Noam Wasserman, a professor at Harvard Business School, studied the careers of 10,000 founders for his book *The Founder's Dilemma*. During his research, he discovered that 65 per cent start-ups fail due to co-founder conflicts. The numbers were higher than the divorce rate in the US. I can vouch for this because I went through a similar experience at Webchutney. I founded the company in 1999 with three colleagues from an ad agency called Grey, where I had worked as an intern for around eight months. One of the co-founders left the start-up within two months and the second one lasted for nine months. Around 2005, we incubated a research firm which went belly-up after a few years because of co-founder issues. With the benefit of hindsight, I agree that start-up failures can also be attributed to co-founder conflicts. Webchutney incubated Adnetwork, which was acquired by Bertelsmann. But it lasted less than six months after the acquisition, again, because of co-founder conflicts. These conflicts have been one of the top reasons even in the start-up companies where I've made investments to date.

The same story repeated itself at Citrus as well. While Jitendra was the person who started the company and Amrish was the angel investor, there was also Satyen Kothari whose name was regularly mentioned in the press as a co-founder. Only the naïve believe everything that they read in the newspapers. Those who did believe the media, never knew the whole truth. Satyen and Amrish had been schoolmates and this acquaintance was the route through which he came on board. According to Jitendra, Satyen did not join Citrus as a co-founder. He was only available in the capacity of a consultant and an advisor as he wasn't even working with them full-time. He would go to the Citrus offices once a month for a few hours, but these visits became more frequent as the business grew.

'I insisted that we should have clarity on how much Satyen should be involved and he agreed to join us full-time. I had no issues with that because he was able to take a few things off my rapidly growing plate. I realised his real intentions quite later. He wanted to take the credit for our success.

He started calling himself a co-founder at Citrus after the company had been in the market for two and a half years already. He began to handle the press while I was busy with business development and operations. I had no idea about what was coming for us in the next few weeks. I would see him in the media seldom never in the office,' clarifies Jitendra as he narrates his side of the story.

Slowly, it dawned on Jitendra that everyone in the industry assumed that Satyen was a co-founder. That is when he had enough of it. He confronted Satyen. Fortunately, Amrish was a board member and also worked full-time at Citrus by then, agreed with Jitendra on the issue and asked Satyen to back off. 'I was relieved for the moment and glad that Amrish chose me over his childhood friend. Satyen seemed to have made his peace and took a backseat,' recalls Jitendra.

How They Almost Blew It

Citrus began the second round of funding for its operations in early 2015. By this time, Ola and Snapdeal had already raised $600 million each. Jitendra and his associates, carried away by the sheer numbers involved in these deals, believed that their valuation should also be in the range of $300–400 million. They thought that their target to raise capital should be approximately $150 million. However, their B2B (Business to Business) model wasn't enough for raising the money. They needed a good consumer-facing proposition. In a moment of desperation and wild optimism, they decided to project Cube as their anchor product. Cube was Citrus's answer to rapidly successful apps like Paytm. Headed by Satyen, they had envisioned Cube as a personal finance manager app. When Jitendra saw the first version of the app, he realised that it was no different than any other recharge app. He admits, 'We had started believing in our bubble. We did not even have 10,000 downloads of Cube, yet suddenly, it was our anchor. We did roadshows in New York, Hong Kong, London, Shanghai, wherever we went to raise funding.' Today, he refers to it as a moment of stupidity.

It is quite natural for entrepreneurs to want the highest valuations for their companies and lately, these valuations have indeed soared. But these sky-high valuations may not always be a good thing for start-ups. In my experience, high start-up valuations are an easy way to distance investors, especially if things don't go according to plan. In situations like that, the investor could become resentful towards the valuation. Furthermore, since the next round of investments requires a lot of traction, it might become difficult for entrepreneurs to attract investors. In such scenarios, investors refuse to meet entrepreneurs. Even if they do meet them, such talks are never taken forward. This happens because the valuation leaves them with an impression that the entrepreneur doesn't know the strengths and vulnerabilities of his own business.

For Jitendra, this reality sunk in after months of unsuccessful meetings with investors all over the world. 'I realised that it wouldn't work because our product was useless,' admits Jitendra. They had only $2 million left in the bank and a four-month runway. Finally, they received a $100 million valuation from an investor who showed interest in their company. It was still a disappointment for them and yet, they had no choice but to keep talking. Eventually, when nothing worked, they went back to Mohit from Sequoia and requested him for more funds. 'Mohit always had confidence in us and said that the funds starvation was a momentary issue. Our business was growing 10–15 per cent every month, so our core business was never questionable. If Mohit had not helped, we would have gone belly-up for sure. He wired the money to us just when we needed it,' says Jitendra.

Most start-ups operate as if they are on a rollercoaster ride. Everything looks great from the top, but on the way down, things begin to look bleak and desolate. Venture capitalists have front row seats on such start-up journeys. The best VCs work through these highs and lows experienced by their portfolio companies. Whenever the start-up encounters a nasty situation, they try to look beyond the immediate issues and focus on the fundamentals. Jitendra came close to blowing it up quite early in the life of his start-up. Although the company was pulled back from the brink of death with the help of timely arrival of funds, Jitendra knew that he had to analyse the factors that had pushed them to the tipping point. 'Cube was trying to compete with Paytm and in hindsight, I think that was a big mistake,' he says without any qualms and continues, 'It was obvious that Cube had been the key distraction over the last eight months. It had taken our focus away from the core business, which was Citrus. It also continued to bleed the company despite our best efforts. We were trying to be BillDesk, Paytm, FreeCharge, and CCAvenue, all at the same time. So I decided that I won't allow a single rupee to be spent on Cube. As the financial in-charge, I simply turned off the tap on it.' Satyen, however, wasn't pleased with the decision and raised this issue with the board. 'This time, it got nastier,' Jitendra recalls, 'Satyen even accused me of being incapable of running the company and laid the claim to be the next CEO for Citrus. I had had enough. I had made a mistake once, I didn't want to repeat it. I told the board to let us both present our cases and then decide. To be honest, I expected the board to provide a middle path. I assumed that their decision would be something like investing $5 million in Cube to give Satyen some runway to prove himself and directing the rest of the freshly-raised capital to the core payments business. I was surprised that the board decided not to invest a penny further in Cube and asked Satyen to leave the company.'

Satyen demanded that he should be handed over Cube as a part of his exit package. The board was more than happy to let Cube go along with Satyen. Citrus, at its core, was a Business to Business model (B2B) company while Cube was a Business to Consumer model (B2C) idea. Why do B2B companies around the world rarely transform into successful B2C companies? The answer is that their business models are significantly different. A successful B2B company is built around technical merit, reasoned product features, large enterprise clients and at the core, a massive sales culture. In case of Citrus, for instance, there was a persistent effort to win the Airtel business, even though it took over a year to make it happen. A successful B2C firm is built around user segments, understanding emotional and rational needs, brand building, user acquisition and the management of multiple distribution networks. They are like chalk and cheese. It's a rare phenomenon to see a company mutate itself from one to the other. Jitendra explains, 'In hindsight, however, I can admit that if the board had decided that I should give him more time and money, the company culture would have turned toxic and we would have eventually run out of money again. We never let it come out in the public domain because we were sensitive to the fact that this uncertainty around the leadership could make clients jittery. We didn't want to sabotage the company's future because of our personal issues.'

Founder conflicts are far more common than people think. In Citrus's case, apart from the fact that their focus turned from their core component and primary B2B model to the B2C product Cube, the conflict between Jitendra and Satyen was probably another reason why they almost blew it. The key to resolving founder conflicts successfully is to agree on a fair process. Sam Altman of Y Combinator said, 'Founder conflicts arise when one of two things happen—either the founders want different things for the company or they want the same thing for themselves. Either way, it is impossible for both parties to get what they want. A decision that makes one party happy is likely to leave the other party fuming. Agreeing on a fair process in advance allows the founders to resolve the conflict (which is essential), but it should be done in a way where both parties can live with the resolution.' Co-founders need to figure out how to have that crucial conversation with each other with integrity and honesty because how they interact with each other will set the tone for larger conversations. They can do it either with integrity or with acrimony. It is anybody's guess as to which is the best way to proceed.

At Webchutney, I've had moments when emotions ran high between my co-founder and me. We found ourselves at opposite ends of an agreement during a critical time. Over the years, I have realised that there is no use in pretending that everything is fine and business is running as usual. I understand that it best to be straightforward in discussions with the core team and the investors and say, 'This is what's going on but I am sure that we will figure out the solution together.' Hence, running a company, in many ways, is not very different from a marriage. You must decide whether you can spend the rest of your life with your chosen partner (or partners). Getting a divorce down the road can often be detrimental for the child, which in this case is the start-up.

Sleeping With the Enemy

One of the biggest mergers in India took place on 14 September 2016 when Naspers' PayU bought Citrus Pay for $130 million in cash. It was revealed that about fifty employees who were allocated ESOPs (Employee Stock Ownership Plan) in the company had a windfall of over $40 crore. Sequoia Capital, Ascent Capital, Japan's Beenos and econtext Asia successfully exited.

Citrus and PayU shared a common vision of building the largest Fintech company in India and saw no harm in their collaboration. The merger was an easy decision for them. The challenge was to convince Citrus's early investors such as Sequoia and Ascent to exit because these investors thought that it was too early for them to do so. Disagreements over the timing of an exit and the value of the exit are common between investors and founders. This type of story rarely gets publicity since founders and investors don't want to criticise each other in public and break the image of happy marriages that they both project in the media. Typically, these situations arise when start-ups get an offer to sell but the founders and venture investors don't agree on whether to take the offer or reject it. These offers, even if relatively small in the investor's view, say $20–30 million, can be life-changing for the founders. But for venture investors, particularly with big funds ($250 million upwards), smaller exits are not appealing. VCs typically want a good venture fund to triple or quadruple their money. In other words, a fund with $250 million investment would have to return $750 million to $1.25 billion from the fund's companies that are acquired in a trade sale or end up being listed. A quadruple return would be about two and a half times distribution to the fund's limited partners after fees to the general partners. So the VCs need to have massive 'home run' exits. For a $250 million fund, VCs would require at least three to four exits of $1 billion or 10 exits of $400 million (Assuming the investor has 20 per cent of the company when they exit).

People have different views on such decision-making. I believe that the founder's opinion should take priority on matters like these, especially the founders who may not come from exceptionally wealthy backgrounds and have not taken money off the table for themselves in the various rounds of financing. Jitendra gives credit where it is due when he says, 'I would give full credit to Sequoia. They go by what founders are convinced about rather than getting into conflicting situations and bullying the start-up. And this is where they supported our decision to part ways and agreed that Naspers was the right choice to take us to the next level.'

REDUX

Like every entrepreneur, Jitendra's journey had had its highs and lows. 'There are two distinct things (that he would have done differently). One, I was slow in hiring. In the first year, I was always trying to balance out revenue and expense and ended up holding back potential growth because I wasn't investing in sales. We had only three sales guys for the first two years,' he ruminates.

The second thing, according to Jitendra, was the idea that became the wallet. 'We were on the cusp of the idea in 2012 when we launched our customer accounts. A user's card, shipping address and purchase history was stored, but we didn't store the balance. We weren't able to see the big picture and decided that if the card pin was not being stored, there was no need to store the balance. Instead of thinking like the customer, we were thinking from a merchant's point of view. We could have flipped this idea into a wallet, way ahead of everyone else, but we failed to see the opportunity. Otherwise, the fate of the company would've been dramatically different,' he says regretfully.

A truly successful entrepreneur is not just a person who comes up with a fresh idea by understanding the pulse and the need of the market but also someone who plants the seeds of that idea and grows it into a tree. He is someone whose focus remains on the bigger picture. He should be able to predict future consumer and market needs correctly and prepare for those eventualities. That is the difference between a *good* and a *great* venture. However, credit should be given where credit is due. Despite missing out on the wallet idea, the Cube struggle and conflicts with Satyen, Jitendra managed to take the company forward and eventually sold big. As an entrepreneur, he managed to successfully carry out his vision without making any compromises by putting Citrus first. Essentially, that is also what makes a great venture. In case of Citrus, it was the founders', investors' and the acquiring firm's faith in the idea and execution of this Fintech company which turned it into a fully grown tree.

DEEPINDER GOYAL

Co-Founder and CEO, Zomato

'Back in the days, one of our competitors spent half of their first round in building an office. I told my team not to worry about them. They were going to last six months at best. I believe that with hot money being easily available, lots of start-ups get their fundamentals wrong. There's no problem in the food-tech space in general. There's a problem with start-ups that are visualising wrong business models. We know it's just a matter of time before everything reboots and the bad apples fall away. But at that moment, it doesn't mean that we can sit tight and not do anything about it. We have to act and move faster. As long as we do that, we will win.'

FROM RAIPUR TO BEIRUT TO OTTAWA, ZOMATO IS arguably the first Indian consumer internet company to go global. It was no small feat for Deepinder Goyal—the *pind da puttar* who claims to have been a rather unremarkable boy from Muktsar, a small town near Bhatinda in Punjab. How this ordinary boy achieved this extraordinary feat is a tale narrated regularly at inspirational sessions at college campuses, in the daydreaming backrooms of budding entrepreneurs and over drinks with friends. Deepinder started Zomato in 2008 with Pankaj Chaddah, a friend and colleague while the two were working at the consulting firm, Bain & Company. They started with the simple idea of a website that would provide scanned menus to users along with contact details of restaurants that took delivery orders over the phone. The users would no longer need to seek and stack up restaurant menus in their drawers as they were easily listed on the website. This clear-cut idea led to the creation of a company which has restaurant listings and review platforms in 70 Indian cities and 24 countries across the globe.

Zomato has been a runaway success when similar platforms such as Burrp (touted as India's answer to Yelp) bit the dust. Burrp was created by Deap Ubhi and Anand Jain, two of the smartest founders in the business, in 2006–07. Because of the founders' reputation as remarkable entrepreneurs, Burrp's sale to BookMyShow at a paltry sum of ₹6.7 lakh was quite tragic and astonishing. The main reason for their failure was that a huge opportunity slipped away from Burrp due to poor timing and bad luck. Though Zomato's initial journey was similar to that of Burrp's, today, they stand on different pedestals. It is fascinating to trace this story of grit and perseverance in the face of all kinds of start-up challenges.

FROM FLUNK TO FANTASTIC!

Deepinder, by his own admission, was a poor student. He repeated the sixth grade after failing and still, showed little improvement in the second innings. To think that such a boy would crack the demanding IIT entrance in a few years is unthinkable and yet, he made it happen. 'I think I became a teacher's social experiment,' Deepinder says with a laugh. During his repeat year, a Malayali teacher came to school and took kindly to Deepinder. He even went out of his way to help Deepinder with his final exams by giving him all the question papers with answers beforehand. 'I came third in class that year. Unfortunately, the teacher couldn't help me much with the Punjabi paper or I would have come first!' Predictably, there was shock and awe at school and Deepinder became the talk of the small town. 'I was thrilled to have this new found attention and had a spring in my step. But just before the next exams, the teacher who had been my Messiah, vanished. No goodbyes. He was just gone. I was stuck. I didn't want to lose my new found fame or hurtle back to the bottom of the class again. So, I began to take my studies seriously,' he narrates, solving the mystery of how the bottom dweller rose to the top of the mountain. 'Thankfully, I managed to get to sixth position in class. From then on, I worked very hard and that mindset finally helped me in cracking the IIT JEE exams as well.' While he learnt to take himself seriously, he also learnt not to cower down easily. This trait helps him cut through the noise and stay unperturbed in the face of extreme professional competition.

The Beginnings

The idea for Zomato was born because of a personal experience. When Deepinder and Pankaj both worked at Bain & Company in 2007, the lunch hour at the canteen was an everyday struggle because the cafeteria was always lagging on the orders. Everyone dashed to avoid the long queue to check the menu before they could order. It never occurred to anyone to print more menu cards till Deepinder and Pankaj scanned the menu and put it up on Bain's intranet. The idea was an instant hit. This minor success gave them the confidence that this idea could be a similar hit across the city. For the next few weeks, they picked up menus from several restaurants and put them up on their website, FoodLet.in (a play on the term, Food Outlet). The website enabled customers to order food online but this feature didn't work well because this was 2007 when no one was using online transactions. Flipkart hadn't been born yet, and sites like Paytm and FreeCharge which facilitate online transactions today, didn't exist either. The venture also became operationally a challenge because of the food delivery feature. It was yet another idea born before its time. Deepinder realised this and concealed the food delivery feature for the time being. At the same time in 2007, the founders also decided to let go of the domain name Food Let which ended with a dot-in and not a dot-com and moved to a new domain called FoodieBay.com.

In hindsight, the first version of Foodie Bay was average in terms of design and user experience. The website had no search functionality. It only contained scanned menu images with the restaurant's contact number. Given that there was no better alternative, users continued to flock the website. Slowly, restaurants started noticing the customer traffic coming in from Foodie Bay and contacted them to advertise on the site.

The website started gaining traction. 'At the end of two years, we were generating a revenue of ₹6 lakh per month with a team of fifteen employees,' recalls Deepinder, 'We were getting by. You see, billing and collections are very different processes. While we had substantial billing, we were collecting only half of it every month.' This reminded me of something that I was told many years ago, 'Businesses don't die because of profit and losses; they mostly die because of cash flow issues.' Fortunately, for Deepinder, Foodie Bay was not in danger of going down the same sunken path.

A Photo Finish: Zomato's First Round of Raising Funds

By 2010, the company began to spread its wings by expanding to other cities. Deepinder was getting ready for their Bengaluru launch when he received an email which said, 'Good stuff with Foodie Bay, would love to chat – Sanjeev.'

'Back in those days,' Deepinder explains, 'we used to get a lot of emails from salespeople. I thought that this must be one of them and didn't give it much thought. But for some reason, that email stuck with me. Nearly three days later, I was still thinking about it. There had been a note of authority in the words. I felt like that the email couldn't have been from a salesman, so I looked at it again and then it hit me. The email was from Sanjeev Bikhchandani, the founder of Naukri.com!' Deepinder replied to that email at 2 a.m. saying, 'Sanjeev, would love to catch up. Please let me know when.' At 6 a.m., he finished up his work and called it a night. At 7 a.m., Sanjeev responded, 'Come and meet me at 9 a.m.' But Deepinder woke up to Sanjeev's email at 1 p.m. Realising that he has missed the bus, he asks if they could reschedule as he had been working all night. Sanjeev responded, 'Come and meet me at 3 p.m.' 'What Sanjeev didn't know was that I was in Gurgaon and he was in Noida. It's a two-hour commute but I somehow managed to get there in time without killing anyone,' chuckles Deepinder.

Sanjeev spent a couple of hours with Deepinder in the Naukri.com office and was convinced of their model. It was similar to the classifieds business that Info Edge had built and executed brilliantly. Sanjeev called in Hitesh Oberoi (his co-founder), Vivek Khare (EVP, Corporate Development) and Ambarish Raghuvanshi (Info Edge's CFO) who grilled Deepinder together for the next few hours. At the end of this intense meeting, Info Edge was ready to invest in his business. Deepinder and Pankaj were already talking to Accel Partners at that time, trying to negotiate a deal for $500,000 for 25 per cent stake in the company. When he mentioned this to Sanjeev, the latter offered him $1 million for 33 per cent. Deepinder went into a quiet contemplation on hearing this. 'Sanjeev was staring at me. So I asked him, "What? You want me to say yes or no now?" And Sanjeev said, "Why not?" I responded, "Well then, okay!" The deal was signed in just six days.'

IGNORANCE IS BLISS AND SOMETIMES A VIRTUE

While Foodie Bay had been moving full steam ahead, especially after the very generous funding, Burrp, which was built on a similar model, was dying a slow death. Deap and Anand after trying to raise money for over three years, had finally sold their company to Infomedia18, a part of Network18 group for a paltry ₹4.25 crore in 2009. Anyone else in Deepinder's shoes would have been bothered by the critical condition of a similar business or worried about meeting the same fate. Fortunately, he was completely ignorant of what Deap and Anand were going through. 'While Burrp was growing in Mumbai, we were focussed on Delhi. We didn't know about their struggles. In hindsight, that was probably a good thing,' he admits, 'Had we known about them, I'm not sure how we would have reacted.'

GOING GLOCAL: *DESI* ZOMATO IN *VIDESHI* MARKETS

After two years of bootstrapping and managing cash flow issues, Deepinder's company had room to grow, breathe and experiment. Sanjeev suggested that they also needed a new name as Foodie Bay could potentially conflict with the eBay trademark. Deepinder and his team had two final options: Zomato and Forkwise. 'I rolled my eyes when I heard Forkwise. It certainly wasn't a clever name to consider. Zomato, however, was a premium domain name and available for about $10,000. Forkwise was available at the usual $6–7. I didn't see any sense in spending so much money on the domain name,' mentions Deepinder. Thankfully, Info Edge's team finally pressured them into going with Zomato. It was time for the scrappy little start-up to become a global company.

'By 2012, we had been in business for almost five years and defeated Burrp, fair and square. We were pretty much the only player in town and our sales were also growing. Slowly, the company turned into a well-oiled machine,' Deepinder mentions, evidently pleased with the way things were moving. But the omnipotent question called 'what next' hung around their heads. Deepinder was convinced that it was still early to get into the online food ordering or table reservations. 'There were only two choices in front of us. One was that we could get into other verticals. We could do reviews and ratings, spas, salons, gyms and enable the discovery of those service providers like we were doing for restaurants and become a horizontal classifieds business. Or we could go global with our restaurant listing business. At that time, the team believed that learning new geographies would be easier than learning new businesses, so we opted for extending the restaurant listing businesses globally,' he says. That's how simple that choice was for them.

UAE (United Arab Emirates) was the first country that they chose to explore. Soon, they landed success in Dubai, which proved to be a giant milestone that set the ball rolling for the company's direction for the next year. It may have seemed surprising that Zomato would choose a small place like Dubai, with a total population of only about 3 million, for its first international launch. But, in this case, the figures can be misleading. 'The ticket sizes for a meal in Dubai are four times to that of India,' Deepinder explains, 'Back then, Dubai's market was almost the same size as that of India for us. People don't get that. You see billion and a half people in India and think that the country's market is large.' In other words, what needs to be taken into consideration is the number of people who connect to the internet and use such online platforms. Zomato had broken even in Dubai within four months of its launch. 'It gave us the confidence that we have a good product on our hands, and we should probably take it to more countries,' Deepinder adds.

With this win, Zomato's global ambitions were on fire. They launched in the UK, Turkey, Brazil, New Zealand, Portugal and several other countries. Some of these countries proved to be challenging markets where they faced strong local competition. This was when Zomato started acquisitions, as Deepinder explains, 'Our restaurant listing business is not that capital intensive. It doesn't take a lot of money for us to launch in new markets. However, if we are going into a market which is already competitive and dominated by a large player, it's tough for us to win that space because of the existing networks that the local businesses have in place.'

Zomato acquired New Zealand's MenuMania within six months of entering the market. 'We hadn't been able to make any headway with the largest player in New Zealand, MenuMania. They were very strong and out of pure frustration, I gave the founder a call in 2014 saying that we are considering buying his company. The founder had been running MenuMania for ten years, hadn't raised any money and was looking for an exit. So he asked me, 'For how much?' Without giving it a second thought, I mentioned a million dollars. And to my surprise, he said, 'Okay, done.' It was literally a two-minute phone call,' Deepinder chuckles. With this first acquisition, they completely switched over all the traffic to Zomato, monopolising the market and leaving the users with no choice but to use their platform. 'We fundamentally believed that we had a better product than any of the local competitors and eventually, as people started liking our product, it worked out. Now, New Zealand's revenue is more than what we paid for the acquisition,' Deepinder adds. Having tasted success so quickly and to such a large extent, Zomato's team was excited by the idea of buying out other monopolised markets, which they did in countries like the Czech Republic and Turkey. Zomato followed its buying spree by taking over Lunchtime in the Czech Republic, Obedovat in Slovakia, Gastronauci in Poland and Cibando in Italy. Since venture capital ecosystems in these countries had not evolved, valuations for market leaders or even monopolies weren't unreasonable. This factor alone helped Zomato roll in and take over. At the same time, working with local founders gave them an insider's view of the place, giving them a jump start. They were able to understand the local needs and demands quickly.

BITING OFF MORE THAN THEY COULD CHEW: SCALING AND ACQUISITIONS

While things looked splendid on the surface, the truth of the matter was that several issues accompanied this massive scaling. 'Dubai's success gave us the false confidence that we could walk into any market, launch our website and win. Moreover, we went crazy after perhaps, launches in ten countries in just six months. We failed in half of them and realised that the one-size-fits-all approach doesn't work when you are launching in multiple markets. We also realised that it is one of the biggest problems of Silicon Valley companies. They actually have a very Bay Area point of view regarding all kinds of products and they want that point of view to fit into our local markets,' laments Deepinder. However, most of the rapidly growing companies are quickly learning to grapple with this. Companies like Uber, for instance, are not just customising their product according to the country, but according to every new city where they launch their services. Zomato picked up the trick of the trade soon enough. As Deepinder puts it, 'Once we started customising the product, we started generating revenues in markets where we had previously failed.'

Investors also continued to back the company. In April 2015, Info Edge led the seventh round of funding with $50 million, and later that year, in September, Temasek led a round of $60 million alongside the existing investor Vy Capital. Armed with the cash, Zomato took its boldest acquisition bet and acquired Urbanspoon for around $52 million. The acquisition of Urbanspoon marked Zomato's entry into the United States, Canada and Australia. The news, as expected, raised plenty of eyebrows. So far, Zomato, a six-year-old start-up, had been playing it safe in smaller markets. This entry into the big leagues meant not just dealing with a mature market but also facing tough competition. Zomato's David had to face the Goliath Yelp, which completely dominated the North American market. This was an eventuality they were aware of, but not necessarily prepared for. At that time, Deepinder admitted in a phone interview to Reuters, 'It's an all-cash deal. We pretty much had to spend all our last round of funding on this and it's a big deal for us.'

When Deepinder acquired Urbanspoon, his eyes were firmly fixed on Canada as well as Australia, where the brand dominated the market. He had never intended to try and beat Yelp on its home turf. 'We had been evaluating entry into several countries. During the vetting process, we knew that Urbanspoon was strong in both Canada and Australia. It was pretty much the monopoly even compared to players like Yelp. We bought Urbanspoon for Canada and Australia, not for the US. The idea was not to go after Yelp. And honestly, it would be stupid to go after them in North America, much like they would be equally silly to come to India and compete with us. The US belongs to them and we know that. Having said that, like all wishful people, we tried to do a few things in the US that didn't work, so we had to pull out.'

On Dealing with Headwinds

While Zomato's team was globetrotting, a lot was changing back in India. In 2014, a couple of ambitious entrepreneurs from Bengaluru launched Swiggy, a young team straight out of IIT-Mumbai launched TinyOwl and raised capital. Deepinder had been tracking Foodpanda since it launched in India in 2012, but with little interest. Food delivery wasn't on Zomato's radar and Deepinder was content with performing better than everyone in the search and discovery business, globally. But things were changing too fast. By 2015, TinyOwl had raised a few million dollars from marquee investors such as Nexus Venture Partners, Matrix and then Sequoia Capital, which was also an investor in Zomato. Foodpanda, which was backed by Rocket Internet, the multi-billion dollar start-up factory from Germany, was on an acquisition spree and had bought TastyKhana and Just Eat India. Zomato had to step up now and bring in the food delivery feature. Without losing any more time, in February 2015, Zomato announced its plans to launch delivery services. It was live in Delhi, Mumbai and Bengaluru within weeks with 2,000 restaurant partners. Zomato announced that it expected to reach 10,000 supported restaurants nationwide within a few months. 'We had a sales team of around 300 in India and 5,000 advertisers. Both Zomato and these partners were aware of the traffic we sent to them, so it was easier for us to analyse and predict the demand and volume that we could generate. We planned the fleets accordingly,' says Deepinder.

GOOD MONEY CHASING BAD EXECUTION

After a heady 2015, when companies were raising massive amounts of capital, the market scenario changed entirely in 2016. The industry was excited about the food tech becoming larger than e-commerce in India and continued to pour millions of dollars into the sector. Food tech, the darling of every VC was predicted to reach $78 billion by 2018, growing at 16 per cent YOY[8]. Soon, the sector was flooded with start-ups with similar models and the results began to show. Of the 105 food tech start-ups launched in India in 2014–15, only 58 were still around by 2016.

---

[8] YOY: Year Over Year

Start-ups like iTiffin, Eazy meals, Zeppery, ZuperMeal, Dazo, SpoonJoy had shut down operations. TinyOwl was in serious trouble while Rocket Internet-backed Foodpanda was struggling to find a buyer who could take the monkey off their backs. Foodpanda had laid off 300 people before the year ended. Even Zomato had begun to struggle. It laid off people and shut operations in markets where it wasn't making any money. In 2015, online ordering was closed in Lucknow, Kochi, Indore, and Coimbatore as the markets were not big enough for Zomato to sustain operations. It was a hyper-funded space and the funding frenzy had impacted Zomato's plans. 'I think most VCs have this illusion that money can solve everything. Sometimes I wish they'd put their money where the mouth is and jump into the game themselves. See if throwing money at the problem, hiring more people to do the tough things or getting their own hands dirty takes them anywhere. They don't realise that there is much more to it than the money that goes behind building companies. I've seen over time that there is a lot of hot money in the market but it remains useless. The bottom line is that hot money hurts healthy companies.

Companies like Zomato that were trying to do the right thing were forced into doing the wrong thing because the short-term implications of hot money are very, very harmful for companies like ours. Stupid investments hurt the ecosystem. It's not about risk and success ratios. So that needs to stop,' Deepinder continues, 'Back in the day, one of our competitors spent half of their first round in building an office. I told my team not to worry about them. They were going to last six months at best. I believe that a lot of start-ups get their fundamentals wrong because of easy availability of hot money. There's no problem in the food-tech space in general. There's a problem with start-ups that are visualising wrong business models. We know that it's just a matter of time before everything reboots and the bad apples fall away. But in that moment, it doesn't mean that we can sit tight and not do anything about it. We have to act and move faster. As long as we do that, we will win.' This was a game that Deepinder and team learnt early on. They knew when to pick their battles and engaged in them only after careful evaluation of markets from time to time. They would have none of the foolish chivalry or swashbuckling. They were not afraid to turn their backs on a fight that they knew they could not win.

'We are happy to run away from any battle that could potentially kill or drain us in the long term,' admits Deepinder, 'We prefer to live to fight another day.' Deepinder owes his company's success to carefully well-laid plans that have no room for ambitious but doomed plans of expansions. This is probably why the company never tried to step into China. 'I understand that it is a huge market, but the four potential competitors have a billion dollars each in the bank. So we stay out of China. There are many other markets where we have a much bigger shot at winning and we are happy with that,' he says.

On Downgrades and Consequences

Valuations—like market sizes—are difficult to place. What must be taken into consideration is not just the population of a country in which the business is being launched (which becomes the 'market') but also other factors such as the strength of its currency, internet penetration and percentage of the population using such platforms. In Zomato's case, for instance, their business is brisk and profitable in a country like Lebanon. But Beirut, another market of Zomato, has only half the number of restaurants that Delhi does. 'The catch is that the value of their currency is four times greater than the Indian rupee. Hence, Beirut's market size becomes twice the size of Delhi,' Deepinder explains, 'but investors have a very different view of such situations. They think that the population is equal to market size. That's not true for our sector. For us, the calculation of the market size is based on the number of restaurants multiplied by the currency strength.'

THE PURSUIT OF VALUATION

The poster boy of the start-up world, Flipkart, was devalued twice in 2016, owing to all the headwinds around the start-up sector. In March, Morgan Stanley cut the firm's valuation by 11 per cent, followed by T Rowe Price a month later, which slashed the value of its investment in Flipkart by 15 per cent. This was a case of investors losing faith in the company's prospects. Then, in May 2016, analysts at HSBC's brokerage arm, HSBC Securities and Capital Markets valued Zomato at $500 million, about 50 per cent lower than what it was valued at in its last funding round in September 2015. The report said, 'We do a DCF (discounted cash flow) and value the business (Zomato) at about 50 per cent lower to the $1 billion valuation. Zomato is present in 23 markets so early on and none is profitable which implies that to address both the investments in last mile delivery and losses in international operations fundraising will be a continuous phenomenon, suggesting current valuations don't make much sense.' The HSBC report argued that the existing revenue stream wasn't working for Zomato. Only about 6–8 per cent restaurants on the platform paid for advertising, while their relatively new food ordering business was at a nascent stage. 'In our view, for Zomato to emerge as a market leader in the restaurant search space, it needs to focus on online food ordering and build last-mile delivery capabilities,' the report concluded.

This report started a tug of war between Deepinder and Mahesh Murthy, the then co-founder of early-stage investment firm Seedfund when Murthy told the news website Quartz, 'There is no doubt that we have been in a valuation bubble. Specifically in the case of Zomato, valuing it at even half-a-billion is ambitious. In the businesses that Zomato is in, the revenue comes from restaurants who advertise and the food delivery part. Both these are low-value and low-margin businesses. So it makes it difficult to believe that with ₹97 crore ($14 million) of revenues, the company is valued at $1 billion.'

The report and Mahesh's interview elicited a long post by Deepinder on Zomato's blog. He wrote, 'Nobody who knows our business has marked down our valuations. Our existing investors are bullish about us and are willing to back us further, if needed. And they have categorically said that our valuations are justified. Especially because we are more than doubling year on year and the next year looks even more exciting for us. But external perceptions of valuations are determined by the state of the market and the availability of facts to the person who is analysing these numbers.'

Mahesh took to Twitter to respond and said, 'So @Zomato took in ₹1,500 crore to do ₹97 crore sales at ₹137 crore loss. If I said that a fixed deposit would've done better, I'd be called a start-up hater :).' Deepinder didn't hold back and replied, '@maheshmurthy I will send you some books to read up on how to build tech businesses with long term profitability. And the book *Venture Capital 101*.' This paved the way for a blog post titled 'From Unicorn to Unicorpse: Zomato Flounders.' Deepinder was predictably offended. 'Flipkart's downgrade came from their own investors, remember? An external analyst reported our devaluation and it is an ethical courtesy to check with the company before publishing a report. They never did. I wrote a post to counter certain points mentioned in HSBC's report but they never responded or corrected their analysis. It is upsetting because it affects the company's morale, turns off prospective employees and the jitteriness creates unnecessary distractions but you know that you can't do much beyond a point. Now, till the valuation is reset in the next round of financing, we have to live with this,' Deepinder concludes.

The change came in swiftly for Zomato in October 2018 when it announced that the company was raising an additional $210 million from Alibaba's payment affiliate, Ant Financial at a valuation of over $2 billion. Till this large round of funding from Ant Financial, Zomato had a history of raising capital from Info Edge. Their long and intense courtship led to an increase in Info Edge's stake in Zomato to 57.9 per cent in 2013. Since Zomato had raised three rounds of financing from them amounting to ₹31 crore—later that year, Sequoia Capital led a ₹220 crore round in the company leading to the dilution of Info Edge's stake. While it's always great validation for a new investor that an existing investor has historically doubled down since the first round of funding, it was surprising that it took Deepinder that long to raise money from a new investor after Info Edge. 'Building a company is teamwork. You need employees aligned to your vision and values and the same is true for investors as well. I was talking to a very prominent VC in 2012. We were discussing Zomato's valuation and were comfortable with $30 million pre-money, while looking to raise $3 million. Citing no rational reason, he offered us $3 million for $25 million pre-money. I wondered why I should agree to that. We had two term sheets from funds that we liked. And from the beginning, we didn't negotiate on valuations.' Deepinder and his team led their first four rounds of funding sans any PowerPoint presentations or any business plans. He explains, 'But that VC went on justifying his ask, suggesting that he will add value and connect us to bigger fish with deeper pockets,' Deepinder recalls the bewildering moment, 'I have a strong belief that if you have the right thing to say, the investors will respond even to your cold emails. If you and your numbers are making sense, anybody will listen to you. So I responded to this investor saying that my team and I don't agree at a $25 million valuation as it makes no sense for us to do it. This was his answer, "Just do it at 25. And let's not tell your team that we did it at 25." And I kept thinking, "What does that even mean?" In the end, we had options to go with multiple investors in all these rounds, but we were just comfortable with Info Edge. In hindsight, I think we're very proud of all the decisions we've made.'

Over the years, Deepinder has built an honest and transparent relationship with his team and his board. 'We are often told to raise money from people who can follow up with much larger rounds later on. That's partly true. If your fundamentals are right, you'll convince those investors eventually. So I don't see my business revolving around how fundraising works. I never built the business thinking that the next round will definitely come in. Because sometimes it doesn't. We have built Zomato thinking that last round of financing is all we have and maybe, the last round of money is all the money we'll ever raise. Also, we never ramp up before the money hits the bank. Till it's in the bank, consider that it hasn't happened.'

Fully Stocked Food Tech Company

The US has many unicorns in the Food Tech space. But three particularly stand out. There is Yelp for restaurant recommendations and listing, OpenTable for restaurant booking management, and Grubhub for restaurant delivery. Zomato plans to be all three. That's ambitious and can be distracting for a company. If the US companies couldn't figure it out to emerge as one dominant player, how was Deepinder hoping to achieve it?

'Yes these companies are in different parts of the value chain and they actually connect the same user and the same merchant. If you dig deeper, you'll realise that they don't need three different products, they only need one product because the first leads to the second and the second to the third. These companies happen to be separate because all of them started at the same time and became so large that they couldn't merge. That's how the US market evolved,' Deepinder shares his observation and he is right. There is a remarkable chance Zomato can be the three-in-one solution that it aims to be. 'We've been strongly successful in a lot of markets and I believe we have a fair shot at building one product which does all these things for our users. It's not going to be easy. It's a very operationally-intensive business. There's a lot of on-ground work to be done,' admits Deepinder.

Dodging Bullets and Preparing for New Wars

A venture capitalist promised Deepinder $50 million to execute 'what Groupon is doing.' Groupon, in its heydays, was the hottest company in the world. A year and five months after being founded, the company cemented its unicorn status in 2010. And the next year, they went public. But Zomato is not Groupon and it has no intention of becoming that either. 'We know what restaurants thought of Groupon, their clones and their customers. They hated them. Groupon customers were deal-seeking bottom feeders who would never come back after using the deal. So restaurants mistreated those customers like second-grade citizens by providing bad service, small and stale portions etc. We had restaurants crying to us about them,' Deepinder reveals. Towards the end of 2018, Zomato's closest rival Swiggy raised a stunning $1 billion led by Naspers and Tencent Holdings. Momentarily, it has surged ahead of Zomato to become the fifth most valuable start-up in India. For a company that was launched in 2014, it's an astonishing feat.

Meanwhile, Uber is also expected to infuse $200 million into its food delivery business, Uber Eats in India. Uber's competitor Ola Cabs that recently acquired Foodpanda, has also jumped on the bandwagon and is anticipating growth in its food delivery business with other players committing $200 million into it. Food delivery battles around the world are long drawn and eventually about the last man standing *with* capital. With Alibaba and Tencent again locking horns outside of China, it looks like it is going to be a head to head battle in India. Over the next two years, food delivery space is bound to become a bloodied field, quite similar to that of e-commerce. Zomato, which has always stood tall in the face of adversities, has quite a few challenges ahead. It remains to be seen how Deepinder will navigate his ship through the storm.

DEEP KALRA

Founder and CEO, MakeMyTrip Limited

'There is never a dull moment in our business. I am glad that I persevered through the dot-com bust, an investor pull-out, industry slowdowns and discount wars with a global giant. It has been an incredible journey so far, but the best is yet to come.'

DEEP COMES WITH AN IMPECCABLE AND IMPRESSIVE educational record. He obtained a bachelor's degree in economics from St. Stephen's College in 1990 and an MBA from IIM Ahmedabad in 1992. He began his career with ABN AMRO Bank before turning into a quasi-entrepreneur in 1995. His first venture, AMF Bowling, introduced pin bowling to India. He enjoyed it for four years and learnt a lot from the experience but as a business, it didn't take off. Deep returned to the corporate world to join GE Money, only to realise that it wasn't what he wanted to do. He concluded that he disliked large companies and decided to explore other options.

In 1999, when he was trying to sell his car, someone told him to list it on AutomartIndia.com. 'So I put it up there, waiting to see what happens. And lo and behold! I received two-three queries and interestingly, two interested parties offered more than ₹10,000–20,000 than what I had been previously offered. One of them showed up the next day, bought the car and gave me a full cheque payment. We sealed the deal and this experience taught me how the internet is all about dis-intermediation,' says Deep. Around that time, Deep had another encounter with the internet. Deep and his wife were expecting their first child and they decided to go to Phuket for a holiday while she could still travel. Having booked tickets through an agent, Deep began to search for affordable hotel accommodation. That process turned out to be frustrating as the travel agent started playing truant and Deep didn't have much time to drop by his office to look at brochures. Finally, when he was pushed to the brink, Deep decided to take matters in his own hands and search for a hotel online. 'I saw two or three sites, and finally landed on AsiaRooms.com. One of the hotels that my agent had referred was called Kokanad Lagoon. When I checked online, the cost of one room was $15 a night and $90 for six nights. I felt that it didn't sound right but when I saw the assurances on the website, said to myself, "What the hell, let's take the chance,"' he shares. Naturally, Deep was apprehensive because if this didn't work out, then he didn't know where he would go with his pregnant wife. 'But to my surprise, it was seamless. No cheating at all. In fact, at the reception, I saw the guest relations staff talking to walk-in customers saying that they could get a better price on online booking. Since there was no mobile internet then, they were navigating visitors to nearby cyber cafés to book online and avail discounts. I couldn't understand *why* until I figured out that they were building their online business and in the process, also building their valuation for investors,' adds Deep.

Deep became more convinced of the opportunities that the internet presented as he spent more time on it. He knew that he was on the cusp of a revolutionary idea, a once-in-a-lifetime opportunity to build a business and he didn't want to let it pass. The idea was a perfect fit for his vision which was to set up a unique organisation with a purpose and a culture where work could be fun. He evaluated the pros and cons but was unable to make up his mind on whether he wanted to set up an online travel company or an online stockbroking firm. Deep says, 'Somewhere along the way, I understood that online stockbroking will ultimately belong to a financial institution. Customers need a lot of trust in where their money is being invested and information on the kind of trading that is going on.' A sound thought process, indeed. It is probably one of the reasons why ICICI Direct has made a mark while Indiabulls, despite being an online stockbroking firm, pivoted into being a real estate developer. Deep and his wife are avid travellers and at the end of the day, the choice was clear. They would work on building an online travel company because this idea excited Deep much more than that of an online stockbroking firm.

Funding and Team Building

In 1999, Deep wrote a business plan and headed to Mumbai to meet Neeraj Bhargava, a partner at e.Ventures which was a bit of a late entrant but a hot fund for start-ups in India. Its limited partners included SoftBank, ePartners and London-based P.K. Mittal, one of the three owners of Ispat Group that had committed over $150 million to India. In the first nine months of their operations, they had already invested $65 million in over 11 companies. 'I met Neeraj at Crossroads Mall in Tardeo and showed him my business plan. I found him to be a genuine and trustworthy man. He was my senior from St. Stephens and a former employee at McKinsey. We signed the deal on a paper napkin,' Deep says. e.Ventures was going to invest $2 million in the company for a 70 per cent stake. Deep would own 25 per cent and 5 per cent would go towards ESOPs. The money would come in two equal tranches in a year.

With that deal in place, Deep now had to build a team while the formal paperwork was underway. New to this field without any previous knowledge sans his personal understanding of travelling for pleasure, Deep knew that he needed to hire experienced employees. He appointed Keyur Joshi for international travel and Ambrish Mahajan for domestic travels. Himanshu Khanna was going to manage the marketing and

Rajesh Magow was handling the finance department. 'We would start around 9–10 a.m. work past midnight. It would be our routine on weekends also. After working like that for four-five months, Himanshu said to Deep in late 1999, 'I can't hack this. My wife is going to leave me if I continue like this.' And he quit. Deep's former colleague, Sachin Bhatia messaged him around this time saying that he was leaving AMF Bowling and that he'd given Deep's reference to his prospective employers. Deep offered Sachin the position of the vice president (marketing). Keyur Joshi was hired while he was travelling to a wedding on a train with his huge Gujarati family. He had a degree in Chemistry and an MBA from the State University of New York. Deep says when Keyur called him, 'All I could hear were songs in the background. The call must have been disconnected ten times. Frustrated, I just sent him a letter saying that he was hired,' Deep laughs. Over the next few days, when the core team began to brainstorm, Deep realised that he wouldn't regret impulsively hiring Keyur. Furthermore, Deep saw so much potential in him that Keyur was made AVP within a week of hiring and VP in his second week at the company. He moved up two positions in two weeks! In twelve months, Deep and his team were meeting all their targets.

How They Almost Blew It

But in March 2000, the dot-com party was ending globally. Deep and his team were blissfully unaware that the dot-com bubble had burst. One single week had changed the fortunes of thousands of start-ups, millions of employees and investors around the world. The events also hit e.Ventures badly. Rupert Murdoch, SoftBank and Ispat Group also got cold feet and decided to exit the country by leaving companies, selling off their stakes to anyone interested and cancelling all future commitments in the portfolio companies. Unaware of any of these disastrous occurrences, Deep was in back in Mumbai to collect the remaining $1 million committed by e.Ventures as the second tranche. Neeraj, however, had other plans. He wanted Deep to repay the previous tranche money and take back the 70 per cent stake that e.Ventures owned in the company. It seemed like the end of the world for Deep. They gave each other a week to figure out how to facilitate these developments.

Back in Delhi, Deep pondered over how to raise the money to return to e.Ventures. Every venture capital firm had sobered down going by the demands of the day and there was no way that a bank would fund a dot-com company. Deep was staring down the barrel of a gun. In desperation, he started reaching out to his friends for advice. 'Thankfully, a dear school friend Sanjay Bansal was in KPMG. I told him about the e.Ventures fiasco, and he asked me to offer them a distress valuation. Following Sanjay's advice, Deep offered a total of ₹46 lakh for the 70 per cent stake to Neeraj. That amount was Deep's entire life savings. Deep was terrified that Neeraj would laugh at him and refuse, but what happened next is a classic example of 'if you never ask, the answer is always no.' e.Ventures agreed to sell the stake back to Deep and took a massive downgrade on the investment. Deep and his team now had 100 per cent ownership of the company but the next few years were going to be full of torment.

Under Pressure

Online travel space had become very competitive in the days of hyper funding in 1999. ICICI Venture had funded My Travel

Genie, Net2travel had some marquee investors and Travel Mart was funded by Citibank. When e.Ventures packed up from India, MakeMyTrip decided to brave out the storm on its own. These were dark times for Deep and his team. Even as the internet industry was reeling under the fund crunch, Net2travel announced in 2000 that it was buying two large offline travel companies, Pearl Travels and Hopp Worldwide in a stock-swap deal. The deal would create an entity with a combined turnover of ₹150 crore. Net2travel became the new media darling.

On the other hand, Deep had asked the senior management to take massive cuts on their salaries, because MMT was still struggling to stay afloat while competitors seemed to be getting close to the finish line. 'It is easy to say these things now, but what helped to keep us going is the fact that we never got paranoid about competition. We were always more obsessed with customer issues. That said, we were aware of our competition although we never tried to become like them. In fact, I have always pushed our top managers to spend one day in the market, every month. They go and talk to customers and small hotels to get feedback and insights. We were too busy on our journey to get worried about getting pushed over by competition,' says Deep. Sure enough, in a few months, Net2travel announced that it was getting acquired by another struggling start-up, Indya.com (funded by Rupert Murdoch) in an all-stock deal. Subsequently, Net2travel also announced that it was calling off its plans to acquire the travel businesses, Pearl Travel and Hopp Worldwide. Indya.com too shut down its operations in the next few years. But that is a story for another chapter.

I have always advised start-up founders that media coverage is mostly overrated. I tell them to ignore it because that coverage consists of a mix of sugar-coated lies touting a start-up as the 'next big thing,' but before we know it, that 'next big thing' dies before its time. There are times in a start-up's journey when everyone keeps talking about their competitors' success charts. They mention how they are absolutely 'crushing it', raising a ton of money, hiring executives from the best business schools in the country, etc. The truth is that those competitors are facing the same issues as your start-up every day. Ultimately, the start-ups that keep their head down and work towards their goals are the ones that eventually succeed. This is not to suggest that one should ignore the competition. To flourish, I recommend that an up and coming start-up should stay on course despite the success or failure of their competitors and completely focus on the execution of their strategies regularly. This is what worked in MMT's case after Net2travel, My Travel Genie and Travel Mart India all folded up, one by one. '2001 to 2003 was just darkness and nothing else. So I told Sachin, Rajesh and Keyur that I would take a 100 per cent cut in my salary and they should figure out the amount of cuts that they can afford. I will convert those cuts into equity. I guess the smartest thing that they did was agreeing to this proposal,' says Deep. This was the moment when the founding team members became actual co-founders in MMT.

A founder is someone willing to let go of a significant portion of their cash compensation in exchange for a good chunk of equity in the company and is expected to play an important role in its ongoing success. When everything around them was going down in ashes, MMT's founding members rose to the challenge and became equal partners in the struggles of the company.

TIME IS AN ILLUSION, *TIMING* IS AN ART[9]

There were plenty of issues plaguing the e-commerce and OTA sector in the early years of the internet such as poor credit card penetration, no internet banking, poor internet connections, unreliable payment gateways, trust issues with online transactions in India and a low user base. People were looking up pricing for hotels, etc. but then asking their offline travel agents to match it. Deep realised it early on that without the cash, India wasn't ready for an online travel portal. Cost of customer acquisition even today remains the largest X factor that makes or breaks an online business. CAC (Cost to Acquire Customers) can be calculated by simply dividing all the costs spent on acquiring more customers (marketing expenses) by the number of customers acquired in the period during which the money was spent. For example, if a company spent $100 on marketing in a year and bagged 100 customers in the same year, their CAC is one dollar. Even today, with relatively easier access to capital, entrepreneurs and their investors get seduced by significant revenue generated by start-ups and all that capital allows undisciplined management teams to dig themselves into trenches because of the mediocre operations.

No matter how brilliant and hard-working the founder is—launching a product in the market too early can lead to the product being stuck in a limbo, waiting for the race to begin. The reverse situation is also worrying. The founders may be stuck in an exhausting fight against innumerable competitors if the product is launched quite late. In short, timing is everything.

An early decision made by the MMT team was to shut down marketing in India and focus on the NRI customers.

---

[9] Emunds, Stefan, *Goodreads*. https://www.goodreads.com/quotes/7191386-time-is-an-illusion-timing-is-an-art

Their last day of Indian marketing was 31 December 2000. Deep divulges, 'Indian customers were only window shoppers back then. There were barely any conversions. Our steady transactions were coming from only the NRI customers, so we decided to focus entirely on that. I learnt to measure the CAC early on and it was simple math for us that our spending on Indian customers was not turning into steady profits. If we hadn't shut down our Indian operations and stopped the cash leak, we could have easily blown it all up and closed down our shop.'

After this bold decision in the aftermath of the 2000 bubble burst, second and third blows came in quick successions with the tragedy of 9/11 in 2001 followed by the scare of the SARS virus epidemic in 2002. Globally, the travel industry was the worst hit business. But these trying times also taught Deep and his team that the NRIs were a resilient lot. Besides, travel wasn't a luxury for NRIs. It was a necessity. Deep explains, 'Young professionals working in the US need to come to India from time to time to meet their parents and vice versa. NRIs with families and new babies meant that parents had to be shipped from India to them. People would get married, so there were logistics around that as well. This was a need. These weren't annual vacations for NRIs.' MakeMyTrip continued to be the one-stop shop for NRIs travelling to and from India for the next four years. Afterwards, they resumed their focus on Indian customers.

A concept in nuclear physics suggests that the minimum amount of fissile material needed to create a self-sustaining nuclear chain reaction is known as critical mass. In the start-up world, critical mass refers to the size that a company needs to reach in order to efficiently and competitively participate in the market. This is also the size that a company must attain to sustain growth and efficiency. By 2005, Deep realised that it was time to reconsider launching India operations. This was also a critical moment for the company. 'In 2005, two things happened, which convinced me that India was ready. First of all, Indian Railways launched IRCTC, which made Indian travellers comfortable with online payments. Full credit for this transition goes to Indian Railways. The second thing was the arrival of low-cost carriers (LCCs), such as Air Deccan and Sahara. They were advertising fares for ₹999. Customers loved the fares but when they went to the websites of these airlines, the sites would often crash because of the traffic. Agents were unwilling to book these flights because there were no profits for them in doing so. We knew that this was the ideal problem to solve through technology and we could easily disintermediate the offline travel agent,'

Deep continues, 'We solved the issue by meshing the fares of LCCs with the global distribution system (GDS). Now, every travel fare was on offer. This was a big hit. It was a game changer because there was a shift in power from the agent to the customer. The customer now had the power to call the shots. We were probably the first online travel agency (OTA) to sell LCCs in the world. As we scaled up the India operations, it made sense to look at funding again.' That's how MMT's business in India finally took off.

On Fundraising and Competition

MMT got term sheets from Sequoia and SAIF Partners in 2005 but it was a tough choice for them. 'The terms were better with Sequoia, but I still went with SAIF. I met Ravi Adusumalli from SAIF through my friend Anand Pathak and we hit it off instantly. He was ready to sign the term sheet immediately.

You should always pick investors who are a) quick decision makers and b) someone you are comfortable with. Sequoia was more process-driven, so I had to go back and forth to Bengaluru a couple of times for all that. For entrepreneurs, time is money,' says Deep.

SAIF invested $10 million in the first round and a total of $25 million in the company, subsequently. Incidentally, just a couple of days before the investment was announced, I received a call from Sachin Bhatia, vice president (marketing) and now, the co-founder of MMT. He wanted to evaluate my company, Webchutney for their creative mandate for the India launch which we bagged a week later. They were also my first clients for viral marketing work. In a relationship that lasted a decade, Webchutney received a number of creative awards in the digital category for the work done with MMT.

The next four to five years were great for MakeMyTrip. Their top line grew twenty times from about $30 million in 2005 to $600 million in 2010. Along the way, they raised a second and third round of funding with Tiger Global (Lee Fixel's first investment in India, Sierra Ventures and Helion Venture Partners as shareholders and investors along with SAIF). But with that, the competition also increased. The major players that were launched in the Indian market included Yatra.com, backed by Norwest Venture Partners, Reliance Technology Ventures and Network18 Group; Cleartrip.com, backed by Sherpalo Ventures and Kleiner Perkins Caufield & Byers; and Sequoia Capital and Battery Ventures-backed Travelguru.com. Bengaluru based Via, backed by NEA Indo US and Sequoia Capital, was another leading player in the business.

Cleartrip was celebrated by the start-up community for their user experience and design, while Yatra was considered the proverbial underdog. 'I don't want to belittle our competitors but Yatra always copied us. That actually helped us in a way because if you have been copying the leader and the leader makes a mistake, you end up copying that too. At our end, we would make sure that our mistakes are corrected but they wouldn't realise the same.' Deep reveals, 'Cleartrip's team and their design is good. Hrush Bhatt (the co-founder of Cleartrip) is brilliant and Stuart (the co-founder and CEO) is also a nice person. But this is a dirty business; not so much the flights' section but managing the hotels is quite stressful. To handle 45,000 hotels, you've got to get your hands dirty because cancellations are real and regular. We've built a robust engine but I don't think they did such a good job in terms of technology versus products. That's only half the job.'

There was a time when Yatra was breathing down MMT's neck in terms of Gross Merchandise Value. For MMT, the situation changed dramatically when the Lehman collapse triggered an economic turmoil, in September 2008. There's a rumour that there was considerable panic in many start-up board rooms including Yatra where the board pushed the company to conserve the $17 million invested by Intel a few months ago. MakeMyTrip had survived the 2000 meltdown and knew better. Fully backed by its investors and the board, it continued to stay on course and increased its lead on Yatra by a mile. After this, Yatra could never catch up to them.

On Listing

Info Edge's Sanjeev Bikhchandani, who was on MMT's board, recommended them to consider an IPO. His venture Naukri.com had been at a similar stage when they went in for an IPO. Sanjeev was Deep's mentor, philosopher and guide. 'I met him when he was a teacher in my CAT classes. He pretty much set the gold standard for corporate governance. He was on the board from 2005 to 2010 but didn't take any remuneration and when we offered stock, he said that it should be issued in Info Edge's name since he was consulting on their time. He drilled a useful statement into our company's core that there is nothing more important than solving the customer's problems. He also helped us expand into the offline market, in 2008. Though our foreign investors baulked at the idea, it helped us gain customer confidence in smaller cities and towns. For their first booking, customers would visit our store and they'd call us the second time. By the third booking, they'd become comfortable enough to move online.'

While they all agreed that it was a good time for a listing in 2009–10, MMT's board was divided on where to list. Info Edge's Sanjeev and Sanjeev Aggarwal from Helion felt it was better to list in India; Tim Guleri from Sierra Ventures and Ravi Adusumalli felt it was better to go for a NASDAQ listing. Deep took a week to discuss this dilemma with several experts including Ajit Balakrishnan of Rediff.com, Akhil Gupta of Airtel, and Mohandas Pai of Infosys—almost everyone who had come out with an IPO—for their expertise in this matter. Deep also spoke to Neil Shen, one of the founders of Ctrip, a Chinese company which had listed in the US, in 2006.

It was clear that investors in the US understood the model well and rewarded growth without being fixated on profitability. Hence, Deep finally decided to list on the NASDAQ. In the run-up to the IPO, Rajesh and Deep travelled all over the US to meet investors. He recalls, 'It was tiring with nearly ten meetings a day but, it was equally exciting to see the response that we were getting. We survived on barely three hours of sleep each day. A night before we were all set to ring the bell at NASDAQ on 13 August 2010, our lawyer got a call by the SEC (US Securities and Exchange Commission) to send information regarding a query. We spent all night digging up the information required and finally, the issue was resolved by 7.30 a.m. We had to be at Times Square at 8.30 a.m. and rushed to be there on time. That was a close call. Once there, we were overwhelmed seeing that the floor was packed with our well-wishers and investors. The stock surged 90 per cent on the listing. Oh, how we partied the next day on a rented yacht! God knows we deserved it!' On 12 August 2010, MMT's market valuation nearly doubled to $902.8 million on its debut trade in the US market. Debut trade shares of the company shot-up by 88.93 per cent over the IPO price of $14 apiece. MMT made $70 million through its first public offering of 5 million shares in the US market and ended its first day of trade at $26.45 per share. The company was valued at $902.84 million at closing that day in contrast to its valuation of $477.87 million a day earlier.

How They Almost Blew It (Again)

India is a very tough market for conducting business. The relentless competition gives you no room to breathe even after decades of battles for cornering consumers. For example, take Airtel's journey—they launched four telecom licences in 1992 and fought a long battle to win across circles by fighting and acquiring competition. Then a few years later, Vodafone UK woke up to the telecom opportunity in India and the battle resumed. Afterwards, Reliance Communications unleashed a pricing war. And just when things started settling down after almost 25 years, Reliance Jio was launched. There wasn't a single dull moment. We witnessed the same situation in the e-commerce space where, even after a decade, the battle between Flipkart,

Amazon and Paytm is still going on. The travel category has been equally aggressive. MakeMyTrip successfully fought the earliest competitors in Net2travel, My Travel Genie etc., and five years later, a new battle began with Yatra, Cleartrip and Via which went on for half a decade. And just when the winner was being announced, Naspers showed up with Ibibo. Naspers is a multinational internet and media group with headquarters in South Africa and offers services in more than 130 countries. In 2001, the then little-known Naspers lucked out by making a $32 million investment in an unknown start-up called Tencent in China. That investment is currently worth over $175 billion. Notably, the market value of its Tencent Holdings was higher than the market capitalisation of Naspers itself. The move has been referred to as one of the most successful venture capital investments of all time. Back in 2007, looking at the success of their investment in Tencent, they started aggressively exploring other emerging markets like India. Ibibo, which was started as a social networking service in 2007 also tried a bunch of other things like e-commerce via Tradus and a gaming company, none of which stuck. Under the leadership of Ashish Kashyap, who was also designated as the co-founder of the group's greenfield operation in India, they pivoted to become an e-commerce and travel organisation. In 2009, Goibibo.com was launched. After a couple of years of revving up its engines, Goibibo hit the accelerator with aggressive discounting and marketing schemes which worked very well with a younger, tech-savvy, transaction-focussed customer. And people in their twenties—interested in spontaneous travelling, planning and saving up for trips—became their customers. So, Ibibo's business model had their market cut out for them.

MMT followed suit and both the companies bled heavily for a few years. Deep acknowledges that MakeMyTrip was completely blindsided about Goibibo for the first two years, and used to think that they were a discount shop. In his talk at a conference called Mobile Sparks in 2016, Deep said, 'We had a lot of scorn for discount shops. We knew you one can't build a business on discounting. But we were wrong.' This perception continued to exist because the MMT team didn't realise how good Goibibo was with technology for more than a year. Deep realised that when he got a chance to look at their extranet app (a solution given to their hotel partners to manage inventory and supply chain). He was blown away by it though some of his team members were in denial. He said in the conference, 'It's human nature to be defensive. My colleagues were defensive and I said that we were behaving like ostriches with our heads buried in the sand.'

Deep recounts, 'It's true that I was dismissive of them. We felt that they were playing the discounting game and not creating any value. But they were aggressive and kept on investing. Their unit economics was terrible but they were a private company, so it didn't matter. The bane of being public is that one investor will say, "Where is the profit?" and the other will say, "Where is the growth?" so we were focussed on balancing both. This was before I saw their extranet. For me, that was the game changer. Someone in my team got access to their extranet. They were changing the slide when I walked in, saw the screen and said, "My God!" For the next few hours, I sat in front of it and thought, "what is this, what is this, what is this?" They had created a fantastic tool. It showed that they knew how to build an extranet. And they made it better than Booking.com. That's when I realised that we must take them seriously.'

In Good Company

In 2015, discount wars were at an all-time peak. It was time to bring in a strategic partner. MMT had a lot of interest from the big boys but decided to go with Ctrip because they had a lot of similar experiences in dealing with choppy markets and discounting wars. In January 2016, CTrip invested $180 million in MMT. 'We were already at loggerheads with Ibibo in the fight for market shares, particularly in the hotel business. I reached out to Naspers through Lee Fixel of Tiger Global to see if we could combine forces instead of bleeding each other, but nothing happened. The service tax case filed against both of our companies in early 2016 brought Ashish Kashyap (Ibibo's co-founder) and me together. It was such a nightmare. I couldn't believe that we as aggregators, were being arm-twisted to pay service tax on hotel bookings. We didn't even get a show cause notice! They came to our office and arrested our vice president (finance) for tax evasion. We fought back hard and eventually won the case in the high court. The judge not only took the Directorate General of Central Excise Intelligence to task for the incident, but he also ordered them to pay the money back with interest. The silver lining of this drama was that it got Ashish and me talking,' Deep reveals.

This hardship brought Deep and Ashish together. They talked, found some middle ground and eventually decided to join hands. It was a scene straight out of the *Mad Men* episode where fierce competitors Don Draper and Ted Chaough combined forces to have a standing chance against the big cats in the ad world. MakeMyTrip acquired 100 per cent of Ibibo and redBus, and Naspers, in turn, got 40 per cent of MakeMyTrip which gave MMT $85 million.

The merger of his home-grown online travel company with the smaller rival, Ashish Kashyap's Ibibo Group has not only been a watershed moment for the Indian online travel industry, but also created a combined entity that leaves little room for a close second. This entity, which will operate as MakeMyTrip, controls about a fifth of the lucrative online air-ticketing segment besides having a substantial presence in the bus, hotel bookings and ride-sharing space.

A year later, Deep knew that he had cut himself an extremely lucrative deal. 'It got the market's approval as the market capitalisation—which was $1.2 billion before the merger—is $3 billion now. So we are moving in the right direction. There is never a dull moment in our business. I always believe that you might regret the things that you don't do in life rather than the decisions you make. I am glad that I persevered through the dot-com burst, an investor pull-out, an industry slowdown and discount wars. It has been an incredible journey so far, but the best is yet to come,' Deep reflects.

Post the Ibibo acquisition, SAIF partners exited MakeMyTrip making an impressive $400 million on their initial investment of $25 million. They pulled off a return that was sixteen times more than their decade-old investment. MMT succeeded where many failed in the Indian start-up ecosystem. Deep continues to ride the waves, cruising on success and keeping his eyes firmly focussed on the next big milestone. In the end, Deep's conviction in the initial idea, patience and perseverance through the stormy days and constant focus on the ultimate goal has led MakeMyTrip to become a solo giant in the online travel industry. The outcome was not bad for an entrepreneur who bet his entire life savings on his idea.

PRADEEP KAR

Founder, Chairman and Managing Director, Microland

When Gary Walrath, Star Group's executive vice president met Pradeep Kar, Kar had no plans in place. All he knew was he needed money. 'He (Gary) asked me how much money was needed. I knew Rediff.com was going to go public and raise about $50 million. So I guessed I needed the same amount to play the game. I had no business plan to support my demand.' Gary shook hands on the deal for a third of the company. It was the largest private equity investment in India in a start-up till date, that too in a company that hadn't even launched.

Before We Begin, We Pivot

'start-up pivoting' is an essential term in the industry, which means changing strategies according to the market assessments and curveballs to turn your venture into a desirable and successful product. When a start-up's original business model isn't working due to various reasons like unviability of the business model or no traction, etc., the founders pivot to another strategy or idea to sustain operations. Arguably, Nokia is the oldest and the most fascinating example of this pivoting. The company—which was a small pulp mill in the small Finnish towns of Tampere and Nokia in 1865–68—went through many pivots over a century to become the telecommunications giant that it is today. In recent history, Twitter was born out of a failed podcasting business called Odeo; Pinterest began as a mobile shopping app called Tote; Paypal originated as Confinity, a method to exchange money via Palm Pilots; Groupon was originally a consumer activist site called The Point; and Android pivoted out of an operating system for cameras.

In the Indian market, Snapdeal became widely known for its pivots. It started as a business called Money Saver in 2007, which sold physical discount coupon books to customers. This model, however, didn't take off, as expected. By 2010, the company observed how the Indian start-ups, one by one, were turning into Groupon clones. By then, Groupon had become the fastest growing company in the US start-up ecosystem. Snapdeal saw an opportunity at that moment when the market was favourable and pivoted into a deals site, the seventh one in India. Within fourteen months of this transformation, they landed investments from Kalaari Capital, Indo-US Ventures, and Nexus and became the kings of the deals business in India. Although the honeymoon period for deals sites all over the world was dying down by the end of 2011, Groupon received a successful IPO but analysts become sceptical of the long term viability of its business model. Snapdeal, on the other hand, decided to ride the waves by pivoting further to an online marketplace model. Clearly, in the Indian start-up scenario, Snapdeal also became the luminary of pivots but, it is not the original emperor of pivoting on home ground. That spot is reserved for Microland, the company that went through multiple pivots since its origin to don the successful avatar that it is now known for.

MICROLAND'S BEGINNINGS

Pradeep Kar landed a job at Wipro straight out of B-school in 1983. Back then, Wipro was known as Western Indian Vegetable Products. Pradeep was sure that it was the right break for him because he knew that regardless of what he did in life, learning about computers was going to be valuable. 'So my decision was simplistic to that extent. It helped that they also paid more so I went with only one thought in my mind, *to learn*. I never dreamt of a career in the IT industry. It is just that I enjoyed it and realised that however intimidating it seems, it isn't exactly rocket science. I decided that I must stay put, which turned out to be a lucky decision,' shares Pradeep. Later he relocated to the US to run Sonata Software for three years. On his return to India, he saw a 'now or never' opportunity in the IT industry and founded Microland as a network integration company in 1989.

Microland facilitated the introduction of several new technologies to the Indian market, namely, Compaq, Cisco, Synoptics, and Netscape. They were the largest and fastest growing computer resellers and software distributors in the country. But when Pradeep saw an opportunity in the emerging internet space in 1998, Microland pivoted from being a hardware trader to a new economy company raising tens of millions of dollars from investors who wanted to get a piece of the pie. Microland built several companies such as Planetasia.com, a leading digital transformation company; Indya.com, a portal that competed with Rediff.com; ITspace.com, a portal specifically for people in Information Technology and media2india.net, the first ad network. It also owned Net Brahma Technologies, a networking software company. By 2011, when the second dot-com burst happened, they had exited all their internet businesses and pivoted into a company that provided remote IT infrastructure management services, globally. In nearly thirty years of its existence, Pradeep Kar's Microland has pivoted thrice. Consequently, many consider Pradeep to be an opportunist who never sticks to one industry for a long while others view him as a visionary who spots opportunities in emerging markets before anyone else. Nandan Nilekani, in a foreword for Microland's coffee table book celebrating its 25 years, compared Microland to 'early seafarers and innovators who have the willingness to take a significant risk.'

When Pradeep returned to India in 1989 and dreamt of setting up an IT company, his goal was to acquire annual revenues of approximately ₹25 crore in five years. His company turned out to be one of the earliest companies to raise venture capital in the country. In June 1989, the European head of Novell NetWare's education arm was visiting Mumbai to explore opportunities in India. Pradeep got this information and wanted to meet him but he had no idea where the man was staying. He called up all the five-star hotels in the city and finally found him at The Leela. He didn't even have business cards yet, so he just went to the hotel's business centre, took plain white cards and typed his name and home address on them. He managed to meet Zbigniew, the gentleman from Novell, and they discussed collaborative possibilities. After a follow-up trip to Milan, Pradeep had signed the first global agreement for Microland. He was only 29 at the time.

In 1990, Microland raised ₹20 lakh from SBI Capital Markets. Dipankar Basu, who eventually became the chairman of SBI, bought into Pradeep's vision. Microland's journey of signing up every major global partner had thus begun. 'I went to the Cisco office in San Jose, seeking a partnership in mid-1993. The Cisco vice president James Richardson confronted me and asked why Cisco should partner with a small company like Microland. Richardson was aware of Tata Group's Tata Consultancy Services (TCS) and said that he would rather go with an equal-sized company for their foray into India,' Pradeep recalls. In response, Pradeep said to the Cisco VP, 'But TCS is not standing at your door, I am.' That response was the reason why Cisco went with him instead of TCS. Microland was still a minor company when it partnered with Compaq. Pradeep faced similar uncertainty while dealing with Compaq as well. He says, 'They had the same query as Richardson. I told them that I don't want to be exclusive. You can sign as many partners as you want and evaluate our performance. If we don't deliver, you can cancel the Microland contract.'

By 1994, Microland had achieved a compounded annual growth rate of 86 per cent and revenues over ₹100 crore, way ahead of Pradeep's original target of ₹25 crore. They were the fastest growing IT company in India, signing up almost every single global giant like Cisco, Compaq, Synoptics, Lotus, Micom, and Check Point Software.

How They Almost Blew It

Behind the curtain, in the mid-90s, there were talks about Microland being more valuable than Infosys Technologies. By 1997–98, it had landed a revenue of ₹180 crore following Infosys which had a revenue turnout of ₹260 crore that year. With the listing of Infosys shares, the IT sector became an exciting arena for Indian investors. Companies like Microland started exploring this growing opportunity. Microland started talks with Enam Securities and SBI Capital Markets, two of the leading IPO advisors. The market was buzzing with the news of Microland's imminent IPO. The IPO was supposed to be a cinch. When Microland was submitting the paperwork with Securities and Exchange Board of India (SEBI), the Pavan Sachdeva scandal broke out. Pavan Sachdeva, MD of the retail company, MS Shoes, had rigged the market by misleading investors. Because of his malicious deeds, markets were completely wiped out and the scandal led to the closure of the Bombay Stock Exchange (BSE)—the country's leading bourse which handles 70 per cent of the market transactions—for three whole days! Investors fled the market. Microland and its aspirational peers seemed to have blown their chance. It would take a long time for the investors to put their faith in the Indian markets again.

Pradeep looks at it differently and says, 'Had we gone public, we would have probably got screwed. Being a publicly-owned company would have taken away our ability to shut down operations and pivot. Three major events occurred in the period, 1995–98. Firstly, the warranties on our products changed from one year to three years, which led to a cut in our margins on revenues. Second, earlier, we were exclusive distributors for Cisco, Compaq and other partners but now multiple distributors had cropped up. The race to the bottom began as the margins dropped and the competition increased. And third, with the arrival of the internet, there was an awareness in customers about what to buy and where to buy it from. The internet had disintermediated the middleman. Keeping all these factors in mind, I knew the winds of change had arrived and we were going to be under threat. The writing on the wall was that it was time for us to pivot.' During this time, several companies which had emerged, like Pertec Computer and Unique Corp, had all shut down their operations. The companies that survived were Wipro and HCL because they had a software business to rely on. 'It's easy to talk about the success of software service companies today, but in those days it could have gone either way,' Pradeep adds.

Faux Pas

Microland's moment of ruining it all comes close to what happened with the company, One97 Communications. I have been acquainted with Vijay Shekhar Sharma since 2008 when I first met him to understand the booming Value Added Services (VAS) business in the telecom sector. Over a decade, Vijay had built a very profitable company by providing services to telecom operators in India in categories like Network VAS, Consumer VAS and Enterprise VAS. Then, he was planning on raising ₹120 crore via an IPO in December 2010. One97's peer, OnMobile had debuted on the stock-market just two years ago with a market capitalisation of over ₹3500 crore. With over 100 million subscribers for its services, including the once wildly popular caller tunes, it had grown rapidly from just over ₹2 crore in income, in 2002, to over ₹500 crore by 2010. Under Arvind Rao, OnMobile had gone international, generating nearly a third of its revenue from over 50 other countries. Around the time when Vijay was planning his IPO, OnMobile was hit by a financial scandal during which its founder, Rao, was ousted from the company.

Things went downhill when annoyed mobile subscribers started complaining that they had been accidentally subscribed to the VAS services and could not unsubscribe from the same. Telecom Regulatory Authority of India (TRAI) decided to act, which made the investors notice and this situation made them nervous. Suddenly, all the VAS companies seemed to be swimming against the tide. This impacted Vijay's plans as well. He was visibly upset back then but was determined to launch a wallet service eventually. He was stunned by Alipay's operations in China. He dropped the IPO plans and went onto launch Paytm. After a few months, when Paytm started gaining massive traction and his plan had worked, he told me, 'OnMobile implosion was the best thing that ever happened to One97.' One97 could have never pivoted the way it did had it been a listed company.

Similarly, the significant delay in the SEBI approval for Microland because of the MS Shoes scandal was a blessing in disguise. In the interim, they received an offer from ILFS and GE Capital who wanted to subscribe to their equity at the planned IPO price. 'We decided to go for it as we had no issue expenses and this decision saved time as well. We were raising ₹16 crore and the IPO marketing expenses itself would have been ₹10 crore. The alternative looked extremely efficient,' Pradeep reveals.

With this fresh infusion of capital, Microland was all set, but the internet was a constant disruptor for their core business as it made information widely available to customers and reduced the margins which bothered Pradeep. His mind was already searching for something new. During this search, he came across a document titled 'The Internet Report', a 300-page document, prepared by Mary Meeker, an analyst at Morgan Stanley, with analysis, graphs and charts predicting the impact of the internet around the world. The report gave her instant recognition as an expert on the internet. It also said that India would have 70 million internet users by 2003. Pradeep's company had some experience in the internet economy through its distribution partnership with Netscape. He saw the opportunity and knew that the gold rush was about to begin. He started studying business models and zeroed in on the world's first internet incubation companies—CMGI, Idea Lab and Internet Capital Group. During their peak years, these companies had incubated and invested in several billion dollar companies like Lycos, AltaVista, Engage, Overture.com, etc. Pradeep decided to pursue this business model. Microland wanted to incubate the internet economy of India, which wasn't an easy feat to achieve. Microland had a large business with over 500 employees and an inventory worth over ₹30 crore that would have to be written off. Pradeep was ready to do that and start all over again.

MICROLAND 2.0: THE BOLDEST PIVOT

Microland, in its new avatar, launched PlanetAsia.com, India's first internet business solutions company. 'Our mandate was simple. There were around 8,000 companies listed in the Indian stock exchanges and most of them would need a website sooner or later. We wanted to build as many of them as possible,' explains Pradeep. Planet Asia was soon building large scalable websites for Encyclopædia Britannica, Sharekhan, British Telecom and publishers like *Hindustan Times*, *Mid Day* and *Stardust*. In its second year, Planet Asia's revenues had grown to over ₹60 crore. While building websites for others, Microland realised opportunities in the portal space and ITSpace.com was launched, which focussed, on technology. Its first digital content venture went live on September 1999. It was considered an early success because most of the heavy internet users were workers in the IT industry. With this, Pradeep thought that he was ready for mainstream portals. Still, in its early days, Rediff.com was the only real competitor in this sector as IndiaWorld was focussing only on NRIs. While Rediff.com was trying to cater to everyone, Pradeep decided that his portal would focus on the youth. 'Remember that there was neither Wi-Fi nor mobiles, tablets, etc. Internet was perceived to be a medium for the young since most users were between the ages of 15–35, and only MTV was tapping into that age group's interests. I had a simple logic that the person who was heading the largest youth media platform in the country had to be my CEO. I showed up at Sunil Lulla's house, had a great conversation with him and he signed up. I used to carry blank offer letters with me, so I wrote his name and salary on one, signed it and gave it to him then and there,' reminisces Pradeep. Soon enough, Alok Sethi joined as the CFO, Neeti Chopra as the head of marketing, and the media veteran from the India Today Group Arun Katiyar, joined as the head of content.

In Microland's coffee table book, Sunil Lulla, the former CEO of Indya.com remembers how Pradeep started a dramatic chain of events by bringing together a dynamic portal with news, sports, Bollywood, mail, entertainment and chat alive, into one website. It also scooped up a seed round from investors like John Sculley, ex-CEO of Apple computers, Vinod Khosla, the super VC from Kleiner Perkins of USA, Rajat Gupta, CEO of consulting major McKinsey, Pavan Nigam, co-founder and CTO of Healtheon and Sanjay Parthasarathy, ex-vice president of Microsoft.

At the same time, News Corp (owned by media mogul Rupert Murdoch) had missed the bus on the dot-com gold rush in the United States and was cautious about not repeating that mistake in India. Internet services company, AOL announced its $160 billion merger with Time Warner. It was the largest merger in corporate history. Star Group's executive vice president Gary Walrath had been asked by Rupert Murdoch to execute an aggressive plan for the Indian market. Gary had read about Pradeep Kar's ambitious plans in India. Gary called up Pradeep who told the Star Group VP that he was too busy to travel for a meeting and asked him to drop by his office. 'I sent a car to pick him up from The Leela hotel,' Pradeep recalls, 'When we met, he asked me how much money was needed. I knew that Rediff.com was about to go public and raise about $50 million. I knew that I needed investment to match that amount to have a fighting chance. I had no business plan to support my demand.' For a third of the company, Gary agreed to invest in Pradeep's company. At that time, it was the largest private equity investment in an Indian technology company that hadn't even proposed a product or a business model to the investor.

Microland's investment-fuelled new-born Indya.com went live in April 2000 with a path-breaking launch campaign. They advertised with the tagline, 'It happens only in Indya' on *The Times of India*'s front page as the first ever four-sheet advertising jacket. The cost of the advertisement was a cool

₹4.5 crore. The company quickly moved into a hyper mode in 2000. Indya's team expanded aggressively, their staff strength reached to 240, around 40 alliances were sewn up, and travel portal Net2travel.com was acquired in a stock swap. Like all portals, their focus was on viewership. An IPO was targeted for December 2000. Microland didn't stop with Indya. It launched media2India, an internet media company that provided research services and produced internet conferences. It also went on to sign up with Jupiter Research and Penton to create India Internet World, launching the Indian franchise of the largest internet exposition platform in the world, besides tying up with DoubleClick for an ad-serving platform. Microland's ecosystem was expanding quickly. Pradeep had no idea that the dot-com bubble had burst in the first quarter of 2000. The opportunist-visionary heedlessly assumed it to be a minor occurrence.

On Life Support: When Microland Blew It (Again)

Quite like what Kryptonite was for Superman, Indya was both the boon and bane of Microland's existence. As the markets turned against the dot-com businesses, Indya.com's burn rate, with its swanky office, large salaries and a huge team became a stressful factor. The situation wasn't improving anywhere else in the world either. On 9 November 2000, Pets.com, a much-hyped company, went out of business only nine months after completing its IPO. By that time, most internet stocks had declined in value by 75 per cent, wiping out 1.755 trillion of market value. In January 2001, just three dot-com companies bought advertising spots during the Super Bowl. These were E-Trade, Monster.com.com, and Yahoo!'s Hot Jobs. The 9/11 attacks accelerated the stock-market drop later that year. Investor confidence was further eroded by several accounting scandals and the resulting bankruptcies caused by events like the Enron scandal. Then in July 2001, Star decided to take over Indya. Pradeep was paid around ₹48 crore (approx. $10 million) at that time for the acquisition. It was also speculated that a large sum of Indya's $53 million war-chest remained unused. They had more than $30 million cash in their bank and Star invested $10 million on top of that to salvage the remains. Star had decided to buy 100 per cent of Indya to make better use of that remaining money.

At the end of October 2001, Sunil Lulla called a meeting of department heads to inform them about downsizing in the company and that he was resigning. Later that day, Gary Walrath, Star Group's executive vice president held a town hall meeting and told the team that it was over. He is reported to have said, 'If six is being invested for every one we earn, then I *have to* make rational business decisions.' That was the situation in the market. Indya had tried to build an expansive kingdom in 18 months, whereas, it had taken Rediff.com four years to do the same. In the process, it had also lost a lot of money and investor confidence.

IT sector was also strapped of cash and struggling to the core. 'We had a shareholders' agreement for $5 million with News Corp. I didn't need the money urgently so I said that I would take the money later. It was a foolish decision because when the downturn happened, they refused to pay. I could have taken the legal route but they are partners in Indya.com, so I decided against it. The lesson here is this, "Never leave the cash on the table,"' says Pradeep as he reflects on the decisions that cost him Indya, the first vertical portal in India. Microland shut down the IT Space in 2001 and exited the conferences. The sale of Planet Asia, Net Brahma and Media2india followed. After raising over $77 million across its ventures in three years, Microland's internet adventure had miserably failed.

MICROLAND 3.0: THE REVIVAL

While evaluating his options, Pradeep realised that he had missed both the software services and the BPO wave. Post this, he decided to focus on the global delivery infrastructure management in the early 2000s. Today, Microland is a company with over $100 million revenue with over 4,000 people managing the Global IT infrastructure remotely from India. It reminds me of how Business to Consumer (B2C) company, Sify went onto become a Business to Business Company (B2B).

'During the second phase of the internet emergence, many suggested that I should resume my journey in the dot-com space but I couldn't see any logic behind that advice. Now, I have embarked on serious business. As you are aware, any sizeable business takes seven to ten years to grow. I saw value in staying rooted in one place. No distractions! Now, I want to build something meaningful and scale-up as I couldn't do with Indya.com. So here I am, telling the naysayers that I won't get distracted anymore. I will build a reasonably good technology services company,' Pradeep concludes.

Today, Microland is churning out a $100 million revenue. It is arguably a unicorn in its space. Finally, his detractors, who assumed that Pradeep never sticks around long enough in a business sphere to grow it, have been proven wrong. Pradeep, the quick thinking visionary, assessed his mistakes, learnt significantly from them and made the most of his second innings, just like a true-blue entrepreneur.

SATYAN GAJWANI

Managing Director and Vice Chairman, Times Internet

'When we acquire a company, one of our conditions states: 'You are not allowed to move into our office. We don't want you to. If we killed your energy by having you come join us and adopt a Times Internet culture, we might as well have just built it ourselves.'

SATYAN GAJWANI IS NOT AN ENTREPRENEUR IN THE traditional sense. He did not set up Times Internet, the company he manages. Indeed, there is no dearth of people who scoff at how the company was handed to him on a platter. It is an easy conclusion to draw because Satyan is married to Trishla Jain, the only daughter of Samir Jain. The Jains can rightfully be called the first family of the Indian media industry. They are the owners of Bennett Coleman and Company Ltd, more commonly known as The Times Group. The behemoth has over 11,000 employees and revenues exceeding $1.5 billion.

So, why should Satyan be included in the esteemed list of entrepreneurs discussed in this book? My rationale for this exception is simple. Because it is Satyan who has made Times Internet what it is today and so, he deserves a spot in the list. Yes, it was already an established company backed by a mega-conglomerate when he became its CEO at the age of 27. But at that time, it was nothing short of a bumbling and antiquated traditional media company struggling to stay relevant by playing catch-up with new upstarts. It evolved into a gigantic digital powerhouse only after Satyan took the reins in his hands. I have followed The Times Group's digital initiatives for a while now, since it was my digital marketing agency's first client in 2000, just a year after the company was launched. Therefore, I've had a ringside view and observed them fumble through the years without a defined vision, rolling through many CEOs and still failing to make it work. Things transformed once Satyan got involved in the company around 2010. Taking over the company at an age when he was unlikely to be taken seriously, his elevation was predictably treated with disdain. Satyan's appointment as the CEO was looked down upon by those unfamiliar with his work experience. There was an assumption that he had no experience about operating businesses in India, but Satyen had been working for the group behind the scenes for nearly four years. I must admit that I was among the dissenters until I discovered that this young man was made of sterner stuff.

It was an anonymous question posted on Quora that completely changed my view. The question read, 'How did Satyan Gajwani become Times Internet CEO at just 27?' Whether asked out of sincerity or malice, it didn't get much attention. But, Satyan's unexpected response to it was rapidly circulated. Here is what he said, 'Yep, this is true. I am married to Trishla Jain, daughter of Samir Jain. And I'm 100 per cent sure that has had a significant impact as to why I'm CEO of Times Internet today. That being said, I would expect that I'll be measured more by what Times Internet is able to accomplish over the next few years, rather than where I am today.' Satyan could have just as easily ignored the post but he chose to respond. I was as impressed as the thousands of users who upvoted his response because business families in India are rarely known for their candour.

Even more unexpected was how Satyan turned the tide in the company's favour. No one had expected the privileged son-in-law to accomplish what he did. Over the last few years, Times Internet has launched a slew of products, has come up with several international collaborations to widen the offering, invested in over fifty earlystage start-ups and made over a dozen acquisitions—the largest being that of MX player in 2018, for over ₹1,000 crore.

Today, the group is spread across forty-odd businesses, including content, utilities, transactions and classifieds, and generates 400 million unique visitors per month, with revenues hitting close to ₹1,000 crore a year. In my opinion, Times Internet is the third-most relevant digital media company in India after Facebook and Google. It is unimaginable for a company to suffer a near-death experience when you have a $1.5 billion annual revenue giant backing you. Nevertheless, Satyan's perspective on the mistakes made by them and the turnaround make for a compelling story.

SWINGING BETWEEN PIONEERING AND PHASING-OUT

When Times Internet launched in 1999, it spun largely around their core property Indiatimes.com. *The Economic Times* was hosted separately. Indiatimes.com was modelled after Yahoo!, which was *the* gateway for internet users at that time. Its ad had a rather cringeworthy jingle with some girls shouting, 'Indiatimes! The i of the internet!' No one was quite sure what it meant. Despite this rather disconcerting display, some of its teams were moving fast. Indiatimes.com was one of the first to launch travel in India at a time when even start-ups like MakeMyTrip had decided to shut down India operations and focus purely on the US-India corridor. Indiatimes.com stepped in and tried to fill the gap. The first ticket I ever booked online was on Indiatimes travel. After the 2008 global financial meltdown—coupled with intense competition from MakeMyTrip, Yatra and Cleartrip—Indiatimes.com shut down its travel section. Similarly, it shut down its e-commerce section in 2016, when e-commerce companies started bleeding money to gain market share. Both categories that Indiatimes. com pioneered have multi-billion dollar winners today. 'I don't know if they (travel and e-commerce) were necessarily built as the best products in their space but they were certainly built as the biggest. They had all the marketing muscle behind them. We spent a lot of energy on a giant marketing campaign to make sure anyone and everyone who wanted to travel knew about it. But maybe we didn't put enough emphasis on things like retention and product flow to make sure that the product experiences were the best,' Satyan explains.

With razor sharp focus on just one vertical and flush with funds, entrepreneurs in travel and e-commerce eventually outperformed Indiatimes.com on the product and user experience. In 2008, MakeMyTrip was preparing for an IPO with a deeper consumer connect, while Indiatimes.com had shuttered down its online travel operations. When Flipkart raised that historic $1 billion from Tiger Global Management, Naspers and Accel Partners in 2015 and was shipping five million units a month, Indiatimes.com knew its shopping vertical wouldn't be able to keep playing catch-up forever and decided to focus on battles that it could win by winding down its e-commerce business.

One major identifiable issue was that Indiatimes.com had been applying 'traditional media business orientations to non-traditional businesses.' Satyan expands on this: 'When the business started to scale-up, our expectation was that it would automatically start generating revenues but we should have pumped more funding into it to make it even bigger.' Despite its experience and muscle might, the company failed to do its due diligence on market-size evaluation. It also didn't acquire an understanding of profitability versus growth. Indiatimes.com continued to deal with it with the traditional perspective that 'businesses make money from the very beginning and they grow as they make money.' This approach proved to be their nemesis.

On his appointment, Satyan implemented a sea of changes in the company's thought processes, strategy and execution.

'The two major changes we made as a company were a) we changed from a media company that used technology into a "product and technology" company that uses media, and b) when we see things thriving or moving well, we double down or triple down on them instead of pushing them to break even like we did in the past,' Satyan reveals.

Consumer internet start-ups have historically always displayed a healthy tension between looking for profits and investing in growth. One can drive profits in any business by not investing in future growth. If further capital is available, it's never a good idea to optimise for cash at the cost of expanding the market. Another reason that Indiatimes.com' sub-divisions of travel and shopping may not have worked well for them is that they were sub-divisions. Businesses that focus on a single product usually have a better chance at succeeding. It is a theory Satyan adheres to. He says, 'Sub-brands work in immature markets. As a market matures, it's easier to build brand association with a standalone product.' For instance, MakeMyTrip works because it feels like a company dedicated to the singular purpose of travel. Whereas Indiatimes Travel feels like a sub-division of something bigger. I do think this outlook hinders the company's ability to grow. Maybe it's an internal orientation of thinking of it as a standalone business and making sure that it is allocated all the resources that it needs as a standalone company.'

Although this theory is yet to be proven, it seems plausible, especially in cases where sub-brands have been unsuccessful. This failure can negatively impact the parent brand as well as its loyalty, trust and business. Bad customer experiences can lead to the tarnishing of the sub-brand and the parent brand's image. For example, if a customer has a bad experience with Indiatimes Travel, it may have a negative impact on how their shopping business is perceived. Armed with this logic, Satyan worked to overcome the shortcomings of the previous model. Indiatimes.com now has separate brand names and identities for each of its businesses. The trade-off is there is no unifying element to hold the various platforms together under the banner of a single brand. It means remarketing and developing a new brand every time, a hurdle that is easily overcome for sub-brands. But Satyan believes that 'the cost savings of sharing a brand are not as great as the benefits of investing more and building a dedicated brand.'

Satyan means to warn against what he refers to as 'over-extending a brand.' A sub-brand can have greater appeal when its feel and flavour is in sync with the leading brand, not when it is meant to have a distinct appeal of its own. Which is probably why the company has been careful to keep brands like its music platform Gaana.com away from obvious associations with the Times brand. Satyan says, 'Times—the brand—stands for trust, integrity, confidence, maturity and sometimes, security. Gaana.com is a music platform. It's for the young. It should feel light, energetic and uplifting. It promotes and emotes a very different message. Were we to build a bank, a Times Bank would probably work because it conveys the trust of our brand, but when we are building a music platform, Times isn't the ideal brand for it. Over-extending your brands, at times, dilutes their impact.'

Lessons Learnt from the 2008 Crisis

Classifieds ads for jobs, matrimony and real estate form a significant part of the revenue for every traditional newspaper publisher. It isn't exactly the business's lifeline, but surely an important and a consistent part of the revenue. A lot of that changed slowly but steadily with the coming of websites such as Naukri.com, BharatMatrimony, Shaadi.com, and 99Acres. After seven to eight years of these start-ups catering to a small online population of 10 to 12 million active users, Monster.com, a global employment website, arrived in India and acquired JobsAhead.com. At the same time, while the newspaper business continued to grow, The Times Group's management had been slacking off. When it woke up, it began to observe the global trends and understood that vertical and horizontal classifieds websites like Monster.com and Craigslist were eating into the traditional newspaper's lunch. The management got busy trying to get its act together, and that's when Times Internet launched TimesJobs.com in 2004 followed by SimplyMarry and MagicBricks.com in 2006. By 2007, Info Edge (which owns Naukri.com, Jeevansathi and 99Acres) had grown from being a ₹3.63-crore turnover company to a ₹84.05-crore company in four years' time at a CAGR[10] of 117 per cent. It also made its public offering that year, with a dramatic debut that saw its stock record a gain of over 90 per cent on day one. BharatMatrimony had raised capital from Canaan Partners and Yahoo! while People Group which owned Shaadi.com and Makaan.com had also raised external capital from WestBridge Capital Partners and others. Online classifieds wasn't exactly a battle of the mighty against the underdogs. At that time, everyone was loaded with ammunition and had enough money to fight it out with each other. With Naukri.com's IPO, it was clear that the opportunity, if executed well, could eventually turn into a multi-billion dollar company. Times stepped on the accelerator by deploying capital and using the multimedia of its own channels, namely outdoor advertising, print and radio assets to thrust forward its online classified properties.

---

[10] Compound Annual Growth Rate

When the Lehman Brothers' bankruptcy hit global economic markets, companies like People Group that owned Shaadi.com & Makaan.com and Matrimony Group which owned BharatMatrimony, ClickJobs, IndiaProperties stopped investing in growth and came to a screeching halt. With investors shying away from making further commitments, each of them experienced their own near-death moments on various levels. Incidentally, when this happened, Satyan had been working with none other than Lehman's equity-trading desk at London. In an interview published in *ForbesIndia*, the magazine claims that as a fall out of Lehman's bankruptcy, BCCL had a month where it witnessed a revenue decline, possibly for the first time in 175 years.[11] In that interview, Satyan talks about his soon-to-be father-in-law's proposal to come and work in India. According to Satyan, 'He [Samir Jain] said that a lot of strategic decisions are going to be made in the next six months that may have long term impact so you [Satyan] should be a part of them.' And so, Satyan moved to India.

By 11 December, MediaNama reported that The Times Group was laying off five per cent of its staff. Times Business Solutions, which was formed in 2005 to build on the online classifieds opportunity and employed a thousand people, suffered the most. The rumoured number of layoffs was about 15–20 per cent. Times was applying the brakes on its classifieds expansions.

'I wasn't in charge of the digital section when all of that happened. But I understood that we were really competitive and pushed the job space in 2006–07. When the recession hit

---

[11] Ajwani, Deepak and Assisi, Charles. 'Satyan Gajwani: Times Group's Digital Navigator', *Forbes India*, 21 November 2012.

in 2008, we pulled back. And though Naukri.com was cautious, it didn't pull back as strongly. We let that gap widen to the point that it has become very hard to compete now. This is what has allowed Naukri.com to be such a great and strong business. We learnt our lesson,' says Satyan. Thus, Times Internet makes it a point to not pull back that easily when the terrain becomes tough. I've seen some start-ups make this fatal mistake. When there is good momentum, the company has a long-term view of the market and sufficient capital to invest, there is no reason for it to hold back. To see a crisis as an opportunity by taking a long-term view of the market is what separates the grain from the chaff.

Times Internet faced a similar crisis when it rolled back on its travel, e-commerce and job properties sections. They allowed the gaps to widen to an extent that taking the leap to the other end became an impossible task. Therefore, when Satyan joined the company, he had his work cut out for him. 'When I came on board in 2011–12, the dilemma in front of me was this, "How do we restore ourselves to the status of a competitive large-scale company in a market that had grown much more competitive than it had been ten years ago?"'

Today, Times Jobs lags behind Naukri.com and possibly LinkedIn as a preferred destination for employers and their prospects. While the matrimonial classifieds battle isn't exactly over, BharatMatrimony has won that race followed by Shaadi.com and Jeevansathi securing spots in the top three. Times Internet's offering SimplyMarry was shut down quietly in 2018. MagicBricks is the last standing classifieds bet for The Times Group, and the latter is bullish about it, unwilling to yield. It is currently engrossed in a neck-to-neck race with 99Acres. Today, MagicBricks is an over-1,400 workforce strong business, with operations across 35 cities.

ACQUISITIONS AND RETAINING TALENT

With Satyan in charge as MD in 2012, Times Internet made a series of acquisitions by buying MensXP that year, CricBuzz, CouponDunia and Dineout in 2014; TaskBucks and Viral Shots in 2015; Willow TV in 2016; and MX Player in 2018. Historically, across the world, most founders quit their company after it's acquired. If one sticks around for a year or two, credit is due to the acquirer. It is not difficult to fathom why a founder quits. An entrepreneur is not used to working for someone else or being told what to do. The entrepreneur creates a company because he or she want to be a leader, and not a follower. So the entrepreneur has a difficult time when the acquiring company tries telling him how to run the business he has created and grown. Moreover, most acquisitions leave no economic incentive or upside for the founders to stay and grow their companies further. But in the case of Times Internet's acquisitions, 11 of the 12 founders whose companies were acquired have stayed on till date, which is a rare and admirable feat.

Satyan credits this to the free hand given to the acquired heads to run their businesses without much interference from the central command. He explains, 'When we acquire a company, one of our conditions is this: "You are not allowed to move into our office. We don't want you to do so. If we killed your energy by having you come join us and adopt the Times Internet culture, we might as well have just built your company ourselves. If we believe that there is something worth acquiring in your business, we want to harness it and juice it as best we can. So whenever you need something from us, give us a call. We will find it, whether it is a marketing resource or access or anything else. But otherwise, keep doing what you're doing and check in with us from time to time. Let us know how things are going and when you need more money. We will figure that out together. Because if we really believe in your skills, competence and work, why the hell would we want to change it?"'

It is a good philosophy to follow. Today, Times Internet's best skill is its ability to harness every entrepreneurial and start-up energy in the business it runs while still leveraging the institutional strengths of the group. Satyan admits that it is the brand's single biggest structural skill. He reflects, 'Many large enterprises can't create entrepreneurial energy and fire in a business. But they have other resources that a standalone company lacks. So usually, the struggle is between scrappy entrepreneurs and huge behemoth corporate. I'd like to think we have the ability to be a little bit of both. We are a combination of the scrappy, focused and hungry entrepreneur armed with the machinery of the large conglomerate.'

Companies that have figured out how to retain their founders can leverage their knowledge and expertise over time and pay much higher acquisition prices than those companies that are afraid that the acquired founders will leave as soon as they can because they hate to get bogged down with the bureaucracy of a big corporation. This strategy proves useful for the acquired business which remains unique in its processing and culture and at the same time, gets infused with the necessary monetary and industrial strength of the large corporation. In short, it is a win-win situation for both parties involved in the acquisition. Clearly, this strategy positioned Satyan as an innovative businessman who didn't push Times Internet to compete with its competitors but used the company's strengths and innovative ideas to create a league of its own.

Lessons from the 2014 Gold Rush: Have Faith in Yourself

Investors reappeared in the start-up ecosystem with a renewed enthusiasm in 2014. SoftBank, Alibaba and Naspers pumped millions of dollars in some freshly minted start-ups, although the classifieds space wasn't affected as far as jobs and matrimonial verticals were concerned. Quikr raised $150 million and with that investment, it was going to build focused verticals across various categories to improve monetisation. A collective of IIT-Mumbai students was raising financing for their new venture, Housing.com and towards the end of 2014, they made the bubble official by raising a whopping $90 million from SoftBank, the leviathan fund, which seems to have access to infinite capital. Info Edge raised ₹700 crore just for 99Acres, announcing its serious intentions to the market. And, for the first time, a rumour spread that Times Internet was seeking to raise external capital to defend its offspring MagicBricks in the real-estate turf.

Satyan confirms this and explains, 'Because we were juggling a lot at Times Internet, we thought that it made sense to raise independent capital for MagicBricks. Housing.com and 99Acres had acquired close to $100 million, Tiger and Google were financing Commonfloor, and Quikr was on its own trip so it was a very threatening time. Now the other side of the story is that every time there was a funding spree, I would ask the head of MagicBricks, "What are they seeing that we don't see?" And his response would be, "Satyan, I am telling you, I know these businesses. They are not substantial. We are building it right, we are doing well and we are going to keep on performing exceptionally. Yes, they are trying to hire our employees by offering them thrice their current salaries. But we will manage it. Let's just stay the course." We did exactly that and he was right. Today, 80 per cent of those companies are just hot air. The only company with strong bones that managed to stick around is 99Acres. They are having the last laugh. We know that battle and we are pretty comfortable with it, even though it was very stressful at that time. It did make us consider the option of raising capital as a defence mechanism just to confirm that we had access to it.'

Every cycle of evolution arrives with favourable and unfavourable changes. A large investment by giants like Tiger and SoftBank is like a double-edged sword. It has made things easier for entrepreneurs but then the investors also expected returns that weren't viable. Nevertheless, fundamentally, now the ecosystem is far more robust with a new start-up sprouting ever so often.

Satyan reflects on the contradictions and says, 'The flip side is that when entrepreneurs get too much credibility too soon, they often end up burning their bridges like Rahul Yadav and some other failed companies did.' Of course, in this case, the bad apple does rot the others. Satyan does admit that 'When the market goes really nuts, it stresses us out because people who shouldn't have as much capital as they do become aggressive in ways that don't necessarily make sense. Rahul Yadav is the perfect example. He didn't really have a substantial business but he was spending ten times more just because he could. Because of the acquired funding of $100 million, with another $500 million quickly following, he had this belief that he could just go ballistic. We, on the other hand, have built our businesses logically and methodically over a longer period of time without jumping into anything.'

I believe, more often than not, the pace at which a start-up burns through its money is often a way to 'fake it till you make it.' It can be impossible to grow a business to scale without deploying the capital you just raised. Think of Flipkart, Zomato, Swiggy and Ola Cabs. But knowing the difference between 'needed' and 'wasteful' spending is crucial, logical and easier said than done because sometimes the entire bubble around the ecosystem doesn't encourage you to exercise restraint.

SMART WAYS OF LOOKING: T-LABS, AN ACCIDENTAL PROFIT CENTRE

In 2011, Satyan oversaw the launch of the very profitable T-Labs, a start-up accelerator. A start-up accelerator is a fixed-term, cohort-based programme that includes seed investment, access to network, and mentorship, ending in a public pitch event or demo day to accelerate growth. T-Labs offered ₹10 lakh financing for 8 per cent equity in a start-up and since its conception, it has supported 57 start-ups in 13 batches. As is the nature of this game, 21 of them have shut down so far, with 27 gathering follow-up investments. But there are also a few start-ups that have gone on to raise financing from top tier VC funds like Tiger Global, Omidyar Network, and Sequoia Capital.

As an experiment, T-Labs gave Times Internet, the opportunity to be part of many different ideas, but it also became an excellent marketing machine. Satyan expands, 'We wanted to reorient Times Internet as a start-up factory rather than a big old corporate. We thought of investing ₹10 lakh in ten companies in a year. That amount comes to ₹1 crore plus related expenses. We knew that we could manage it as a marketing expense. Of course, the entrepreneurs running those start-ups didn't think of it that way. They felt like it was the beginning of a new era in the start-up ecosystem. Just one or two of the investments in T-labs have returned five to six times the entire investment till date, so it's been very lucrative for us on a small scale. We make sure that it grows because it gives us a really strong connection to the entrepreneurial and start-up ecosystem and a very good pulse of the market.'

Now T-Labs offers over ₹50 lakh in seed capital for 8–10 per cent of the company. It's better than most angel fundraises for a start-up as it provides meaningful cash flow, access to our network and mentoring for a small percentage. Between Tiger Global-backed Inshorts, Omidyar-backed Pratilipi, Sequoia Capital-backed Happay, and Blume Ventures-backed Data Weave, the portfolio has raised over $50 million. It has exited seven ventures and has had three exits so far.

Satyan's story reminds me of a book written by Louis V. Gerstner, Jr., the chairman and CEO of IBM from April 1993 until March 2002, titled *Who Says Elephants Can't Dance?* The book is an account of IBM's historic turnaround under Gerstner. When he joined the company, the computer industry had changed so rapidly that IBM was on its way to losing $16 billion. The company was on a watchlist for extinction as it became a victim of its enormous size that made it difficult to change alongside a partisan corporate culture. He led IBM from the brink of bankruptcy and obscurity back to the forefront of the technology business. Similarly, Times Internet was riding into the sunset for almost a decade before Satyan's vision changed everything for the company. Eventually, Times Internet did not jump into the gold rush but managed to remain sustainable, while others burnt out in quick succession. It managed this because instead of making rash decisions, it trusted its own strategies despite the changing facets of the market. As a big and experienced player, it turned into a facilitator for budding start-ups instead of creating more verticals to compete with them. The fluctuations in the start-up ecosystem did make it nervous but even so, having faith in its work was the reason why Times Internet made it. Satyan took firm charge of the company, and as the MD, he developed a vision and an execution strategy, completely changed the corporate culture, quickly adapted in the face of adversities and implemented lessons learnt from errors. Today, he is the head of a completely reinvented Times Internet.

RAJESH JAIN

Founder and CEO, IndiaWorld
Communications Limited

'Rajesh, you keep your mouth shut about the price. I will negotiate. I will get this done.' After their meeting with Ramaraj, Rajesh was asked to fly to Hyderabad to meet Ramalinga Raju, the founder of Satyam computers, which was a significant shareholder in Sify. The meeting went on for hours and at 2 a.m. in the morning, Rajesh called Bhavana. 'Hemendra bhai has quoted ₹500 crore for our company. But Sify doesn't want to invest, they want to buy the whole thing.' 'It was surreal,' Rajesh recalls. 'In just ten days, our valuation on paper (with the Mail.com offer) had gone from ₹170 crore to ₹500 crore in cash. The entire credit for which went to Hemendra Bhai.'

ON 13 DECEMBER 1999, I WAS PREPARING TO OPEN Webchutney's first office in the dusty Malviya Nagar in Delhi when my father showed me a newspaper article that left me stunned. This was the day that the tiny geeky internet world in India became a chic entity that went on to be wooed by the Silicon Valley. The news article was about the acquisition of IndiaWorld Communications by Satyam Infoway, i.e., Sify, in an all-cash deal. Satyam paid $40 million upfront to the IndiaWorld promoter Rajesh Jain, an amount that included a caution deposit of $12 million. Satyam would pay the remaining part of the $115 million by 30 June 2000. The deal value for the four-year-old IndiaWorld was at about ₹499 crore.

This event changed not only the fortunes of IndiaWorld and Satyam, but also the small fish in the pond such as my company, Webchutney. Over the past year, my partner and I had been busy building brochure-ware websites for exporters who had found that an internet presence was becoming increasingly essential for their businesses overseas. After this news spread—and it did spread like wildfire in our world—we began to receive calls from everyone who thought that they could pull off a feat similar to that of IndiaWorld. Since we had been pretty much the only player in town at that point, it led to a substantial boom in our business, and as a result, portals became the new thing in India.

When It All Began

To chart out the journey of IndiaWorld's success, one must go back to the beginning. Rajesh Jains's start-up story is not that different from many other start-up successes that we've already talked about. In 1994, Rajesh Jain hit rock-bottom and assumed that he was a failed entrepreneur. The medical technology business that he had founded with Sanjay Jain had tanked after two years of pounding the pavement. At the time of launching the business—Rajesh, with his coveted IIT and US education, a comfortable family life and a father who was willing to support his dream—thought of himself as the cat's whiskers. But two years down the line, he was nothing but a desperate feline foraging through leftovers. 'My world was collapsing and nothing was working out,' he reminisces in his slick office at Peninsula Towers, in Lower Parel, Mumbai. Post this realisation, Rajesh took some time off from work and headed to San Francisco, where he stayed at the apartment of a batchmate from IIT. This was the time of the Bulletin Board System, popularly known as BBS. It was the first forum to dial into and exchange messages with other users and could also be used to download software. But it was a text-based system and the experience was not all that appealing for an average user. Around this time, a little known company, Mosaic Communications Corporation based out of Mountain View California, launched Mosaic Netscape 0.9, the first web browser that democratised internet users around the world. These were the early years and Yahoo!, eBay and Google hadn't come into the picture yet. Rajesh was toying with a couple of other ideas, but having read an article in *The New York Times* about how Netscape Communications 'had been developing enhanced versions of a hugely successful program called Mosaic that lets people jump between computers around the world merely by clicking on screen icons' and seeing Mosaic at work, he knew he had found a simple but extremely useful idea. Rajesh shares the origin of his idea, 'While I was in the US, I found it very hard to get news about India. Newspapers would take up to ten days to arrive! So, I decided I would head back to India and set up an information marketplace for NRIs.' His plan was to take syndicated content from leading publications from around the country and compile it all on a single portal to become the go-to destination for NRIs around the world. This is how Indiaworld.com was born.

Rajesh came back to India and discussed this idea with Sanjay. They decided to let go of the first venture as well as most of their team because they had limited funds. Eventually, Sanjay left too, went on to join Google and later became the chief product officer at Aadhar. Since resources were limited, Rajesh's wife Bhavana—who was then completing her Chartered Accountancy—decided to help him out. Then, he got to work. Rajesh says, 'I wrote letters to around fifty media companies, newspapers and magazines to introduce our website and request content for it. Only two people responded.' But the ones who go back to Rajesh were icons in the media industry. One was the famed cartoonist R.K. Laxman and the other was the media magnate Aroon Purie—founder, publisher and editor-in-chief of the India Today Group. Loaded with an MVP,[12] Rajesh and Bhavana's team launched IndiaWorld.com in March 1995, only a week after the launch of Yang and Filo's Yahoo! in the US.

Rajesh knew that Laxman's cartoons and the content from *India Today* were going to be a knockout. He leveraged these names with other content providers and soon, IndiaWorld had content from *The Indian Express*, *The Times of India*, *Hindustan Times* and tech-oriented publications like *Data Quest* amongst many others. Rajesh adds, 'We had a small team. We would take

---

[12] Minimum Viable Product

stories and put them up. We also uploaded stock quotes from Merrill Lynch at the end of day. We would email the headlines to our subscribers. It was my job to look at the newspapers every morning and type the headlines. We would update the news section using the evening news from Doordarshan. It worked perfectly because our Indians subscribers in America would just be waking up and we were delivering to them the latest news.' Their content providers gradually increased to nearly thirty, even though he was not paying any of them a lot. Laxman's cartoons became very popular. Since online advertising didn't exactly exist at this point, Rajesh decided to create a subscription model for $59 per year for full access for all the content while some of the content would remain free. 'I thought people in India pay ₹2 for a newspaper every day, so the NRI subscribers should be able to cough up $59 a year. Otherwise, how would I make money?' Rajesh reasons. While the IndiaWorld team was enjoying their initial success, they had no clue that they were not the only ones who got the memo on the launch of Netscape. Ajit Balakrishnan of Rediff. com, Pradeep Kar of Microland and R. Ramaraj of Sify were all working on creating the next e-fix.

Within a few weeks of launching the subscription model, Rajesh was gripped by the worry that the numbers weren't adding up. He reduced the subscription cost to a meagre $20. It took him another eighteen months to understand why the model wasn't working. 'We got one subscription from General Electric in the US, which had a lot of NRI employees. I figured out that everyone was sharing the same password. The bottom line was that it was impossible to get Indians to pay for subscriptions,' Rajesh says. But in an interesting turn, IndiaWorld started receiving queries from companies to build their websites. Rajesh put a neat price on this service.

He recalls, 'We charged ₹5,000 for a page. When we got our first order from the advertising agency, Ogilvy & Mather, we charged them ₹15,000 for three pages. Then we had Boyden, the advisory firm, as our client but one of our biggest clients was Kotak Securities. They wanted a full website and a portfolio manager because they, too, were focusing on NRIs. That gave us monetary relief. We kept the costs low by hiring ten employees in our office at Nariman Point and using our server from the US to host the pages. Life was good.'

Till it wasn't.

How They Almost Blew It

IndiaWorld was managing well for two years and finally breaking even when the axe fell and everything came to a halt. The row of dominoes started falling right after a small dispute with the vendor who hosted their domain, Indiaworld.com in 1997. The situation escalated to the level that IndiaWorld was locked out of its own domain. They lost the domain where they had painstakingly garnered traffic for more than two years. Being early, naive players in the field, they had never bothered to get the domain name registered. It was a massive setback because it meant that they would have to start again from scratch. Rajesh remembers the incident like it were yesterday and recalls the helpless moment when he told himself, 'It's over. We've blown it.'

Rajesh tried to pursue the matter in court but withdrew the case on realising that it would only mean loss of precious time and money. To minimise damages, he registered a new domain name, Indiaworld.co.in, and discovered that VSNL, the only vendor equipped to handle their domain, was very accommodating. VSNL didn't have a policy regarding pricing back then, so they let Rajesh run the website for free till a pricing framework could be officially established. With a fresh domain, IndiaWorld was back in business in two days. At least that's what Rajesh thought. After weeks of waiting, Rajesh discovered the enormity of the damage done by the US host. The numbers barely moved on the new domain.

Rajesh says, 'The problem was our new domain because everyone was a using a dot-com domain in those days. The damage was irreversible as we lost a lot of traffic,' he says. At their wits' end, the husband-wife duo kept the idea mills running to find a way out of this cul-de-sac. Eventually, they came up with an idea that was going to change their lives once again. They decided to use Hindi names with a dot-com for the domain, and by the end of their brainstorming session, they had nearly forty names ready to be registered—Samachar for news, Khel for sports, Khoj for search and directory services, and Bawarchi for the recipe directory. Rajesh says, 'Unlike Yahoo!, which was under a single domain, we decided to create separate vertical domains with names that were easy to remember. So within three to four months, we launched Khoj. com, Khel.com, Samachar.com, etc., and this worked brilliantly. Of the thirteen websites we launched, Samachar, Khel, Khoj, and Bawarchi were quite successful.'

Rajesh and Bhavana kept the business within the family to control the costs. Rajesh's cousin, also an employee at IndiaWorld, developed a crawler that would collect the links for all the newspaper websites and bring them together on a single page. This turned Samachar into a gateway for all the newspaper websites. The cost was almost nothing because it took them only one host page to create this. Thousands of NRIs in the US started flocking to their website every morning for their daily dose of desi news. This patronage was followed by advertisers, mostly telecom companies who were peddling plans for overseas calls to India. IndiaWorld's cash-generating website development business was also booming. They had acquired 200 corporate customers ranging from Tata Sons and Aditya Birla to RBI, ICICI, IndusInd Bank and Kotak Mahindra. The business was profitable and growing, even though it was still small in scale. Rajesh regained confidence and was content in his small corner office at Nariman Point because of the realisation that he and his wife had finally built the perfect lifestyle business that they could run for life.

JACK AND JILL NEVER REACHED THE HILL: MULTIPLE REJECTIONS FROM INVESTORS

However, back in Silicon Valley, where Rajesh had first had his epiphany, things had changed dramatically. On 9 August 1995, when the sixteen-month-old Silicon Valley start-up Netscape tried to go public, demand for its shares rose to such dizzying peaks that trading couldn't open for nearly two hours that morning. The stock, which had been priced at $28 per share, zoomed to $75 within the day. It was the spark that triggered the wildfire of the internet boom. Within the next few months, Yahoo!, a company built on the back of the browser revolution, raised approximately $3 million from Sequoia Capital. On 12 April 1996, Yahoo! issued its IPO raising $33.8 million by selling 2.6 million shares at the opening bid of $13 each. Within an hour of the offering, the shares shot up to $43. Moreover, just a week before these events, Excite and Lycos, Yahoo!'s primary competitors in the portal space, had also launched successful IPOs. The great American IPO party had officially begun, and the frenzy was about to spread to every corner of the world. Everyone wanted a piece of the portal pie.

The internet frenzy reached Indian shores when the biggest venture funds from the US arrived to discover the Yahoo! of the Ganges. Companies like Warburg Pincus, Intel, Draper Fischer Juvertson (which had cracked stellar deals with its investments in both Hotmail and RocketMail) and JP Morgan Chase lined up for the Indian market. Ironically, at that point, there were only two gigs in town that fit their national hunt, IndiaWorld and Rediff.com. Both of them were trying to outrun each other for the first spot.

Even though IndiaWorld had clocked in ₹3 crore in revenue that year, Rajesh was worried about his competition, Rediff.com. He says, 'They had deep pockets and I couldn't spend as much on advertising or things such as acquiring expensive talent. My father also advised me to avoid taking money from outside.'

He would probably have been complacent in the organic growth and success of his venture if it weren't for the frenzied environment that made venture capital available for the first time to start-ups in India and was luring entrepreneurs to raise external capital and think big. It was never Rajesh's plan to raise capital, though he couldn't help but jump on the bandwagon. He had limited choices. It was either jumping into the well or being steamrolled by those who were raising capital. But as they say, if wishes were horses, pigs would fly. It was Rediff.com and not IndiaWorld that checked all the boxes for a VC investor. Rediff.com's founder, Ajit Balakrishnan, was experienced and successful, they had a great team consisting of the best journalists and media experts, and they had invested in technology. Given these facts, anyone else in that position would have also chosen Rediff.com over IndiaWorld.

Rajesh is still displeased about the experience, even though it was a long time ago. Nearly every investor asked him this one question: 'Where is your management team?' It was a vicious circle as he needed money to hire the desired team but couldn't get the required money without having a desirable team to show off to the investors. All he could say to the investors was this, 'I don't have the money to hire expensive experts. Our team consists of me, my wife and my cousin who handles the technical aspects. We all work from a tiny office at Nariman Point.' Most conversations ended then and there. The other obstacle was their inability to project their future prospects. During Intel's evaluation of IndiaWorld and Rediff.com, their first question to both was, 'What is your five-year plan?' Rajesh didn't have one. The meeting didn't take long to wrap up after this admittance. The same thing happened when they met the Bank of America. Rajesh wanted a valuation of $13 million but they refused. After months of dialogue, Rajesh was further aggravated by their sudden demand for a micro-plan focusing on the next three years. For Rajesh, this harrowing conversation was the last one he had with an investor. He was wallowing in self-doubt and paranoia when the three investors that had met Rajesh—Intel, Draper International and Warburg Pincus—all went on to invest in Rediff.com. Ajit was having a field day with enough funds to execute his plans but he is gracious enough to admit that he was doing nothing spectacular as compared to IndiaWorld. 'I was a little older than Rajesh, that's all,' Ajit says.

Bhavana Jain, however, was well aware that the problem ran deeper than that and accurately says, 'They [Rediff.com] knew how to package themselves while we were really naive. We couldn't present ourselves as remarkable to the investor. We didn't have a PR Agency. No one was writing articles about us in the media and our success record wasn't even close to that of Ajit's. Without the capital to grow, we would just remain a small fish in the pond and that was worth nothing.'

The Historic Acquisition

While IndiaWorld was struggling to acquire any capital, in Hyderabad, R. Ramaraj had done a successful IPO on NASDAQ for his ISP business. Post the IPO, when he came back and studied more about the market, he realised that one of the reasons why he had done well in the United States was because companies like his were in short supply. But compared to the Chinese companies that were hitting the billion dollar market capitalisation, he had to be content with only a third of that amount. For instance, China.com, a Hong Kong-based internet portal company, made a hugely successful IPO in July at $20 that year. When Ramaraj looked them up, they were trading at around $95. Ramaraj wondered why Chinese companies were valued better than Indian ones when they had similar demographics. He figured out that the markets didn't understand the opportunity in India as much as they did in China. He decided that he had to bring the market's attention to this region. He had to do something outlandish, like making a large acquisition.

Meanwhile, back in Mumbai, Rajesh bumped into Ajay Garg who was working at DSP Merill Lynch. The Merill Lynch office was in the same building as IndiaWorld. 'We were probably acquainted with each other, having met in the lift of the building. He was curious about our internet business and I was wondering whether I needed someone like him to advise on this increasingly frustrating fundraising process even though, at that time, we were kind of sure that the Bank of America deal would close,' says Rajesh .

Bhavna adds, 'Ajay kept in touch even though we hadn't shown much interest; at that time, we were counting on the Bank of America deal. Sometimes, the world works in mysterious ways. Ajay never gave up on Rajesh and both got along well. Ajay jumped at the opportunity to introduce us to Hemendra bhai when the Bank of America deal failed.'

Hemendra Kothari was at the helm of DSP Merrill Lynch. Rajesh had no better ideas so he met Ajay's boss, Hemendra Kothari, to introduce him to IndiaWorld. To Rajesh's surprise, Hemendra took an interest in his venture and instructed a core team that included Saurabh Agarwal (now CFO at Tata Sons), Amit Chandra (from Bain) and Ajay to explore possibilities with IndiaWorld and see if they could help the company in raising some money. They started discussing the possibility of a valuation of ₹90 crore, but Rajesh kept getting stonewalled because of his inability to draw a larger vision for his small firm of fewer than twenty employees and pitch it as *the* futuristic new-age company from India. One day, Hemendra Kothari summoned Rajesh to his office. Without wasting any time, Hemendra pulled out an envelope from his drawer and said, 'Rajesh, your problem is that you don't want to think big. Take this cheque from me. This solves your funding issue. Now go and think big. It is your choice whether you want to deposit this cheque but I am asking you to think big for your own sake.' Rajesh recalls, 'I opened the envelope to look at its contents. It was a personal cheque for ₹2 crore. Hemendra Bhai had handed me that cheque without any terms or an agreement. I couldn't believe it. It gave me such confidence! I don't think anyone else in this country would've done something like that.'

That cheque made all the difference. Despite the previous rejections and failed deals, by September 1999, IndiaWorld had two new deals on the table. The first one was from

Mail.com.[13] The Mail.com founders spent a lot of their time and funds to register and promote 544 domains, and later, began to buy domain names from other companies. Their idea was to invest $40 million in stock for IndiaWorld and within six months, do another IPO with India.com. The other interested investor was the homegrown Sify. As a two-year old company, Sify had already raised $72 million at a $350-million valuation. But Ramaraj was not going to stop at that. He had tried to strike a deal with Rediff.com but had been snubbed by Ajit. Consequently, he was still hunting for the golden egg—something that would announce to the world that he and Sify had truly arrived. At this time, DSP Merill Lynch's team, headed by Hemendra Kothari, spoke to Ramaraj. 'He [Ramaraj] wasn't interested in how much revenue IndiaWorld had earned, considering our bootstrapping. I don't think he was looking at IndiaWorld's current strength. He was interested in how Sify could make it marketable,' says Rajesh. It helped that Ramaraj liked some of IndiaWorld's portals like Khel.com. There was one dedicated employee who sat in front of a TV and constantly updated the sports data, which contributed to its immense popularity.

Bhavana recalls how Hemendra Kothari summoned both her and Rajesh to his office before their meeting with Sify. He said, 'Rajesh, keep your mouth shut about the price. I will negotiate. I will get this done.' After their meeting with Ramaraj, Rajesh was asked to fly to Hyderabad to meet Ramalinga Raju, the founder of Satyam Computers, who was a significant shareholder in Sify. The meeting went on for hours and at 2 a.m. in the morning, Rajesh called Bhavana. 'Hemendra bhai

---

[13] Mail.com was founded in 1995 as Vanity Mail Services by Gerald Gorman, an investment banker, and Gary Millin, a student Harvard Business School.

has quoted ₹500 crore for our company but Sify doesn't want to invest. They want to buy the whole thing.' 'It was surreal,' Rajesh recalls. 'In just ten days, our valuation on paper (with the Mail.com offer) had gone from $40 million to $115 million in cash. The entire credit for this went to Hemendra Bhai.'

While Sify conducted its due diligence, Rajesh and Bhavna had mixed feelings about the deal. They had never thought about selling the company. They wanted to grow it steadily. However, given the circumstances and the increasing competition, they had been forced to raise capital and were now looking at a possible buyout.

The company had been their brainchild, which they had slowly and lovingly nurtured into a robust enterprise. Rajesh and Bhavana felt the empty nest syndrome at the prospect of handing it over to someone else. Their friend, Late Rajjat Barjatya, who was the MD and CEO of Rajshri Media, helped put things in perspective for them. Over steaming pots of kadhai paneer, dal makhani and buttered naans at their favourite restaurant, Copper Chimney, in Worli, Barjatya convinced them to sell it. 'You can create ten more companies if you get this money. Quit this talk about "my baby" because it's just emotional tomfoolery,' he told them. 'He made us realise that we had to it let it go,' Rajesh smiles.

And the rest, as they say, is history. A press conference organised by DSP Merrill Lynch officially announced that Sify was buying out IndiaWorld for ₹499 crore in an all-cash deal. Sify paid ₹170 crore to Rajesh upfront, which included a caution deposit of ₹50 crore, acquiring 24.5 per cent. Sify had to pay the remaining amount by 30 June 2000.

For a company that had revenues of barely ₹3 crore, this move seemed suicidal. Sify had just raised $72 million from the markets and had decided to spend $115 million in acquiring a full-fledged company, valuing it at 160 times the revenue. Most people weren't sure about how the cookie would crumble. Naysayers were already spelling doom and declaring it the peak of the dot-com bubble.

'Everybody looked at what we got out of it, but nobody looked at Sify. Overnight, that announcement had raised Sify's market capitalisation from $350 million to $1 billion. And since they didn't have the money to pay up, they had already applied to go back to the market, which they did in February 2000, barely three months after announcing the acquisition. This time, they raised the $160 million at an over-$8-billion market cap,' Rajesh recalls.

This was the time when the dot-com could do no wrong. AOL had a stunning development when it announced plans to acquire Time Warner Inc. for roughly $182 billion in stock and debt, creating a digital-media powerhouse with the potential to reach every American in one form or another. The combination immediately boosted a market capitalisation of $350 billion and an annual revenue stream topping $30 billion. Many thought that the merger was a brilliant move and worried that their own companies were being left behind. AOL's sky-high stock-market valuation, bid-up by investors looking for a windfall, made the young company more valuable in market cap terms than many other blue chips. Its acquisition of Time Warner came at a most opportune time.

For Ramaraj, it was a masterstroke fuelled by the freak AOL event in distant America. Sify's market cap went up from $350 million to $8 billion, and they had already spent $115 million! For clueless investors in the US, Sify became India's AOL. The obscene acquisition price of IndiaWorld paid for itself sooner than you could say dot-com!

It is another matter that the dot-com bubble burst within months after the deal closed and the economy went into recession. Advertising dollars evaporated and AOL was forced to take a goodwill write-off of nearly $99 billion in 2002, an astonishing sum that shook even the business-hardened writers of *The Wall Street Journal*. AOL was also losing both subscribers and subscription revenue. The total value of the AOL stock tanked from $226 billion to about $20 billion. It's now known as the worst deal ever made in corporate history. But everyone lives and learns.

However for Rajesh and Bhavana Jain, the timely buyout made them fortune's favoured children. It could have all gone downhill for IndiaWorld in the era of the internet bubble burst, but their smart choice to let go at the right time made all the difference.

SAHIL BARUA

CEO and Co-Founder, Delhivery

'A bad piece of advice that we got from our investors was that we should be a lot more visible in the media. We had just raised Series B and everyone recommended that we get out there and do a huge PR push about what we were building. So, we spent about a year investing in PR only to realise there is literally no advantage in doing this. One moment, we had reporters building us up as the next amazing start-up of India and then suddenly, when we had to let go of staff, they started saying that this is the end of our run. The reality was neither of those two spectrums. We realised that it was best to not say a word to the press because it wasn't going to pay our bills. We had created a monster by focusing on PR.'

IF YOU LIVE IN INDIA, CHANCES ARE THAT YOU HAVE not only heard of Delhivery but also used their services at some point in the last seven years. From delivering food and flowers during their initial run to becoming one of the largest logistics companies with a reach in over 1,200 cities, Sahil Barua and his team proved that where there's a package, there's a way to deliver it. They started with humble beginnings from a rundown space in early 2011, went on to acquire a high-rise, swanky building in the upmarket Gurugram. It was a classic tale of finding the right idea at the right time, but it was also their willingness to take on the challenge that proved to be instrumental in their journey.

Paul Graham, the co-founder of Y Combinator, talks about a phenomena called 'Schlep Blindness'. According to him, there is no dearth of great start-up ideas. They lie unnoticed right under our noses. One reason that we refuse to see them is that they are tedious and involve unpleasant tasks. Of course, this isn't something that is just limited to start-ups; for instance, even though most people are aware of the benefits of exercising, they choose not to do it. It is a decision made by the unconscious brain because it wants to reduce workload. The minds in the e-commerce industry worked in a similar fashion. The idea of e-commerce had been evolving in India for several years from the days of Rediff.com, Indiatimes.com and eBay at the start of the new millennium, and began to peak when Flipkart, Snapdeal and Fashion And You took over the online shopping space. One thing that hadn't changed was the e-commerce delivery space. It was the companies built during the pre-internet era that were doing the actual door-to-door delivery of purchases. Enough people saw the opportunity here, but chickened out because it's a demanding and tedious business. India has over 19,000 serviceable pin codes and the work would require massive infrastructural assembly, from setting up warehouses, air and surface transport; having a workforce that would do the actual work on the ground; and the most challenging of it all, cash on delivery (COD)—nasty operations but that is exactly why it made e-commerce delivery such a valuable enterprise.

On that note, Sahil Barua and his team must be given due credit for taking the bull by its horns. They not only took up the challenge but also delivered! From launching Delhivery as a hyper-local delivery business, they quickly escalated it into a logistics business that has become a massive success. Sahil's family wouldn't have accepted anything less from him. He comes from a prodigious background as his father is a professor at IIM Ahmedabad and his mother is a doctor. Sahil himself graduated from IIM Bangalore, was the gold medallist in his batch, and featured on the Director's Merit List. He is from the batch of 2008, which graduated just a few months shy of the Lehman Brothers collapse. Their placements had been fantastic and Sahil had landed a job with the consulting firm, Bain & Company, first in London and then in New Delhi, where he met his future co-founders, Suraj Saharan and Mohit Tandon. Mohit and Suraj who worked in the same company had already decided to quit. Sahil, too, left the job without a concrete plan. He had been helping the two write their applications for business school when they came up with the idea of Delhivery to deliver food from restaurants, which was a first in 2011.

A lot of start-up ideas generated in India are usually knockoffs of something original in the US, which is not necessarily a bad thing. For instance, Deep Kalra got the idea for MakeMyTrip while booking tickets on AsiaRooms.com, Ashish Hemrajani was getting drunk in South Africa when he heard a radio spot about a website where you could book concert tickets and that's how BookMyShow was born. But Delhivery was an original idea, not just in India but in the world. Standalone food delivery companies didn't exist anywhere. In fact, Postmates, the American unicorn start-up which delivers food, groceries and alcohol, started operations only in May 2011, two months after Delhivery, and their Series A only came in 2013, two years later.

Sahil's inspiration was as *desi* as it gets. 'We knew Deepinder and Chadha (co-founders of Zomato) from Bain. They had a business that was growing well, their investors seemed to have confidence in them and they were expanding to new cities. I was in talks with them to see if they had a role for me at Zomato. Then, a passionate debate around online ordering led me to the idea of delivering food from restaurants, which no one was doing at that time. And that's how we started Delhivery. Our model was very simple: we would get an order from a restaurant, which could come from Zomato or from anywhere else, the client would call us, our delivery man would pick up the parcel and deliver it within half an hour. That's what Suraj, Mohit and I did for the first five months.' The other two co-founders, Bhavesh Maglani and Kapil Bharati joined a few months later. Partnering with Bhavesh was the result of a friendship forged in a drunken stupor coupled with Delhivery's desperate need for a coder. Kapil made a lateral move as he joined their team from another start-up. By the time this team got together, the three founding musketeers, Sahil, Suraj and Mohit, had already chanced upon an interesting new opportunity that e-commerce had to offer. Sahil recalls, 'It was a series of happy accidents.

We thought we would use e-commerce deliveries to fill the buffer time between lunch and dinner. Moreover, Urban Touch and HealthKart had just opened in Gurugram, which was great for us because we would deliver lunch and dinner and in between that time, we began to deliver their orders too. At that time, we thought that e-commerce would be the smaller of the two businesses. It was a side gig at best. Then we met Anshoo Sharma, whom we knew from Bain. He had started magicpin, a hyper-local discovery platform. He advised us to bet bigger on e-commerce. That's how we got into it. Otherwise, we would have been out of business a long time ago.'

In many ways, this proved to be a turning point for them. After staying on course as a hyper-local business, wanting to move into e-commerce was a decision that needed precision, planning and an awareness of the market and their competitors. The Delhivery founders did their research and discovered that the incumbents in the logistics space didn't care much about e-commerce. They had their decades-old models and processes in place. E-commerce was a minuscule part of their total business with very different processes. A typical courier company like DTDC did evening pickups and morning deliveries, but an e-commerce company would deliver round the clock. Unlike regular deliveries, lots of e-commerce companies have easy returns and trial-and-buy schemes that makes e-commerce delivery time longer and complicated due to reverse logistics. Another difference was that courier companies don't handle cash collections whereas in an e-commerce business, nearly 70 per cent of the orders are COD.

The fog was beginning to lift but Delhivery was still unclear about where they stood in the milieu. There were two main ends of the spectrum. On one end were companies like DTDC that picked up and delivered minor parcels such as letters, greeting cards, documents, etc., and charged a minimal fee for it. On the other end were companies, such as Blue Dart, that were blending a retail courier business with an essentially B2B business designed around moving consignments by air. Their architecture was complex as they had collection centres, delivery centres, and hubs in-between. There were also companies like Safex and Gati that fell somewhere in-between but they had no interest in e-commerce. By analysing big companies like Blue Dart, Sahil figured out that they were not particularly excited about e-commerce. For them, it would just remain a small fish in the pond. Clearly, they had not been able to gauge the future of the industry—not at that point anyway. They also figured out that Blue Dart would be too expensive for e-commerce players and the DTDC model was not going to work either, because it would be impossible for them to deliver a parcel for ₹10. Furthermore, neither of these companies provided any visibility on the status of a delivery. There was no way a client could track the order, since their updating systems worked manually with pen and paper. Clearly, there was no online tracking system.

Delhivery cracked the code by realising early on that cash on delivery (COD) was the key to most e-commerce businesses as nearly 70 per cent of the orders were paid for when the product was delivered to the customer. As Sahil says, 'We realised that in this space, we are not only a logistics company but also a payment gateway. And whatever little the people-in-charge were doing, it would take them at least thirty days to return cash. We decided that it could be done in two days.' Cutting down the payment reconciliation time with the e-commerce players was every CFO's dream come true.

Having figured out how they could use the loopholes in the business to their advantage by providing customers what they needed, they went the extra mile by charting down their course of action for the foreseeable future. 'Having a plan on how the model would evolve, the time it would take, the optimisation channels and opportunities we could use has held us in good stead all this while. We took a lot of time to put it all together but we wrote down the backend architecture of the model and how it would work.'

On Fundraising

For the first fifteen months, the five core members kept the company afloat using their own money by bringing in ₹10 lakh each. Abhishek Goyal, who eventually founded Tracxn, was running Urban Touch and invested another ₹10 lakh. With a corpus fund of ₹60 lakh, Delhivery began its operations and made its first delivery in March 2011. 'Surprisingly, we still had cash in the bank when we raised our first funds; there was still some balance left over from the ₹60 lakh. Times also gave us ₹6.7 crore in May 2012. They were also our first e-commerce clients outside Urban Touch and HealthKart,' Sahil informs.

It Was Crazy!

No new venture is complete without its own set of idiosyncrasies. It is like taking care of a new-born child, where each day brings a new set of challenges, laughter and tears. And like a proud parent, no entrepreneur can ever stop talking about his or her start-up baby. There are memorable moments, peculiar pauses and then some crazy days. Some are entirely outlandish, such as the one about Frederick Smith who launched Federal Express (FedEx) in 1971. He was nearly bankrupt within three years of starting the company due to the rising fuel costs. With only $5,000 left in the company, Smith threw all caution to the wind as things couldn't get any worse. He took off to Vegas and did what people do in Vegas. He blew up those funds on blackjack. As they say, Fortune favours the bold. Smith got lucky and FedEx acquired $32,000 to keep the company alive. Similarly, Mark Benioff, one of the founders of Salesforce, is famous for coming up with audacious marketing strategies, especially those that target his competitors. He once orchestrated a fake protest at a Siebel Systems conference with picket signs, chanting and even a fake TV crew. This drummed up a lot of attention for Salesforce at his rival's expense. On another occasion, Benioff arranged to rent an airport's entire taxi fleet right before another Siebel event was about to be held nearby. He then had his employees pitch their sales to the participants taking the cabs all the way to the event, much to Siebel's displeasure.

Delhivery's days didn't go by without its own share of crazy moments. Some were epic enough to land one of its founders in jail. The incident relates to a time when the team suspected that one of its centres in Lucknow was cash rolling. Sahil explains, 'For example, as a delivery boy, I collect one lakh rupees in COD in one day. I do that and then keep ₹20,000 aside. Tomorrow, I'll again collect a lakh, take ₹20,000 from that, add it to the first day's collection and deposit it. It is easy for a dishonest person to do this and once they begin, it is easy for them to believe that they can do it forever if they keep taking small amounts. That is called cash rolling.' Delhivery has now created a system that makes cash rolling impossible, although this was not always the case. 'The problem started when someone got ambitious and started dabbling in higher amounts,' Sahil recalls, 'In 2012, we had a suspicion that someone had been rolling cash. So Bhavesh went to investigate the issue because he was the one running operations. He figured out that some inventory and cash had gone missing. To follow due process, he decided to go to the police to let them know that there had been a robbery in our branch. Meanwhile, the actual culprits, who were possibly a big organised group, realising that Bhavesh was going to the police station, had informed them that the person arriving to file the complaint was the thief himself. The strange thing is that the police believed their story, so the minute Bhavesh landed at the station, he was held for investigation.' Meanwhile the rest of the team at Delhivery was blissfully unaware of the drama unveiling in Lucknow. They were in Mumbai meeting up with New Enterprise Associates (NEA) for fundraising. The head of the Lucknow operations got them on the phone right in the middle of the meeting, yelling frantically that the cops had arrested Bhavesh. That's when Sahil called up Gautam Sinha at Times Internet and narrated the incident. The kind folks at *The Times of India* got in touch with the police and Bhavesh was released five hours later.

Sahil has so many of these anecdotes that one could go on and on but the one of the rogue driver takes the cake. 'We had just raised money from Times Internet, our first institutional round. One of our vendor drivers apparently took drugs that night, before driving a vehicle back to our office in Malviya Nagar. Something snapped in his head en route and he suddenly went berserk. He made one of our employees—who was in the truck with him—get off and tried to kill him by banging him into a wall. Then, he proceeded to break into a house and ransack it. He even broke their fridge and then ran out of the house. By this time, an alarm had been raised and the fellow was surrounded by a crowd. Suraj, Bhavesh and I were chilling with a few beers in the faraway Gurugram, happy about the funds raised, when we got a call regarding this incident. We rushed there to find no fewer than 2,000 people at the scene while the driver was still running a riot. There were now three vehicles full of policemen and it turns out that the man whose house he had ransacked was our landlord! Eventually, the police restrained him, but not before he had bitten one policeman and torn off the pants of another. After a commotion that lasted nearly two hours, they managed to grab him and put him in the escort vehicle to take him to the hospital. We had to buy the landlord a new fridge.' Delhivery might have had its share of crazy, but it was this incident that really made them wonder what they had gotten themselves into!

How They Almost Blew It

In its different rounds of financing, Delhivery acquired funding from Nexus Partners and Multiples but afterwards, they quickly ran out of cash. This was around June 2014. The founders had to use a part of the money raised from Nexus Partners to pay for prior liabilities. 'It was utter stupidity. Our business was growing faster than we had expected but we didn't tighten the working capital cycle fast enough. We were fast and loose with our money at that point because we decided that we should expand it by giving the vendors a thirty-day credit. If you divided the capital that we had raised by our burn rate, you would say that we still had fifteen months of capital in hand. But we realised that we wouldn't even be able to meet payroll in 72 hours. We were negotiating a term sheet from Multiples Asset Management, but term sheets are non-binding and the process takes two to three months before cash hits the bank. We very nearly blew it at that point,' remarks Sahil.

Fortunately, Multiples was supportive when informed of their emergency and assured them that they wouldn't walk away from the deal but that they would need to manage the interim period with due diligence. 'Had Multiples chickened out on realising that these stupid guys are going belly up, we would have been finished,' Sahil adds. He rightly points out that things can get messy without warning. At times, it is difficult for founders to see such trouble snowballing towards them. 'We went to our vendors and told them the truth. The vendors rose to the occasion and solved issues with us like partners. One asked not to be paid for ninety days, others like HomeShop18 gave us money in advance so we just about made it. It took us a year to recover as a company and the scars are still there. Other than that, we've never been in a situation where we might go out of business even though we have done a lot of stupid things,' he says.

But Delhivery did have a second moment when they almost blew it. At this time, the dot-com space was riding on the wave of successful e-ventures, investors, entrepreneurs and trade pundits, and everyone seemed confident about the internet business. These ventures had become the darlings of investors by 2014–15, leading to market comparisons with the dot-com bubble of 2000. Tech investors in the US, Europe and Asia that had either missed out on Alibaba or had hit the jackpot were doubling down on Indian e-commerce companies. In 2014, investors ploughed in more than $4 billion in internet businesses, with Flipkart, Snapdeal, Ola Cabs and Zomato leading the show. Their valuations jumped four to five times. Not wanting to be left behind, Delhivery decided to focus on growth at any cost. In fact, since it was 2014 and the euphoria was just beginning to unfold, they were actively advised to expand. Delhivery had just raised around $35 million from Multiples Alternate Asset Management, led by Renuka Ramnath, and were anticipating a growth explosion in the market. Sahil admits, 'While we aren't a particularly excitable bunch of guys, it was hard not to be swept away by the growth wave.'

Every e-commerce business, at least the ones that mattered, seemed to be booming. Flipkart told them that they were getting a million orders per day. Snapdeal made a similar claim. It looked like the great Indian shopping festival had just begun and Delhivery felt the need to increase their capacity to deliver. 'We went from 6,000 to 20,000 employees in the space of five months to brace ourselves for the peak-season,' Sahil reveals. What they could not have predicted was that the peak season sales wouldn't play out as expected. Their business headcount cost remained fixed and their cash burn ballooned from ₹2 crore to ₹30 crore in those five months. They had raised ₹200 crore from Multiples, but at a cost of burning out ₹30 crore per month, they were staring at a six-month runway at best. They had to make a quick decision. 'We went full throttle that month but luckily, our pullback was swift. Unfortunately, we had to immediately lay off a majority of people that we were recent hires. It caused unimaginable damage to our reputation and is another scar that has remained for so long that even today, when we say we want to hire, head hunters come back and say, "I am going to double, triple, quadruple check every single number before I put a guy on the ground." That's how bad it was.'

He doesn't even need the benefit of hindsight to admit that expanding at that rapid pace was a blunder. 'It was a huge mistake at the board level, and when I say board, I mean that the founders were complicit since we make up 40 per cent of the board. We listened to people doling out advice, agreed that it was a great idea and acted on it.' While he has his regrets, there are also valuable lessons learnt. They now know better than to jump the gun and never put any plan into action unless they are confident of its outcome. It's commonly said that 'being an entrepreneur is a bit like having a child.' All of a sudden, everyone from your neighbours to your relatives will start giving you advice on how to take care of your start-up. Google the phrase 'advice to entrepreneurs' and you will find thousands of pieces written about this. That brings us to the challenge of choosing the right advice that fits the context of a business and weeding out the ones that don't.

Sahil shares, 'A bad piece of advice that we got from our investors was that we should be a lot more visible in the media. We had just raised Series B and everyone recommended that we get out there and do a huge PR push about what we were building. So, we spent about a year investing in PR only to realise there is literally no advantage in doing this. One moment, we had reporters building us up as the next amazing start-up of India and then suddenly, when we had to let go of staff, they started saying that this is the end of our run. The reality was neither of those two spectrums. We realised that it was best to not say a word to the press because it was not going to pay our bills. We had created a monster by focusing on PR.'

The other harmful advice that they had been given was to go global but thankfully, they pulled the plug on it quite early. 'Zomato was going outside India and that hit us for a brief moment. There was no dearth of people encouraging us to go for it. They talked about big opportunities in the Middle East and we got carried away. We built a warehouse in Dubai. Fortunately, it was a small variable cost and not a major investment. We sunk nearly ₹50 lakh in it in terms of infrastructure set-up, and about ₹5 lakh per month on rentals. That year, we didn't make a single rupee on the revenue. It was a bad advice. We realised that going global is extremely relevant to the context of a business. It may work for some but doesn't work for everyone,' Sahil laments, 'We've learnt to not get swept away anymore.'

TREADING THROUGH THE 2014–15 FUNDING FRENZY

Many entrepreneurs, including the ones discussed in the book, have raised capital at high valuations. But when it started to pipe down, even leading companies like Flipkart and Ola Cabs faced the heat. In early 2017, it was reported that Ola's parent company ANI Technologies Private Limited had received a sum of $260 million (₹1,675 crore) from SoftBank. This was at a valuation of $3 billion in a down round. The fundraising was done at a lower valuation than the previous round of funding, which had pegged Ola at $4.5 billion. A down round occurs in private financing when investors purchase stock or convertible bonds from a company at a lower valuation than the preceding round. Flipkart, too, had a tumultuous 2016. Many of their investors lowered the value of its investments several times. A mutual fund managed by Fidelity lowered the valuation of its investment in Flipkart by almost 36 per cent. And finally, it was reported that after struggling for a while, Flipkart raised a total of $1 billion, but this was secured at a down round that valued the company at $10 billion. At its peak, it was valued at $15 billion. Thus, valuations had drastically changed.

'To be honest, I think valuations are still out of control. You will realise that India is a deceptive market if you do your math. It looks much larger than it actually is. You run out of the addressable market reasonably fast. The assumption that 200 million Indians will magically switch to online shopping in three to four years was a fallacy. Those who do not make purchases online have several reasons for doing so. Language barrier is the reason why so many people are willing to be on

Facebook but don't want to make purchases online. Specifically, the issue is that they face language barriers while searching for a product online. We haven't solved this problem yet. So it is true that valuations continue to be too high. And that's the reason for the bubble burst. Good businesses, given the right capital and valuations at the right time, will be successful in five to six years. The larger issue is the capital overhang that ends up killing the start-up. Many drown under its weight,' explains Sahil. Indeed, Capital or Private Equity overhang means that when an investment is put in a company, a certain amount is kept aside to either use in a limited time frame or return to the investor. No entrepreneur wants to return that amount so they burn it out rather quickly, which ends up drowning the start-up since the focus shifts from potential growth to capital spending by opening new ways of expenditure. It is not a sustainable model and so it becomes the anchor pulling down the ship to its doom. Justin Kan, the founder of Twitch.tv and partner at Y Combinator has famously said, 'No matter how much you raise at your company, you'll end up spending it in twelve to twenty-four months.'[14] Venture capitalist Mark Suster wrote on his blog, 'I was always fond of saying this about fundraising, "When the hors d'oeuvres tray is passed, take two and put one in your pocket for later. Just don't take the whole tray." My analogy was that there are markets where it's relatively easier to raise capital and therefore you should take a little bit more but you should create a budget where you only spend 70 per cent of what you raise on a pace of 18 months. But people never do.'

Regarding the investment decision-making, many entrepreneurs take the route that suggests 'grab as much

---

[14] Suster, Mark. "Why Raising Too Much Money Can Harm Your Start-Up", *Medium.com*, 30 June 2016. https://bothsidesofthetable.com/why-raising-too-much-money-can-harm-your-startup-5adc112e1259

as you can, move faster and worry less about fundraising'
without realising the truth in Justin's words. Most end up in
the market again to raise more money. Needless to say, it is a
painful process. In the marketplace, venture capitals are the
buyers and entrepreneurs are the sellers. The only proof of
your progress is how much further you've gotten since the last
round of funding and how the company was evaluated in the
previous round. If you over-committed and under-delivered
the last time, you are likely to get into trouble. You are lucky
if you can even get a down round. But the problem is that
everybody hates down rounds. Employees are demoralised
because the value of their ESOPs does not look as pretty.
Early financiers feel betrayed that you didn't do enough to
protect their interests. The whole process becomes downright
messy and destructive for a start-up.

'We experienced this ourselves in the previous round of
funding,' Sahil says. 'Apart from Tiger Global, we had another
term sheet from Ontario Teachers' Pension Fund. Their term
sheet was better than Tiger Global in terms of valuation.
Ontario gave us a term sheet for investing $150 million at a pre-
money valuation of $450 Million. Tiger's offer was $85 million
at 283 pre-money. We went with the Tiger term sheet because
we thought the Ontario term sheet was too aggressive. We
didn't believe we were worth $600 million post-money and we
actually wrote back to them saying that. This is a scary process
because they will revisit the value of this investment in two
years and hold us accountable if the valuation hasn't doubled by
then. The board will have a field day and we will end up being
devastated. We put our foot down, which shocked Ontario's
team. When we raised the Tiger Global round at a modest and
realistic valuation, we were happy and relieved since it sounded
just about right. Also, the reality was that we had raised this

round with Tiger Global within nine months of our previous round with Multiples Asset Management, which valued us at around $100 million. Even the Tiger Global funding had been quite expensive but fortunately all of it worked out because our business grew between this round and next one. So, by the time we went for the next round of funding, our valuations had normalised.' Though Sahil believes that keeping expectations and valuations realistic is a method to avoid a downfall, he feels that the market is still in a bubble as India continues to remain a deceptively tough arena.

The Way Ahead

A successful IPO not only provides access to public capital markets, unlocking wealth for investors, promoters and employees eligible under the company's stock option pool, but also helps in establishing robust governance structures and finance processes.

An IPO is both a massive milestone for any company and a very challenging undertaking. It requires the company to create new systems, identify and address talent gaps, manage the regulatory reviews and build credibility with analysts and investors, all while running the business. CFOs who have experienced IPOs recommend the founders to be prepared with the process team two years in advance. The founders of Delhivery are now working their way towards an IPO.

'When we started Delhivery, we had a clear vision that we wanted to build a business that would go public. Going public creates a larger market interest in the company, evolving from being the concern of just the private investors and the founders. We had been harbouring the ambition to go public from the beginning because we've always envisioned this as *our* business, not something that we would eventually sell off to someone. Also, to be honest, we always found fundraising difficult. It's always been hard to explain to investors why our business is exciting and why they should give us money at any valuation. We also have a fairly wide stock-option plan, nearly 40 per cent of the management, which is nearly 800 people are in our option plan. The only way you can keep your direct cost of operations manageable is by using stock options. Secondly, there are no listed stocks in logistics. The first company to go public in this space will be the national consolidator of this space in India. I think there would be a good demand for our stocks. We've got decent stories to tell the markets about why we are raising the money. We are operating in a business where, historically, compliance has been low and logistics companies are no longer viewed as part of a dirty industry. There is value in saying that we are a professionally managed, well-governed company. Then, I can hopefully go to Walmart and say, "Sign us on as a partner." They are not willing to do that just yet. If you are a listed company, you are considered kosher,' Sahil concludes.

Of all the start-ups stories I've collected for this book, I found Delhivery to be the most intimidating business because it is such a daring endeavour in all aspects, from dealing with blue-collar employees to potential frauds and errors. It is a massive undertaking and requires a braveheart to not just begin it but stick with it till the end.

As I was writing this chapter, media reported that Delhivery could become the newest entrant to India's unicorn club as it is in talks to raise $450 million from SoftBank. This would mean a 25-per-cent jump in its valuation since its previous funding round, which saw the entry of Carlyle Group as an investor. On reading this news, I was again reminded of the Paul Grahm note that suggested that because everyone's scared of the schlep (i.e., the road not taken), the spoils double for those who do take it. And so, as the meme goes, keep calm and schlep on, which might as well be Delhivery's tagline because schlepping has clearly been their forte.

ALOK MITTAL

Co-Founder, JobsAhead.com

'Lesson number one, don't rack up costs till the committed investment is in the bank. Lesson number two, in tough times, be very realistic about the revenue and costs. One more lesson learnt: never be in a hurry to sell a company that's profitably growing three to four times a year.'

THE YEAR 2004 WAS A GROUNDBREAKING YEAR IN THE Indian start-up ecosystem. It was preceded by four years of prolonged drought since the dot-com bubble burst. By then, hundreds of start-ups littered the dot-com graveyard. The dry spell seemed to be finally over. Baazee, an auctions platform, was acquired by eBay. The next acquisition was JobsAhead.com by Monster.com for $10 million. Not a large amount by today's standards but at that time, this acquisition broke the curse that had made it difficult for Indian start-ups to exist. JobsAhead.com—founded by Alok Mittal and Puneet Dalmia—stood out amongst from other ventures for a particular reason. It had been a profitable company at the time of its sale which is rare even today. While the ₹40-crore exit was celebrated in 2004 by the entire ecosystem—within two years, Naukri.com, its arch nemesis, went public. Today, it has a market capitalisation of over $3 billion. In hindsight, Alok and Puneet's decision to exit was a bad one, but Alok says that he has made peace with that decision and is happy if his experience helps someone in making a wise decision. It is undeniable that this acquisition ended the monetary dearth and revived the Indian start-up ecosystem. But how JobsAhead.com achieved this success is a journey worth exploring.

THE QUICK STARTERS

Alok and Puneet met when both of them were students at IIT Delhi. Puneet went on to pursue a business degree at IIM Bangalore and Alok completed his MS and Management of

Technology programmes from UC Berkeley. He came back to join Hughes India in Bengaluru, with a clear intention of starting up on his own at some point. He hadn't given much thought to the internet because his focus was on the software services business. He had stayed in touch with Puneet and one day, received an email from him. In it, Puneet had outlined opportunities in the Indian internet space and asked whether Alok would be interested in a partnership. Puneet came to Alok's house in Bengaluru to discuss the contours of what they could possibly do. Before they could zero in on a particular idea, they had finalised that they would work in the online space. Alok quit his job within a week and in a month, he was in Delhi with Puneet to figure out their next step.

Alok says, 'We scanned the market to find out what was working around the world and which business models could work in India. Within a month, we were clear that our predominant audience in India would be the youth. We had seen the success of iVillage as it was a great example of how you could have a specific target audience, which in this case was women, instead of a large base across genders, nationalities or age. So in our mind, we had decided on having youth as the audience and a vortal (vertical portal) as the theme. We wanted to build a one-stop shop for the younger generation of Indians, which would revolve around jobs, fashion, dating, relationships and e-commerce. We raised an angel round from Puneet's family and in three months, launched Zip Ahead in November 1999.'

They spent some of that money on advertising and started getting good traction. Soon, Ashish Dhawan's Chrysalis Capital—one of the earliest funds focused on Indian start-ups—invested ₹11 crore in Zip Ahead. Since the jobs section could be monetised first, they hired a sales team. In a couple of months, everyone realised that the traffic mostly engaged with the jobs section and Ashish proposed that they spin it out as a separate business. Without much deliberation, by mid-January 2001, they had their spin-off business called JobsAhead.com. By March, JobsAhead.com went live and they launched an aggressive marketing campaign to attract resumes by rolling out a three-month free trial option for corporates. 'We had 3,000 signups from corporates by the end of the 90-day period,' Alok recalls that they were even ready to upstage Naukri.com. 'When the free trial expired and the paid plans came into play, we had ₹20 lakh of revenue coming in. Along with that, we had investors who were discussing a $20-million term sheet with us. Life was good.'

How They Almost Blew It but Learnt Their Lessons

In March 2000, by the time they launched JobsAhead.com, NASDAQ had begun to slide and the dot-com crash followed, contrary to the market whispers that it was just a temporary global correction.

The term sheet discussion dragged on for much longer than they had anticipated. It hadn't fallen through but it was certainly taking time. Young start-up founders tend to be overly optimistic without sufficient caution. Assuming that the term sheet would go through at some point soon, JobsAhead. com increased their staff, moved into a posh office and kept spending money and resources on running Zip Ahead. With revenues close to only about ₹20–25 lakh per month, their cost of running the business stood at ₹1 crore. And then, the term sheet vanished. The deal had been called off. 'We got a reality check when it happened. We quickly got down to how much more revenue we ought to generate and how much cost-cutting was required. We came to the conclusion that we could reduce costs to ₹60 lakh per month and in three months, grow the revenue accordingly. We assumed that it would do the trick. So we did our first round of layoffs in March 2001 and switched to a basic office. We capped the money allocation to Zip Ahead at ₹1 crore and decided to focus only on JobsAhead. com. After two months, while costs had been cut, the needle on the revenue board had barely moved. We were still making only ₹20–25 lakh. We decided to reset expectations for the next three months to ₹40 lakh for costs and ₹40 lakh for the revenue,' Alok explains.

Unfortunately, more bad news was to follow. First, the telecom bubble burst in the US and then 9/11 happened. That tragedy impacted all kinds of businesses on a global scale. Even the Information Technology Enabled Services (ITES), which constituted almost 60 per cent of the jobs classifieds revenue in India, suffered from the after effects.

'Now we were staring at a dead end with only three months of cash left in the bank. We told ourselves to assume that our last round of financing was the only financing we would ever raise and decided to work sustainably. We took large salary cuts, reduced our staff again and forced the company to become profitable.' Alok explains that this was a time of lessons for Alok and Puneet, 'Lesson number one, don't rack up costs till the committed investment is in the bank. Lesson number two, in tough times, be very realistic about the revenue and costs.' By end of 2001, JobsAhead.com had forced itself into profitability. It was going to survive the dot-com winter.

Slowly, the dot-com wheel started turning again. In 2002, JobsAhead.com grew ten times in terms of sales and profitability. By 2003, they had added ₹4 crore to their bottom line, their team size was back to the pre-lay off number of around 135 and they had hired a CEO, Rajiv Puri, who had previously worked for Xerox. They were rolling along merrily when the global giant of jobs market, Monster.com, arrived in India and proposed to acquire JobsAhead.com. Monster.com acquired JobsAhead.com for ₹40 crore. This newly combined entity claimed nearly 60 per cent stake of the market share, twice the size of Naukri.com. 'And at that time, it looked like a fantastic outcome. But if you look at it in hindsight, it wasn't,' Alok rues.

Info Edge's Naukri.com and JobsAhead.com were competing neck-to-neck in revenues. JobsAhead.com also had a superior product in terms of interface and technology. However, post the JobsAhead.com acquisition by Monster.com, Info Edge debuted on the Bombay Stock Exchange and turned into a ₹1,000-crore company. Considering how things moved for other portals in the same space, the decision to sell off a profitable and well-oiled business was unfathomable. Was it desperation for cash or a fatigue brought on by the challenging journey? 'It wasn't fatigue. The painful period only lasted from March to December 2000. We acted swiftly in that period. To be clear, Puneet and I have never regretted the decision to sell early. But to give credit where it's due, we didn't envision that JobsAhead.com could turn into a ₹100-crore revenue generating company anytime soon. Even though we were growing three to four times year by year, we were caught by our conservatism despite having seen the trend lines. We thought that growth was happening because of our small base. We didn't really see it the way Naukri.com's founders did despite being in the same league before our acquisition and their IPO. Since its debut on the stock exchange, Naukri.com's standalone revenues are now close to ₹800 crore a year. Had we been aware of this outcome beforehand, we would not have sold JobsAhead.com. From that perspective, it does look like an awful decision,' Alok says. JobsAhead.com's promoters and investors made the mistake of not evaluating the market properly. They thought that their business would only grow the usual 40 per cent year over year, which meant they would be about thrice their size in five years. Alok admits to the error, saying, 'One more lesson learnt: never be in a hurry to sell a company that's profitably growing three to four times a year.'

For entrepreneurs, knowing when to sell is always a tough question. The founders of Snapchat refused to sell to Facebook even for multibillion dollars. Was it a bold decision or a blunder? When Instagram was acquired, everyone thought that Facebook had overpaid and that the Instagram founders were fortunate. Facebook has completely turned things around by monetising and turning Instagram into a profit-churning machine. Eventually, all successful entrepreneurs confront the situation. Most face pressure from investors and employees who want liquidity. But the choices also involve ambition and the fatigue that comes with chasing success. It marks the difference between initial dreams and the harsh on-ground reality. To sell or not to sell is never an obvious choice.

'Another reason for having done what we did—and it's something that I've understood only now—is that we underestimated our own potential. As a result, we hired a lot of the management, including our CEO, from outside. The initial days of hiring experienced management weighed on the cost factor, so there are mixed feelings about that now. Today, I do believe that we should have run the company ourselves for longer. I am not suggesting that hiring external talent is never a great idea, but it should have boundaries. Because we had little experience in running a business, hiring someone experienced was supposed to help but it really didn't. I believe that not all great business leaders in the corporate world make good start-up CEOs. Entrepreneurs with limited skills can do far better and stay on course for a longer period. We made the decision to sell for the right reasons but the outcome could have been different. So that was another lesson that we learnt,' says Alok, who seems to have earned more wisdom than wealth from this experience.

Whether founders make for great CEOs has been a never-ending debate. There is a camp that believes that founders make the best CEOs. This is true of founders like Mark Zuckerberg, Jeff Bezos and Reed Hastings. Contradicting this are studies like the one by World Management Survey that provides a detailed review of more than 13,000 mid- to large-sized companies in 32 countries. According to the review, firms led by original founders were 9.4 per cent less productive on average and had consistently lower management scores, which typically rose once the founder-CEO was replaced.

Alok continues, 'Back then, getting the deal done was a victory for us. We may feel whatever we do in retrospect but at that time, we were proud that we had built something that a global giant was acquiring. It seemed like a very positive outcome. Our employees also made money as we had doubled the ESOP pool from 6 to 12 per cent.

The Monster.com Acquisition: A Win for Employees, Shareholders and the Competitor

Every acquisition is done with the intent of becoming a bigger powerhouse in an industry that revolves around opportunities. However, time and again, executives face major stumbling blocks after the deal is consummated. Cultural clashes and turf wars can prevent post-integration plans from being properly executed. Different systems and processes, dilution of a company's brand, overestimation of synergies and a lack of understanding of the target firm's business, can all work towards destroying the very reason for its acquisition. The JobsAhead.com acquisition by Monster.com demonstrated exactly that.

The acquisition had promised or at least intended to fully upstage Naukri.com. With Monster.com's global might and potential investments, JobsAhead.com could have left the competition far behind. But what happened next was exactly the opposite of JobsAhead.com's expectations. Monster.com messed up royally and lost its focus immediately afterwards. Naukri.com raced ahead and made the combined Monster.com-JobsAhead.com entity a distant number two in a span of two years. According to rumours, Monster.com underinvested in the brand, realigning the key sales territories from JobsAhead.com to Monster.com and that possibly became one of the reasons for its failure.

'There were twists and turns. Monster.com was run by Arun Tadanki, who was our marketing head in 2000. He left JobsAhead.com, joined Monster.com and eventually came back to acquire us. For reasons outside of his control, Monster.com was going through trying times globally and they didn't invest in anything behind the brand. They were treating India as a cash-generating machine rather than investing the profits back into the company. They used India's profits to subsidise those funds into their global brand. But Arun wasn't partial to Monster.com employees. He had respect for our team because he had been a part of our original set-up. In fact, for the longest time, he fought with the global team of Monster.com to let our product engine run both sites. He believed our engine was superior to the global one that we were being forced to use. But that didn't materialise.

That killed our brand, the product and the combined potential. So yes, one of the best things that happened to Naukri.com was our acquisition,' Alok concludes.

Post JobsAhead.com, Alok joined Canaan partners and made some good investments in Car Trade, Matrimony.com and Mindtree. He has recently started Indifi, a Fin-tech company helping small businesses with loans. Its first seed investors included his friend Puneet Dalmia and Alok Tadanki. Indifi recently raised $10 million from Omidyar Network in its Series A round—the same number at which he and Puneet had exited from their previous start-up almost twelve years ago.

Hindsight can be a blessing or a curse depending on how long you lament over it. Either you can learn your lessons from the past decisions or keep brooding over past choices. As discussed in this chapter, the founders of JobsAhead.com chose to learn valuable lessons that sometimes take years for entrepreneurs to realise. They are moving forward with new ventures loaded with essential wisdom from their years at JobsAhead.com. Their acquisition is an example that if you learn from your mistakes, the maiden venture need not be the last one.

R. RAMARAJ

Founder and CEO, Sify

'We lobbied and got the licences issued. But the government did what it always does. It opened the floodgates a tad bit unnecessarily and issued 600 licences. Suddenly, the game was all about who rolled-out quicker and executed the fastest. Thankfully, we had done most of our legwork work beforehand.'

RAMARAJ FOUNDED SIFY, INDIA'S FIRST PRIVATE internet service provider (ISP), in 1997 and partnered with Satyam Computers as an investor. It was also the first internet start-up from India that became a decacorn, a term used for companies valued over $10 billion when listed. Sify is known for making the most audacious acquisition that cost it nearly ₹500 crore. It acquired a small company called IndiaWorld, whose turnover was just ₹3 crore. This acquisition officially flagged off the dot-com mania in India but within a period of 18 months, Sify crashed after being devalued at $70 million. They lost over $11 billion of market capitalisation in less than two years. If these numbers are any indication, Ramaraj's ride with Sify is certainly not for the faint-hearted.

On Chancing Upon the ISP Opportunity

Before Sify, Ramaraj thrived in the telecom industry. During 1992–96, he was supervising Sterling Cellular, which had successfully bid for the Delhi Circle licence when mobile phone technology was introduced in India. Later, Sterling was acquired by Essar Group and eventually became Vodafone. After this stint, Ramaraj had a chance meeting with Ramalinga Raju, the founder of Satyam computers, who had taken Satyam public in 1992. Raju was now eyeing the lucrative telecom licences. Ramaraj was advising Raju on the same. As luck would have it, they didn't win any of the next circle bids but Raju still wanted to collaborate with Ramaraj on something.

Raju had a sketchy idea. He wanted to launch a Reuters-like service in India. Ramaraj wasn't exactly thrilled about it but decided to do his homework. He started holding exploratory meetings with similar service providers like Bloomberg and Australian Associated Press, which were keen to enter India. To size up the market further, Ramaraj also decided to meet some of Reuters' customers in India.

Ramaraj remembers the feedback from Reuters' customers. 'No one had any issues with the content provided by Reuters but their major concern was that the connectivity pipe was terrible. Internet connectivity was a very disappointing affair in India. So I thought that if I could build the information highway, I could then build any content layer on top for those who use my pipe. That would make me a powerful gatekeeper. And since I had just come out of the cellular industry, it looked like the next big thing to do. Almost overnight, we switched the plan from being a content business to being the connectivity providers.'

It was easier said than done, though. The government was still discussing its ISP policy and there was no way to get a licence for TCP/IP (the internet protocol suite) in the country. VSNL had started internet services just a year ago with some moderate success. Ramaraj began the operations from the ground up by creating an association of interested companies that wanted to apply for ISP licences and spent his days in Delhi lobbying the government. It was a déjà vu moment for him as he had done this before in his telecom days.

He recalls, 'We lobbied and got the licences issued. But the government did what it always does. It opened the floodgates a tad bit unnecessarily and issued 600 licences. Suddenly, the game was all about who rolled-out quicker and executed the fastest. Thankfully, we had done most of our legwork work beforehand. We had already tied up with a US-based ISP called CompuServe. The company wanted to have an offshoot in India for its multinational customers. So when tied up, we were handed over a global standard specification and introduced to all their tried and tested gold-standard vendors. CompuServe had both B2B and B2C customers. When we launched the network, we had their B2B paying customers from day one. With rolling revenues from the first day and world-class infrastructure, we were now focused on winning B2C customers.'

The Launch of Satyam Online

Clifford Stoll, a US-based author and engineer, infamously called internet to be a 'passing fad' in 1995. Google didn't exist back then and this prompted AOL to come up with a simple, old-fashioned idea. They put free trail floppy discs—which eventually became CDs—in every mailbox in America. They bet on the assumption that with the free CD in hand, almost everyone would give it a go and then hopefully, be hooked to the internet and turn into a paying customer. Steve Case, the founder and CEO of AOL, claimed that when they went public in 1992, they had just about 200,000 subscribers. Thanks to this strategy, they acquired over 25 million subscribers in a decade, with a market capitalisation of over $100 billion.

Ramaraj knew that to scale in India, he would need to use the same strategy without wasting any time. They decided to use the CD route as a way to distribute the prepaid packs by the hour. Luckily, he managed to convince the then Chief Minister of Andhra Pradesh, Chandrababu Naidu and Prime Minister Atal Bihari Vajpayee to launch this plan during Hyderabad's 'Hi-Tech City Launch'. It was an ambitious project by the state government to position Hyderabad as the IT capital of India. Next day, the front-page news in dailies carried a picture of the Sify

CD launch. 'Unfortunately for the Chief Minister, the original "Hi-Tech City" story ended up on page 5.' Ramaraj laughs.

'We quickly mushroomed in eight to twelve cities. Then, we hit upon an issue. The infrastructure business needs constant capital infusion to grow. Satyam's own mothership, the IT services business, was growing fast too and they had a limit on how much they could invest. On the other hand, I didn't want to dilute either. I preferred debt. I wanted to conserve my equity in the company.'

On the Famed IPO

In 1999, the concept of venture capitalism knocked on the Indian doors. Whatever risk capital was available, it was from companies trotting around like VCs, but behaving like banks with a risk-aversion. Also, the cheque sizes back then were small. Sify needed tens of millions of dollars to fulfil its ambition. The current funds couldn't satisfy that appetite. Ramaraj needed an alternative to raise capital.

Then on 11 March 1999, Infosys became the first Indian company to debut on the NASDAQ roster and raised $50 million. Promoters of other IT companies, market participants and fund managers heralded the listing as a positive and path-breaking achievement, and as a result, expected many Indian companies to list on NASDAQ. Ramaraj, like many entrepreneurs at that time, wasn't aware of NASDAQ as an alternative to raising funds. He did extensive research and realised that certain Chinese and Israeli companies were listed on it. Optimism returned to his team. He says, 'We believed that we could try. Luckily, our auditors were KPMG, who had previously assisted Infosys to get listed so we had their experience on our side.'

Afterwards, Ramaraj needed a reputed investment banker to turn this into a reality. A company that wishes to raise money from investors through the stock-market must hire a merchant bank to implement and underwrite the whole process. Ramaraj zeroed in on Merrill Lynch after conversations with many bankers. In October 1999, Sify became a listed company on NASDAQ in a short period of eight months. At a valuation of $350 million, Sify raised $72 million. It was a higher valuation and fundraise than Infosys. Sify was the new Indian ambassador on NASDAQ.

The Massive Indian Acquisition

Ramaraj was back in his office with plenty of cash. After reaching the international milestone, Sify's focus returned to growing the business. But something continued to bother Ramaraj. He explains, 'When I came back and looked at all the Chinese companies on NASDAQ like China.com and NetEase, they were all well over a billion dollars. I wondered why we got the short end of the stick. India had a similar population and demographic, therefore, a similar opportunity. What I realised is that US investors didn't understand India because we hadn't done enough to convince them that Sify was a well-deserving candidate. We had the capability to achieve a status similar to that of our Chinese counterparts.' This epiphany was a defining moment for Ramaraj, who realised that he had to do something unimaginable, something 'large' in order to catch the attention of the US investors. The likely thing to be done, given the circumstances, was to make a 'meaningful acquisition'. He adds, 'AOL had successfully built a hybrid model for subscription and an advertising model around its portal. I needed a stronger contender and began to evaluate companies. I knew that if

I made a small move of ₹10–15 crore, it wouldn't move the needle on Sify's fortunes. I could have got IndiaWorld for that amount, but it wouldn't have changed anything. So we ended up paying $100 million.'

On 29 November 1999, all the newspaper headlines across the country screamed, 'Sify acquires IndiaWorld for ₹499 crore.' IndiaWorld Communications was acquired from its founder Rajesh Jain in all-cash deal. Satyam paid $40 million to Jain, which included a caution deposit of $12 million. The remaining $115 million were going to be transferred by 30 June 2000.

With the acquisition, Ramaraj announced to the world that much like AOL in the US, he had massive ambitions to build a content layer on top of his connectivity pipe. He wasn't going to be satisfied with just subscription revenues from internet services. Like AOL, he wanted to scoop up most of the advertising dollars that were going to be spent online.

Everyone in the business was concerned about whether Sify had made the right decision by paying ₹499 crore for a paltry net profit of ₹27 lakh. Ramaraj defended the decision in the press. 'The acquisition would be a good strategic fit for Satyam Infoway's portal business, adding a large overseas Indian audience to the large India-based audience that satyamonline. com currently enjoys. The combined portal network is expected to be a mega portal for audiences from everywhere interested in India.' Indeed, many journalists, when they read the press release, believed there had been a mistake in the numbers. It was certainly an atrocious amount to be paid to a company that obviously did not deserve it at that point in time.

It is something that bothers Ramaraj even after two decades and he says, 'Listen, everybody looked at what Rajesh was getting. I was tired of the articles that were being written. They thought that I didn't know what I was doing or whether it was a clean transaction. There was all sorts of nonsense being written. But nobody reported what my move did to the Sify stocks. Our market capitalisation went from $350 million to one billion overnight.' I had missed this tiny detail like many others.

The deal had tranches. Sify had acquired a 24.5 per cent stake in IndiaWorld for ₹122.20 crore and paid a deposit of ₹51.30 crore to acquire an option to buy the remaining 75.5 per cent on paying ₹325.40 crore before 30 June 2000. Ramaraj had only raised $72 million from the market. It needed time to generate the rest of the cash.

'I had already applied to raise funds again from NASDAQ. By the time we did that, it was February and in a matter of three months, our market capitalisation had shot up from $1 billion to $8 billion. We raised about $160 million in the second round. This time, it was so much easier.'

Technically, Ramaraj had paid less than 2 per cent of Sify's stock to acquire IndiaWorld and fire up investors' imagination from a $350-million market capitalisation to $8 billion, in just a few months. Investors believed that the deal had been a bargain for Sify and the company's growth strategy was absolutely believable. Betting on IndiaWorld had clearly paid off.

It was equally astonishing that Ramaraj had considered IndiaWorld when Rediff.com was alive and kicking. IndiaWorld was meant for NRIs, but it barely got any traction from India. Rediff.com, on the other hand, was dedicated to the domestic audience.

Ramaraj recalls, 'Ajit was my senior from college so I had called him up and asked him whether he would like to part of Sify.' Ajit is known to have notorious reactions towards conversations that revolve around acquisitions of his companies. Rediffusion, the advertising agency he had co-founded in the 1980s, remains independent even today, despite many global networks having approached him over the years. 'He called me names and hung up!' Ramaraj reveals with a chuckle.

How Ramaraj Blew It!

Globally, market euphoria towards internet stocks had fuelled the dot-com bubble from 1995 to 2000. It was a historic economic bubble. NASDAQ included many internet-based companies, which peaked on 10 March 2000. It was like the flame that burns the brightest before its final hour. After hitting the peak, NASDAQ crashed. The dot-com crash, which lasted from 11 March 2000 to 9 October 2002, was the period of immense gloom that led to the annihilation of many promising companies such as the online shopping portals Pets.com, WebVan.com and Boo.com, as well as communication companies such as WorldCom, NorthPoint Communications and Global Crossing. Every major company back then, including Amazon and eBay, were stripped off their billions of dollars of capitalisation. It was obvious that the crash had also affected Sify. But it was uncanny that Ramaraj seemed to have foreseen this possibility. He said, 'From February 1999, when I knew nothing about NASDAQ, to being listed by October 1999 followed by a fundraiser, the entire experience was surreal. But at the peak of all this, I knew one thing for sure. We didn't know how long it was going to last. We had a window within which we had to use the currency as it wouldn't last forever. And then in January 2000, AOL was bought by Time Warner for $162 billion.'

The deal marked a major turning point in the media industry, highlighting the massive power and value that internet companies like AOL had built in a relatively short time. Through this deal, AOL shareholders now owned 55 per cent of the combined entity, even though Time Warner's revenues of $26.8 billion dwarfed AOL's $4.8 billion. 'I had it in my mind that I wanted to buy a ₹1,000-crore revenue company overseas. A potential acquisition of that size would come at a fraction of our market capitalisation, which had crossed $11.5 billion (in excess of ₹50,000 crore). I looked overseas, since revenues are meaningful there as compared to India. And in the normal course of events, I would have gone to Merrill Lynch, my tried-and-tested bankers. But unfortunately, I made the mistake of going to a large consulting company.' It proved to be a costly mistake. 'Those guys know how to keep your ego flying and have very little to show for it. So I met all their partners in different parts of the world. I travelled around the planet for six months with them. And in the end, there was no deal. By then, NASDAQ was in a tailspin and nobody wanted our stock because the sentiment had changed. If I had gone with a pure merchant banker, I would have had a deal. We had an opportunity in sight but missed out on grabbing it. Everything else we moved on, we clinched. This one, we screwed up.'

It was a mistake one would not expect from someone of Ramaraj's status. The consulting company had been circling around to learn about the internet. 'I think they had a mandate from Reliance to learn about the internet and go back to advise them. So, all of them were in my face including their country head and all the US partners. Everybody was hounding me. The consultants have a way of putting you on a pedestal and you get screwed. I thought that with their global network, we would close faster than a banker. I completely screwed up.' He adds, 'While there is a lot of grunt work in both industries, in banking, it's more quantitative and no one cares about offering "strategic insight" and putting things in quadrants. They just focus on getting the deal done.'

Sify, over the next few months, tumbled from its peak market capitalisation of $11.5 billion down to a mere $70 million. The amount was less than what it had coughed up for IndiaWorld and a bit shy of what it raised in its IPO. It took Ramaraj nearly five years to make a slow and painful turnaround.

Now that the investors had fled the dot-com scene, Sify was sitting on India's largest private internet network, covering 220 cities with more than four lakh subscribers. But B2C had become a challenge because VSNL continued to ensure there was no level playing field between private ISPs and itself. The slow growth and negative realisation in the retail business were partly offset by Sify's quick ramp-up of its corporate business, including data-network services and e-consulting. It had a list of 500-odd corporate customers including bigwigs such as Procter & Gamble, Lucent, Gillette India, HDFC Bank, UTI Bank and Maruti. In 2001, three-quarters of its top line was being generated from B2B businesses.

In 2005, Satyam Computers announced that it was divesting its shares in Sify, amounting to almost 32 per cent, to Silicon Valley entrepreneur, Raju Vegesna. Satyam's journey with Sify was over. Within a year, Sify reported revenues of $28.74 million for the quarter ending in June 2006. The revenues were up by 29.1 per cent compared to the same quarter in 2005. It reported that the cash profit in adjusted EBITA[15] terms for the quarter was $4.03 million. The company ended the quarter with a cash balance of $55.27 million after capital expenditures of $6.7 million. Five years down the line, Ramaraj had kept the ship cruising and shored it to safety. But that same day, Ramaraj also announced that he was giving up his position as the captain.

---

[15] Earnings before interest, tax, depreciation and amortisation.

Three years later, Ramaraj's former partner, Ramalinga Raju of Satyam Computers, was involved in one of India's biggest accounting scandals. He resigned after confessing that he had manipulated Satyam's accounts to embezzle ₹14,162 crore in several forms. Ramaraj declined to talk about Raju and the scandal, stating that right after the IPO and its success, Sify had gradually distanced itself from Satyam, in terms of not only ownership but also business and management interests. He says, 'We were at an arm's length from each other.'

What started out as a pure-play internet firm, ended up as a company focused more on areas such as enterprise solutions, infrastructure management and IP telephony. Today, its market capitalisation stands at $270 million. But its share price languishes at $1.5 from its peak of nearly $400 two decades ago. A classic case of the mighty having fallen. And yet, Ramaraj's instinctual decisions served him well—from finding an industry-wide need in the IP telephony, lobbying for it and creating uproar over the huge acquisition of IndiaWorld. The only time his instincts failed him was when the US-based consulting firm took him on a ride, but he persisted and gave up on his position as the CEO only when that one mistake, which reduced the company's value during the dot-com crash, had been rectified. Ramaraj retired from Sify like a graceful captain whose journey—full of lessons, instinctual decisions, owning up to and mending mistakes—serves as an inspiration for anyone who wants to build the next big start-up.

GIRISH MATHRUBOOTHAM

Co-Founder and CEO, Freshworks Inc.

'When we started with Freshdesk, our whole plan was that Version 1 was going to be the first stop. We aimed to build a complete solution for the customer's journey to eventually create a unified product. If we go back to 2005 and look at some of the products that we were using, we had Ericsson, Motorola, LG or Samsung for mobile phones, Canon, Nikon or Kodak for cameras, and Sandisk or Transcend for MP3s, Sony or Samsung for DVD players and Tom Tom or Garmin for GPS. Now, I want you to pause for a minute and think about these product categories. Each one of these categories was distinct. A lot of research and innovation had gone into building these products. As customers, we all assumed that we needed to buy all these products. Now I want you to take that analogy and apply it to business software. Imagine an iPhone moment in business software.'

India's First Official SaaS Unicorn

UNTIL A FEW DECADES AGO, NO ONE HAD IMAGINED that software would one day be sold not like a licence for perpetuity model but as a service. Software, nowadays, comes as a 'pay as you go' service. SaaS (software as a service) cannot be downloaded or sucked out of a CD ROM to your computer, it doesn't break your bank anymore, and it is updated and improved all the time as certain remote updates take place nearly every week. It's been almost seven decades since the computer was invented, four and a half decades since the invention of the microprocessor and a little more than two decades since the beginning of commercial internet. Considering these, SaaS is a revolution that has been slow in the making, but it's time has finally arrived.

In the late nineties, Marc Benioff, the founder of Salesforce.com, triggered the 'software-as-a-service' wave, enabling enterprise customers to buy software as part of their monthly subscription plans without creating a deep hole in their pockets.

Today, many new-age smart companies have almost zero paper process. The paperless office—imagined decades ago—is slowly becoming a reality. These companies use SaaS subscription services for almost all functions, processes and tools that they need to run their business: email, customer relationship management tools, internal communication and collaboration tool, document storage, accounting software, expense reporting, video conferencing and much more. It is a paperless world.

The entire SaaS provider market could be divided into two: Horizontal SaaS providers and Vertical SaaS providers. Horizontal SaaS focuses on departments within the organisation (such as HR, admin and payroll) and spread across industries. Vertical SaaS focuses on a particular industry rather than individual departments within organisations.

FusionCharts, based in Kolkata, was the first Indian SaaS start-up that I heard of. It was founded by a sixteen-year-old Pallav Nadhani, who probably sensed an opportunity to make some pocket money. As the name suggests, FusionCharts turned boring basic excel charts into beautiful and easy-to-use interactive charts. My first impression of this venture was 'Sweet, not bad for a sixteen-year old.' Ten years later, it claimed to have 20,000 paying customers and 4,50,000 users in 118 countries, powering more than a billion charts per month and generating $7 million in annual revenues. It didn't take long for my reaction to morph from 'sweet' to 'Oh, my God!' Though Pallav's story, fascinating as it is, couldn't be chronicled in this book, I hope that someday, he'll tell that story himself. Here, I am going to narrate the story of Girish Mathrubootham, CEO and co-founder of Freshworks, which is one of the biggest SaaS start-ups from India and surely the most visible one. Even in today's era, when a lot of SaaS companies in India are still struggling to convince VCs to believe in their model, Girish and his co-founder Shan have raised $250 million from marquee investors like Sequoia Capital and Accel Partners as well as Capital G, the VC wing of Alphabet Inc., Google's parent company, which focuses on late-stage start-ups. He is also one of the few co-founders who has never had a real 'blew it' moment in his professional career.

The First Adventure

Born and brought up in Trichy, Tamil Nadu, Girish studied engineering in Chennai. He claims that he was an average student. He completed his formal education with an MBA from the University of Chennai. His first experience as an entrepreneur was as a Java tutor to his friends in Chennai, where he eventually started a formal training institute teaching Java to CS aspirants. After 2001, when everything changed in the IT world, 'dot-com' became a bad word. To make matters worse, new emerging technologies such as C# (pronounced as C sharp), backed by Microsoft within its .NET Initiative, were causing confusion within the tech community, where mastering languages eventually became imperative.

Girish remembers, 'I was off to a good start but within a year, I found myself trying to convince the developer community about Java's relevance. People started believing that C# was the next big thing and Java was no longer relevant. The critical lesson that I learnt back then was that it's easier to sell a product that people already believe in than trying to evangelise the need for a different product. I think that's a fundamental lesson and it has served me well in my career. So, it's important to identify a booming market where you can ride the wave and then build something that everybody wants rather than attempting to create a new need. That said, you have to innovate on the product and be better than the competition. For example, companies around the world are already aware that they need a CRM solution. You don't have to go around explaining why they need CRM. You just need to convince them that you have the best solution to the problem they are trying to solve. Bottom line is that for you to be successful, it is much easier to go with the tide than against it.' Wisely enough, Girish folded up his first venture and went on to work with AdventNet (now known as Zoho) from 2001 to 2010. Coincidentally, Zoho and Freshworks are currently the two Indian SaaS unicorns based out of Chennai. Girish joined them as the lead engineer pre-sales and moved to product management in a year.

The Beginnings of Freshworks

In seven years, Girish had established himself as a valuable team member at AdventNet. In 2008, the company decided to send Girish to Austin to set up an office. One of their flagship products, Manage Engine, was doing well and had grown a sizeable revenue. The founders wanted Girish to strengthen analyst relationships with Gartner, Forrester, etc. to further establish the product as a leader in that vertical and hire more sales and marketing resources.

Soon, the financial services firm Lehman Brothers filed for bankruptcy in September 2008, changing everything. It remains the largest bankruptcy filing in the US history till date. Lehman had holdings of over $600 billion in assets. The worldview of every professional, company and country went into a toxic negative spiral. All of AdventNet's plans were put on hold. In April 2009, Girish spoke to his boss Sridhar Vembu and told him that he was bored of waiting for the environment to change. He recalls, 'I told him that the environment is bad, we are not hiring and I understand that. Why not allow me to head back to India and scale the venture from there as it would be much better ROI (Return on Investment) for the company. I was back in Chennai by June but by then my team had really stepped up and was running on autopilot. I was suddenly a member of the management team, which I found extremely boring. My job was to attend meetings and resolve conflicts and disputes. I am the guy who loves getting his hands dirty so this new role wasn't for me.'

Incidentally, the idea of Freshworks germinated in his mind while he was in the process of returning from Austin to Chennai. It so happened that his forty-inch LCD TV was damaged while being shipped back to India. When months of trying to get in touch with the relevant people at the insurance and shipping companies yielded no results, a frustrated Girish took to Return to India, a forum that provides an interactive platform for Indians worldwide. His intention was to warn others about not using the company's services but what happened next was unexpected. 'To my surprise, the very next day, the president of the insurance company apologised on the forum for the harassment caused and a day later, the money was in my bank.' This was Girish's 'Eureka!' moment. 'One of the things I had been building at Zoho was a muti-channel help desk. Back in the day, it meant that the customer could contact a company to complain or seek help via phone, chat, website or email. Now, I saw a new channel emerge—an online forum that could force an unresponsive company to respond immediately. Suddenly, power had shifted from the company to the client. Listening and responding to customers was no longer a customer-support issue; it could potentially be a marketing issue since not responding or addressing a customer's concern could lead to poor marketing for the company and cause a severe loss in its client base. The forum had forced the company to do the right thing,' explains Girish.

Girish started researching this sliver of an idea and saw the beginnings of a similar change on popular blogs platforms like YouTube and to some extent, Facebook. He started brewing plans for a new-age help desk with a fresh perspective. Hence the name, 'Freshdesk'. The real punch in the idea landed sometime in May 2010 while browsing through Hacker News (HN), a social news website focusing on technology and entrepreneurship, run by start-up incubator Y Combinator.

'I saw this article about Zendesk raising their prices 60 to 300 per cent and how their users were unhappy about it,' Girish says. One comment, in particular, caught Girish's eye. This HN community member was furious and had posted something like, 'We ended up using eSupport (which is a complete piece of shit).' Whenever I read something like this I can't help but think, 'here is a potential customer' for whoever can get this right, and at the right price. It seems like there is still a huge opening in this market for someone to come in and take all of Zendesk's and eSupport's customers. 'That comment was like a slap on my face,' Girish later wrote on the Freshworks official blog. 'Here was an opportunity sitting right in front of me. I had the domain knowledge and I knew that a massive transition to cloud computing is happening. The *spidey sense* in me told me that I should throw my hat into the ring. That was the exact moment that I decided that I should build something in the customer-support market delivered as SaaS. The next few weeks were actually pretty stressful. I couldn't sleep because of the excitement and the fear (school fees, home mortgage, etc.). I had not talked to anyone (not even my wife) about the idea but I was researching all the companies in that space. The time had come when I needed a co-founder. I talked to my good friend and colleague of several years, Shan, who is a great techie and he immediately agreed.' And this is how Freshdesk was officially born. In its first avatar, it was a SaaS-based social customer service platform that enabled small- and medium-sized businesses to roll out a professional and modern customer support system.

On Financing

Girish admits that he knew nothing about fundraising in the beginning and had never met a venture capitalist in his life. His friends from engineering and later, during his MBA, Rajesh Rajasekar and Ravi Raman, who had backed his failed Java-training institute, returned to invest in Freshdesk by putting in ₹25,000 each. While Girish had about ₹30 lakh in savings, thanks to his US stint with AdventNet, every penny from his friends helped. Girish had written a blog post for a contest by AppSumo, a daily deals site for digitally delivered goods and services. The contest was on the subject of building a lean start-up. While Girish didn't win the contest, the post went viral on Hacker News.

His product was not ready, yet he earned a few hundred sign-ups. Anand Daniel of Accel Partners happened to see the blog post and connected with Girish. Girish admits, 'Our timing led to some dumb luck. A couple of years ago, nobody wanted to come to Chennai, especially to meet some boring help desk company. Most investors may have preferred to fly to a city where they could have more than one meeting, so I can imagine them cancelling meetings in Chennai. But by the time we launched, SaaS was coming of age, so at least a few Venture Capitalists were scouting.' Soon, they got Atwell College from Australia onboard as their first customer, who committed after testing out Freshdesk's trial version. 'We got six more customers from four different continents, but none from India. We knew we were building an international tech company from day one,' Girish reveals. In 2011, Girish participated in the Microsoft BizSpark contest and won the first prize of $40,000. Freshworks was the finalist in another event called

Unplugged. These achievements helped the start-up garner investor interest. Anand Daniel, a VC at Accel partners, referred Freshdesk to their newest partner, Shekhar Kirani, who was scouting for his debut deal. A wonderfully written profile of Girish and Freshdesk on the popular website Factor Daily noted the developments between Accel and Girish, 'He (Shekhar Kirani) hopped on a plane to Chennai sometime in January 2011 and went to check out Freshdesk. The first thing that hit Kirani when he got to Freshdesk's 700 square feet office, in a place called Kilkattalai in Chennai, was the furniture. Kirani recalls, 'They had really "mixed" furniture. The chairs didn't match the table, which in turn didn't go with the other stuff in terms of colour and design,' he recalls. 'But all six of the desks had a Mac each. It signalled to me that these guys knew where to spend their money.' After a few weeks, Girish met Sameer Gandhi, a partner from Accel's San Francisco office in Bengaluru when he was visiting on a business trip. 'If he had walked into my office in the Valley, I would have ensured that he walked out with a cheque,' Gandhi told Kirani after the meeting. In particular, Girish's storytelling, combined with the market opportunity to disrupt an established incumbent like Zendesk, impressed the early investors. On 1 December 2011, Freshdesk announced that it had raised $1 million from Accel Partners with Shekhar Kirani joining the Freshdesk board.

An Expert's Guide to Turning a Freak Accusation into a Huge Marketing Opportunity

Just a day after announcing their million-dollar financing, Freshdesk had a crisis on hand. On 2 December, noted cloud analyst and blogger Ben Kepes tweeted, 'Seems to me that #Freshdesk is an unethical troll trying to cash in on #Zendesk's good name. But that could just be me …'[16]

Girish recalls the incident, 'Initially, I was taken aback. Where was this coming from? Why was this blogger suddenly making a statement out of nowhere, attacking us and calling us a rip-off? No sensible blogger would do that. Because for all you know, we could be a client in the future. I went and checked whether he had signed up to take Freshdesk for a spin before making the judgement. He had not! So, I went ahead and asked him why, instead of signing up and giving an objective review like any good analyst would, he had chosen to make a judgement like that?' Ben Kepes didn't have an answer since he hadn't expected Girish to take this head on. Girish continues, 'So he came up with the lamest answer possible, which is that our name also has 'desk' in it.'

Ben accused the Freshdesk founders of piggybacking on Zendesk's name. He had tagged both Girish and Mikkel Svane, the CEO of Zendesk, in his tweet. Within minutes, one of Ben Kepes's Twitter followers, Christian Marth, continued the attack by calling Freshdesk founders, a 'bunch of Indian cowboys'. Girish was convinced that taking them head-on was the only way to go and he replied, 'Making an unsolicited attack on our nationality reflects badly on you not us. We're Indian and proud of that.' By then, Zendesk's CEO Mikkel Savane had decided to jump in and added fuel to the fire. He replied to Ben Kepes, 'You know what they are. Imitation is the sincerest form of WAIT-WHAT-A-FREAKING-RIP-OFF!'

Girish and his team had taken enough of it. It was no secret that the idea of Freshdesk had been born out of the frustration

---

[16] The tweets are archived here: http://ripoffornot.org/.

of Zendesk's customers, who were seeking a better, more affordable alternative. Freshdesk immediately put up a website exposing how Zendesk was a customer of Ben Kepes's services as a blogger. The page noted that there were several help desk companies around the world with the word 'desk' in their name and wondered whether Zendesk was plain frustrated about their Accel fundraise and the fact that customers were switching to Freshdesk. Clearly, Zendesk was irked that Freshdesk wasn't just an annoying fruit fly that would eventually go away. With financing and customer traction in place, they were going after Zendesk with all their might. This action on Freshdesk's part to expose the intentions of a global player went viral. It was perhaps the first viral marketing campaign for a B2B company in India. 'At the end of it, the lesson we taught everyone is to never attack a small guy who's got nothing to lose.' Girish chuckles. Another mistake that Zendesk made was publicly acknowledging that the 'cowboy' Freshdesk was comparable to their company, instantly cementing the credentials of the six-month-old start-up.

On Ambition and Being Bank-Rolled

Just a few months after the slugfest with the Zendesk CEO and his biased followers, Freshdesk had 700 signed customers and announced a $5-million financing round led by Tiger Global in April 2012, with participation from existing investor, Accel. Notably, this was Tiger's first B2B investment in India. It was uncharacteristic of Tiger Global, which was busy pumping truckloads of money in Indian consumer start-ups like Myntra, Flipkart, Ola, and ShopClues, to consider a B2B company. In an Ask Me Anything (AMA) with the website Inc42, Girish explained how this happened, 'I met Tiger Global's Lee Fixel in a hotel lobby with an iPad and I walked him through the story. The next day, I think I was in Bengaluru pitching to another VC when he called and made an offer on the phone. He just said, "Girish, if you like it, we will shake hands in the air and we can skip the term sheet and move directly into due diligence." He added that the offer was one of the highest amongst those received from Indian VCs.' Everybody was asking the Freshdesk founders for excel sheets and numbers, but Tiger Global made them a much bigger offer without looking at their performance. Lee told Girish, 'If you look at the business numbers, there is nothing much to bet on. I am just betting on you, since you have been there, done that.'

Amidst all of this, Tiger Global hired a company in Mumbai that contacted all of Freshdesk's two-hundred-odd customers. Tiger Global wanted to conduct a survey to gauge what Freshdesk's customers liked about its product, what they didn't like, whether they would refer Freshdesk to others, how the company could address to their further requirements, etc. 'The survey report was overwhelmingly positive. I think 96 per cent of the survey respondents actually said they would recommend us to their friends and all the demands were added features like an iPhone app, reporting, and so on,' Girish added. Girish was amused by the effort Tiger Global made to understand Freshdesk's perception in the market and its customers' needs. He said that it was the first and only time when he saw a VC actually carry out a full-blown analysis by talking to all of a company's customers and carrying out a survey. From that Series B round, Freshdesk went onto raise another five rounds of financing that led to the infusion of $250 million, the last one being in July 2018, which raised $100 million from Sequoia, Accel and Capital G, valuing the company at over $1.5 billion.

Girish and his team were also now more ambitious than ever. As they were expanding their portfolio of products from an integrated CRM suite to other domains, they decided to rebrand the company to FreshWorks immediately. In a blog post, Girish wrote, 'In 2010, we started Freshdesk as a 'fresh help desk' with a dream to make a dent in the world of customer support. While Freshdesk continues to grow exponentially, as a company, we [have] moved beyond customer service by offering innovative products in the ITSM, CRM and call centre domains. As we expand our vision and build more exciting products, we believe that this is the right time to create a new brand that allows us to tell our multi-product story better…. Today, I'm happy to announce that we are rebranding the company as Freshworks. We're not in this just to change the way businesses do customer support, but to refresh the way they do business. Our goal is to build a company that is loved by employees, customers and shareholders alike.'

To give you a comparison, Zendesk had raised less $100 million before its IPO and was valued at $900 million at their IPO in 2014. That said, today, Zendesk is a public company and has a seen its market capitalisation climb up to well over $5 billion. Clearly, Freshworks investors believe its fate will be similar, if not grander. While the Freshworks valuation is worth celebrating, it is also worrisome. A few years ago, $100 million in revenue served the ultimate goal for the software and SaaS start-ups. Today, many companies are in that revenue zone but are completely in a time warp. They just aren't growing. With stalled or marginal growth year after year, there is neither any chance to go public nor any interested buyers. These companies are the zombies of the Silicon Valley. In the process of building a multi-billion dollar software or SaaS company, generating large revenues is not the only goal. The checkboxes have changed. There is also a need to come up with great year-over-year growth. If not 100 per cent, then at least 30–40 per cent with a large untapped potential market. Hence a higher growth rate is the key to keep the desired valuation promise. Markets no longer reward revenue alone; it must be accompanied by continued growth. Freshworks faces a similar challenge. How big can the company get? Has the company set a high bar for itself? How does it plan to sustain its mind-boggling valuation? How far can a help desk company grow?

Girish explains, 'When we started with Freshdesk, our whole plan was that Version 1 was going to be the first stop. We aimed to build a complete solution for the customer's journey to eventually create a unified product. If we go back to 2005 and look at some of the products that we were using, we had Ericsson, Motorola, LG or Samsung for mobile phones, Canon, Nikon or Kodak for cameras, and Sandisk or Transcend for MP3s, Sony or Samsung for DVD players and Tom Tom or Garmin for GPS. Now, I want you to pause for a minute and think about these product categories. Each one of these categories was distinct. A lot of research and innovation had gone into building these products. As customers, we all assumed that we needed to buy all these products. Now I want you to take that analogy and apply it to business software. Imagine an iPhone moment in business software. Today, customers want to buy different products to serve different needs. So if somebody wants customer support, they search and buy Freshdesk or some other solution. If a customer wants a sales CRM software, he will search for one and buy it. Ditto for marketing automation. Today, customers believe that they need to buy all these different categories and then they are also forced to make the software work together. So they hire developers to try and connect everything and make it work together. Turns out that it's not a very efficient method.'

'That is exactly the question we have asked ourselves. "How can we create one experience, which gives a superior customer engagement platform to our customers?" What if I can give you a platform where you can understand everything about your customer from marketing to sales to support to chat to phone calls? What if a business knows which marketing campaigns the customer responded to, what they did on the website, which whitepaper id they downloaded? Did they talk about us on social media? Are they happy or unhappy? Did they send support tickets? Did they respond to a survey and said they were unhappy? What did the company talk to them about during the phone calls, emails or in the chat conversations? Can a business find all this information in one place? If the business software had an iPhone moment and we could mash all these software and the functions they provide and stitch them into one unified view, won't it be an obvious advantage over having to go to a lot of different places to get that? Imagine all that fragmented data that can be brought together.' Girish says, 'So if you really think about the everyday usage scenario like, let's say, a support person is actually working on a ticket and they need information about the customer, what have they purchased, how valuable they are to our business. If the salesperson is negotiating a contract, then he should know if this customer sent a support ticket and is not happy so that is not the best time to renegotiate the contract. So you can imagine all these scenarios across marketing and sales, and support the context of what the customer is feeling momentarily.' Girish isn't off the mark. That is exactly what companies today are looking for: to figure out where they stand in their relationship with the customer. It is what helps them make strategic decisions.

Moreover, such seamless integration makes the need for expensive consultants redundant. In the scenario that Girish envisages, sales teams, marketing teams, support teams, product managers, security experts, data centre guys and IT guys all work together to make the customer happy. 'Which is why we think of Freshworks now as a customer engagement platform,' Girish says with a smile.

SaaS's Secret Sauce

The SaaS model—when working right—is a dream come true. In an ideal scenario, predictable revenues recur each month, there is lower customer attrition if the product is sticky and it locks down users while customers continue to increase. This leads to quick progress in the business along with oh-so-sexy gross margins. The result is a cash register that does not stop ringing, followed by superb valuations. But I am aware of many entrepreneurs in the SaaS business who have struggled to get beyond a couple of million dollars in revenue despite being in the business for years. While building a global business from India looks extremely lucrative, the fact is that 90 per cent of SaaS start-ups eventually fail or report zero growth.

Having burnt my fingers by investing in a B2B SaaS company, I know that we had made the classic mistake of confusing a few early adopters with a real large market. Also, I knew Freshworks had made a string of acquisitions over the years by taking in smaller, struggling SaaS companies ,mostly as an acquisition-hire. The long list includes Airwoot, Framebench, Konotor, Frilp, 1Click, Chatmity, Pipemonk and Joe Hukum. While Girish acknowledges that most of the acquisitions were to get the brilliantly talented co-founders on board, a few were taken in to roll out separate products in the Freshworks suite or add some capability to an existing product. SaaS is an exciting world on the face of it. Everyone believes that there are hundreds of opportunities that can be turned into a successful business. But considering the high rate of failure in SaaS companies, anyone who wants to enter the space would probably benefit from the lens with which Girish evaluates SaaS opportunities.

'On the face of it, it's very simple,' Girish says. 'What we understood is that you have to map your solution to the global search volume on that problem. You need to innovate on a product for which there is an existing and pressing demand. My favourite analogy is when a customer walks into a store wanting to buy a washing machine. They aren't at a stage where they can define the solution by saying, "I need to figure out a way to remove dirt from my shirt." They are likely to say, "I want an IFB Senorita, 6.5 kilograms, front load washing machine." Now, after they have stated this, the sales person has a chance to either sell the client whichever model they are looking for or convince them to buy a different model, by saying, "Why don't you consider the new LG model, which is much quieter?" The same analogy applies to business software. When thinking of building a SaaS product, we know the customer is knowledgeable about the pain point that they are facing and are looking for a solution already. The customer knows what they want. So they are searching online with a clear expectation and a checklist of what features should be there in the solutions that they are evaluating. Now, when they discover us, it's our job to convince them that they have come to the right place. That, I believe, is where most SaaS start-ups fail. You have to cater to an already large market, lure the prospect with a superior aesthetic experience, and as soon as the prospect signs up for a trial, make them feel that the product is intuitive and ensure that they choose it on their own. DIY (Do-It-Yourself) is key in SaaS, so is competitive pricing.' Girish believes that the fate of a SaaS start-up depends on the choice of the market, product architecture, pricing, aesthetics and intuitiveness. They must all work in tandem for one to win. Missing any one of these means the product is dead on arrival.

In January 2019, Girish, along with two other SaaS founders, announced a conclave called SaaSBooMi in Chennai. The organisers claim that the conclave will see over 300 founders of SaaS firms and that, it is expected to give an impetus to the sector. 'That is SaaSBooMi for you. This is our pay-it-forward contribution to the ecosystem. This is how great ecosystems like Silicon Valley were built,' Girish told the media. It takes grand ambition to have the vision to create such an opportunity as SaaSBooMi, which is set to be Asia's largest SaaS conference. Girish is an exemplary entrepreneur for anyone interested in learning how to act on their ideas promptly and gather the guts to follow through. Sometimes, in the start-up world, once you spot an opportunity, acting as fast as a cheetah is the only right move you need.

AFTERWORD

The entrepreneurial journeys discussed in this book have highlighted stories of various Indian start-ups that managed to survive the turbulent years of the internet world. From early visionaries like Sanjeev Bikhchandani to young blood like Ashish Hemrajani, they discovered the potential for growth in the dot-com business and created products that met the needs of the average Indian. We no longer need to wait in queues in the sweltering heat or pouring rain to get event tickets. We don't have to roam from one corner of the city to the next with a broker in tow to look for an affordable house in a secure neighbourhood. Even food reaches our doorstep in less than half an hour if we are in no mood to go to the restaurant. Moreover, the roller-coaster ride of finding a life-partner or a love interest is also at the tips of our fingers today, thanks to the entrepreneurs who persevered and believed in their companies.

Just as I began writing this book, there seemed to be a new undercurrent in the start-up world. It is the quiet before the storm—the advent of the Chinese invasion of the Indian start-up ecosystem. From a financial point of view, China's two biggest companies, Alibaba and Tencent, had begun pouring significant amounts of money into start-ups, grabbing big seats at the table where Tiger Global and SoftBank had been leading in a duopoly. By betting hundreds of millions of dollars, Alibaba bought its way into Snapdeal, Paytm, Bigbasket, Xpressbees.com and Zomato. Tencent invested in Gaana.com, Swiggy, Flipkart, Ola Cabs and Byju's in major deals across the sector.

And it wasn't just the money from these two. A report by the website FactorDaily said, 'The number of Chinese apps in the top 100 Google Play Store apps has reached 44 by the end of 2018. The year 2018 may well be remembered as the year when Chinese start-ups landed on Indian shores to compete with us.'[17] These start-ups include Helo, SHAREit, TikTok, Bigo Live, BeautyPlus, Xender, CamScanner and PUBG. They are heavily focussed on the millions of internet users in India rolling in from tier-three markets and beyond. It's almost sad to see Indian start-ups failing to grow during our own wave of economic boom.

That said, India now stands at fourth place in global unicorn ranking, after the US, China and UK and it looks like it's going to get better. As I was writing the final chapters of the book, it seemed likely that BigBasket, Byju's, Delhivery, Rivigo, BookMyShow and Druva would join the unicorn club soon.

But it has now become imperative to look at the small businesses that are growing profitably online rather than these coveted unicorns. These fast-growing businesses include the merchants on Flipkart and Amazon as well as some of the direct-to-consumer brands that are emerging in India. Start-

---

[17] Shaikh, Shadma. 'The Chinese Takeover of the Indian App Ecosystem, *FactorDaily*, 2 January 2019. https://factordaily.com/the-chinese-takeover-of-indian-app-ecosystem.

ups growing steadily and sustainably without millions of dollars of financing like Bhane, Bombay Shaving Company, Chomp, Daily Objects, Korra, Nicobar, Scarters, all indicate a different side of this story. This new generation of digitally native brands is aiming to shake up traditional retail. New-age e-commerce companies build, market, sell and ship their products themselves, without middlemen, changing the way people shop. Through this process, these brands—spanning from cosmetics to technology—are radically changing consumer preferences and expectations.

We have seen a wave of new internet users in the post-Jio world. None of the legacy start-ups had these audiences—the lower middle-class Indian households—in mind when they started. Their challenges and needs that can be solved using technology gives us new opportunities, but I guess it also requires a completely new set of start-up entrepreneurs who can become these problem-solvers. India's start-up potential in the next few decades is truly limitless. There is no better time to be an entrepreneur in our history, and I look forward to the next generation of titans who take on this journey.

www.ingramcontent.com/pod-product-compliance
Lightning Source LLC
LaVergne TN
LVHW020315200726
843507LV00012B/2104